# Pervasive Intelligence – From Architectures to Sustainable Edge AI Systems-of-Systems

**RIVER PUBLISHERS SERIES IN COMMUNICATIONS AND NETWORKING**



The "River Publishers Series in Communications and Networking" is a series of comprehensive academic and professional books which focus on communication and network systems. Topics range from the theory and use of systems involving all terminals, computers, and information processors to wired and wireless networks and network layouts, protocols, architectures, and implementations. Also covered are developments stemming from new market demands in systems, products, and technologies such as personal communications services, multimedia systems, enterprise networks, and optical communications.

The series includes research monographs, edited volumes, handbooks and textbooks, providing professionals, researchers, educators, and advanced students in the field with an invaluable insight into the latest research and developments.

Topics included in this series include:

- Communication theory
- Multimedia systems
- Network architecture
- Optical communications
- Personal communication services
- Telecoms networks
- Wifi network protocols

For a list of other books in this series, visit www.riverpublishers.com

# Pervasive Intelligence – From Architectures to Sustainable Edge AI Systems-of-Systems


**Editor**

**Ovidiu Vermesan**
SINTEF, Norway

**Luca Valcarenghi**
Scuola Superiore Sant'Anna, Italy



River Publishers

Routledge
Taylor & Francis Group
NEW YORK AND LONDON

**Published 2026 by River Publishers**
River Publishers
Broagervej 10, 9260 Gistrup, Denmark
www.riverpublishers.com

**Distributed exclusively by Routledge**
605 Third Avenue, New York, NY 10017, USA
4 Park Square, Milton Park, Abingdon, Oxon OX14 4RN

*Pervasive Intelligence – From Architectures to Sustainable Edge AI Systems-of-Systems* / by Ovidiu Vermesan, Luca Valcarenghi.

Routledge is an imprint of the Taylor & Francis Group, an informa business

ISBN 978-87-4381-519-8 (hardback)
ISBN 978-87-4381-522-8 (online)
ISBN 978-87-4381-521-1 (master ebook)
ISBN 978-87-438-1524-2 (ePub)

DOI: 10.1201/9788743815211



Printed on acid-free paper.

## Dedication

"I know that I am intelligent, because I know that I know nothing."
– Socrates

"Creativity is intelligence having fun."
– Albert Einstein

"Never confuse motion with action."
– Ernest Hemingway

## Acknowledgement

The editors would like to thank all the contributors for their support in the planning and preparation of this book. The recommendations and opinions expressed in the book are those of the editors, authors, and contributors and do not necessarily represent those of any organizations, employers, or companies.

Ovidiu Vermesan
Luca Valcarenghi

# Contents

# Preface

**Edge AI - The intersection of Imagination and Execution**

This book explores the critical developments driving the next generation of edge artificial intelligence (AI). The following chapters delve into the core technological foundations, system architectures, and advanced algorithms that enable these innovations, while also addressing the complex engineering challenges inherent to the field. As edge AI increasingly transforms industrial sectors, this collection provides a comprehensive look at how intelligent systems can achieve autonomous, efficient, and sustainable operation across a wide variety of heterogeneous devices and dynamic physical environments. The summaries below offer a detailed roadmap of the specific topics and insights covered in each chapter.

**Chapter 1 - Edge AI System-of-Systems Reference Architecture: Engineering Foundations and Multi-Dimensional Views**
The opening chapter defines the conceptual and engineering foundations of edge AI systems. Edge AI results from merging IoT, edge computing, artificial intelligence, agentic AI, and embodied generative intelligence. These systems function within real-world constraints. The chapter asserts that edge AI is an evolving ecosystem, interconnected hardware, software, data, models, and communications, rather than isolated devices or algorithms.

To address the growing complexity of these environments, the chapter proposes a standardised, application-agnostic reference architecture. The architecture introduces a common taxonomy (a standardised way to classify and define components and concepts) and an engineering framework (a structured set of guidelines and best practices for system development). It is designed to support interoperability (systems working together), reuse (using components in different contexts), trustworthiness (reliability and security), and system validation (confirming systems function as intended). The discussion is organised around quality properties (measurable system characteristics), layered technology stacks (arrangements of technologies in tiers), and edge-to-cloud processing continua (data processing spanning from edge devices to cloud servers). The chapter also introduces a quad-optimisation paradigm (approach to balance four key objectives) for balancing competing objectives, such as performance (system speed and efficiency), energy efficiency (minimising power usage), trustworthiness, and operational adaptability (ability to respond to changing conditions).

**Chapter 2 - Towards Smart and Adaptive Agents for Active Sensing on Edge Devices**

This chapter discusses the limits of TinyML (machine learning models for tiny, low-power devices) and deep learning on edge devices (with restricted memory or processing power). While TinyML enables neural networks on such hardware, the authors argue that current methods lack adaptive reasoning (real-time decision adjustment) and environmental awareness (recognising changing conditions).

To overcome these limitations, the chapter presents an agentic active-sensing system based on active inference principles. The proposed system combines perception and planning directly on edge devices. This enables autonomous decision-making in dynamic environments. A practical implementation is demonstrated through a saccadic camera agent running on an NVIDIA Jetson device. The agent can control camera movements in a human-like manner. The work highlights how compact, real-time intelligent agents can support robotics and surveillance applications. They do so while maintaining low memory and computational requirements.

**Chapter 3 - Prediction of Neural Network Latency on Embedded GPU Accelerators**

This chapter focuses on predicting neural network latency on embedded GPU platforms such as NVIDIA Jetson devices. Accurate latency estimation is essential for designing real-time AI systems where timing, energy consumption, and resource utilisation are critical.

The authors introduce a layer-wise latency prediction model. Here, 'layer-wise latency' refers to the time it takes for each individual layer of a neural network to execute. The model uses neural network parameters, such as the number of layers and neurons, and hardware metrics, such as processor speed and memory usage, to estimate execution performance. The results demonstrate that accurate predictions can be achieved with minimal measurements and low computational overhead, making the process computationally efficient. The study reveals that relatively small parameter changes, such as adjusting the number of neurons, can significantly reduce latency. The chapter emphasises the importance of hardware-aware AI optimisation, which involves tailoring AI models to specific hardware to improve performance. It demonstrates how predictive performance models can accelerate the design of embedded AI applications, or AI software designed to run on devices with limited computing capability.

**Chapter 4 - Closing the Gap Between AI Models and Silicon: Application Deployment for Next-Generation Edge Accelerators**

This chapter examines the deployment pipeline for connecting machine learning models to specialised edge AI silicon accelerators, chips designed to efficiently process AI tasks at the network's edge. The authors present a complete workflow for deploying deep neural networksâĂŤalgorithms modelled after the human brain to recognise patterns, onto the J3DAI low-power accelerator. This accelerator is integrated into a 3D-stacked CMOS image sensor, a technology that layers image sensors and circuitry to optimise performance and space.

The chapter outlines the process from PyTorch model training to quantisation, optimisation, and binary generation with the Aidge framework. It covers hardware-accurate simulation to assess performance before silicon fabrication. Key deployment considerations include quantisation trade-offs, tiling strategies, and hardware-software co-design. The chapter shows how future edge AI accelerators can enable real-time vision processing at the sensor level.

**Chapter 5 - Multichannel Speech Enhancement Under Low-Latency Constraints: Balancing Quality and Computational Cost**

This chapter investigates speech enhancement methods designed for real-time and embedded environments. The authors compare three representative approaches: FaSNet-TAC, neural MVDR, and Tango, analysing their performance under strict latency constraints.

The study analyses trade-offs between enhancement quality, computational cost, and latency. Results reveal that context length greatly impacts speech enhancement. Architectures vary in robustness under constraints: Tango excels in low-latency scenarios, while FaSNet-TAC is more sensitive to reduced context. The chapter offers key insights for designing practical edge AI speech-processing systems.

**Chapter 6 - Pareto Optimal Benchmarking of AI Models on ARM Cortex Processors for Sustainable Embedded Systems**

This chapter presents a benchmarking framework for evaluating AI models on ARM Cortex embedded processors. The focus is placed on balancing energy efficiency, accuracy, and computational requirements to support sustainable AI deployment.

Automated benchmarking of Cortex-M0+, M4, and M7 processors reveals Pareto-optimal trade-offs between inference performance and resource consumption. Results show that different processors are optimal for specific inference scenarios. The work offers developers practical guidelines for selecting combinations that maximise performance while minimising energy use in embedded AI systems.

**Chapter 7 - Improving Classifier Latency at the Edge through ARM Helium**

This chapter explores the use of ARM Helium vector extensions to accelerate machine learning inference on low-power microcontrollers. By exploiting SIMD-based processing on Cortex-M processors, the study demonstrates measurable reductions in classifier latency.

The authors implement and evaluate a dedicated SIMD-based inference kernel on STM32 hardware. They use multiple benchmark datasets. The results confirm that vector extensions can significantly improve inference efficiency on constrained devices. The chapter highlights the growing importance of hardware acceleration techniques in enabling advanced AI functionality directly on microcontrollers.

**Chapter 8 - Structural Sensitive-Attribute Leakage in Face Recognition Embeddings for Edge AI Deployments**

This chapter addresses privacy and trustworthiness concerns related to edge-deployed face recognition systems. The authors investigate how facial embeddings from modern recognition systems can unintentionally reveal sensitive demographic attributes. These attributes include gender, age, and race.

The study shows that demographic leakage persists across datasets and deployments, indicating that demographic information is embedded within representations. The chapter evaluates mitigation methods, such as image blurring, and discusses trade-offs between recognition performance and privacy. It highlights the need for stronger safeguards and ethical considerations in edge AI with biometric data.

**Chapter 9 - tinyHLS, a Python-based Hardware Compiler for 1D and 2D Convolutional Neural Networks**

This chapter introduces tinyHLS, an open-source Python-based hardware compiler. It automatically generates HDL accelerators for convolutional neural networks. The framework simplifies the translation of TensorFlow Keras models into FPGA-compatible hardware implementations.

The chapter presents a smart-farming workflow for orange detection. Hardware-specialised CNN accelerators enable low-latency, low-power inference for edge AI. Automated hardware generation tools reduce development complexity and speed embedded AI deployment.

**Chapter 10 - Fair AI Experimentation on Edge Device Clusters via Distributed Orchestration in dAIEdge-VLab**

This chapter focuses on distributed orchestration and scheduling for clusters of heterogeneous edge devices used in AI experimentation and benchmarking. Managing distributed resources fairly and efficiently becomes increasingly important as edge AI infrastructure scales and complexity grows.

The authors propose a distributed orchestration framework integrating resource awareness, task prioritisation, and fairness. Built with Nomad and Consul in dAIEdge-VLab, it enables scalable, decentralised AI experiments. The chapter emphasises the role of orchestration technologies in federated learning, distributed benchmarking, and edge AI research.

**Chapter 11 - Physics-Informed Kalman Filtering for Multi-Step Bias Correction in Indoor Temperature Forecasting**

The final chapter presents a hybrid machine learning and physics-informed forecasting approach. It is designed for predicting indoor temperatures in winery environments. Accurate temperature forecasting is challenging because of thermal inertia and uncertainties in environmental conditions.

The solution combines autoregressive machine learning models with a two-state kinematic Kalman filter to track prediction error and thermodynamic drift velocity. This improves long-term prediction stability and realism while accounting for physical dynamics. The chapter shows how combining AI, domain knowledge, and state estimation improves reliability in real-world edge AI forecasting.

# List of Figures

# List of Tables

# List of Contributors

**Abate, Lorenzo,** *Università degli Studi di Napoli Federico II, Italy*

**Amft, Oliver,** *Intelligent Embedded Systems (IES) - Lab, University of Freiburg, Germany; Hahn-Schickard, Germany*

**Auzanneau, Fabrice,** *Université Paris-Saclay, CEA-List, France*

**Barbareschi, Mario,** *Università degli Studi di Napoli Federico II, Italy*

**Benslimane, Zahra,** *Université Paris-Saclay, CEA-List, France*

**Braun, Silke,** *Infineon Technologies Austria AG, Austria*

**Cardinali, Matteo,** *AGRICOLUS, Italy*

**Chersi, Fabian,** *Université Paris-Saclay, CEA-List, France*

**Coppola, Marcello,** *STMicroelectronics, France*

**Daoutis, Georgios,** *Hellenic Mediterranean University, Greece*

**Divernois, Margaux,** *HES-SO, Switzerland*

**Dubbelman, Gijs,** *Eindhoven University of Technology, Netherlands*

**Dupertuis, Baptiste,** *HES-SO, Switzerland*

**Emmanuele, Antonio,** *Università degli Studi di Napoli Federico II, Italy*

**Farrugia, Axel,** *Université Paris-Saclay, CEA-List, France*

**Favre, Dorvan,** *HES-SO, Switzerland*

**Gaede, Raphael,** *Fraunhofer IMS, Germany*

**Helms, Domenik,** *German Aerospace Center (DLR), Germany*

**Hoyer, Ingo,** *Fraunhofer IMS, Germany*

**Huguenin, Maïck,** *HES-SO, Switzerland*

**Jain, Pranay,** *Fraunhofer Institute for Integrated Circuits IIS, Germany; Intelligent Embedded Systems (IES) - Lab, University of Freiburg, Germany*

**Jovančević, Igor,** *Computer Science Center, University of Montenegro, Montenegro; Fain Tech, Montenegro*

**Köber, Göran,** *Intelligent Embedded Systems (IES) - Lab, University of Freiburg, Germany*

**Kappert, Holger,** *Fraunhofer IMS, Germany*

**Kasper, Maximilian,** *Fraunhofer Institute for Integrated Circuits IIS, Germany*

**Klös, Verena,** *Carl von Ossietzky Universität Oldenburg, Germany*

**Kornaros, George,** *Hellenic Mediterranean University, Greece*

**Linnartz, Jean-Paul,** *Eindhoven University of Technology, Netherlands*

**Liu, Erica,** *Eindhoven University of Technology, Netherlands*

**Milazzo, Filippo,** *AGRICOLUS, Italy*

**Millet, Raphael,** *Université Paris-Saclay, CEA-List, France*

**Milović, Nikola,** *Fain Tech, Montenegro*

**Moineau, Cyril,** *Université Paris-Saclay, CEA-List, France*

**Olivares, Enrique Orozco,** *Eindhoven University of Technology, Netherlands*

**Osterwind, Adrian,** *German Aerospace Center (DLR), Germany*

**Pazos, Nuria,** *HES-SO, Switzerland*

**Pižurica, Nikola,** *Computer Science Center, University of Montenegro, Montenegro*

**Plinge, Axel,** *Fraunhofer Institute for Integrated Circuits IIS, Germany*

**Poreba, Martyna,** *Université Paris-Saclay, CEA-List, France*

**Prado, Miguel de,** *VERSES, USA*

**Pype, Patrick,** *NXP Semiconductors, Belgium*

**Rebstein, Grégoire,** *HES-SO, Switzerland*

**Rolfes, Carsten,** *Fraunhofer IMS, Germany*

**Roscini, Mauro,** *AGRICOLUS, Italy*

**Seidl, Karsten,** *Fraunhofer IMS, Germany; University of Duisburg-Essen, Germany*

**Serizel, Romain,** *Université de Lorraine, INRIA, LORIA, France*

**Seuss, Dominik,** *Fraunhofer Institute for Integrated Circuits IIS, Germany; Center for Artificial Intelligence and Robotics (CAIRO), Technische Hochschule Würzburg-Schweinfurt, Germany*

**Szczepanski, Michal,** *Université Paris-Saclay, CEA-List, France*

**Tain, Benoit,** *Université Paris-Saclay, CEA-List, France*

**Thuries, Sebastien,** *Université Paris-Saclay, CEA-List, France*

**Tomoutzoglou, Othon,** *Neotera, Italy*

**Verbelen, Tim,** *VERSES, USA*

**Vermesan, Ovidiu,** *SINTEF AS, Norway*

**Vyas, Devendra,** *VERSES, USA*

# 1

# Edge AI System-of-Systems Reference Architecture Engineering Foundations and Multi-Dimensional Views

**Ovidiu Vermesan[1], Marcello Coppola[2], Silke Braun[3], and Patrick Pype[4]**

[1]SINTEF AS, Norway
[2]STMicroelectronics, France
[3]Infineon Technologies Austria AG, Austria
[4]NXP Semiconductors, Belgium

## Abstract

Edge AI systems are emerging from the convergence of IoT, edge computing, AI, agentic AI, and embodied, physical generative edge AI delivering adaptive, autonomous behaviour under physical, cyber, and operational constraints while remaining trustworthy. This article frames edge AI as a complex system-of-systems in which hardware, software, models, and data continuously co-evolve across heterogeneous "multi-X" environments: multiple systems, modalities, and agents distributed from the edge to the cloud. The article argues that as edge AI technologies are maturing, there is a need for a standardised, application-agnostic reference architecture to provide a shared lexicon and taxonomy, reduce integration errors, and expose opportunities for reusable assets and productive interoperability and standardisation. The paper grounds this need in systems engineering and introduces a quad-optimisation paradigm for balancing competing objectives during design and operation. The article presents a design framework and a multi-dimensional architecture organised into three complementary views: quality properties for trustworthiness and dependability, a layered technology stack within each tier, and a processing continuum that partitions intelligence across edge-to-cloud tiers. Finally, the article discusses value creation, interoperability, and how a

DOI: 10.1201/9788743815211-1

common baseline supports the development of complex edge AI systems-of-systems and their verification, validation, testing and benchmarking.

**Keywords:** edge AI, edge AI systems reference architecture, generative edge AI, agentic edge AI, embodied edge AI, physical edge AI.

## 1.1 Edge AI as a Complex System-of-Systems

Edge AI systems represent a class of engineered systems arising from the deep convergence of the Internet of Things (IoT), edge computing paradigms, Artificial Intelligence (AI), generative AI (GenAI), AI agents, and agentic AI architectures as represented in Figure 1.1. Edge AI systems operate continuously under stringent physical, cyber, and operational constraints while remaining highly adaptive, autonomous, and thoroughly trustworthy [14].

From a rigorous systems engineering perspective, this technological convergence produces a highly complex system-of-systems (SoS). Within this SoS, hardware modules, software components, deployed AI models, and real-time data are tightly coupled and continuously evolving together.

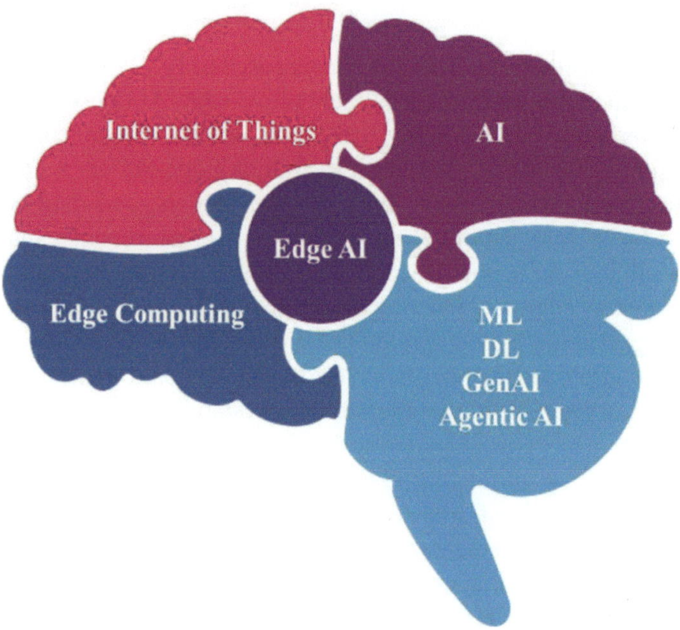


**Figure 1.1** Edge AI as a complex system-of-systems.

This intrinsic, compounding complexity creates an interlinked scientific and engineering rationale for developing a standardised, application-agnostic reference architecture tailored for edge AI environments.

Traditional systems engineering principles emphasise abstraction, clear separation of concerns, requirements traceability, and comprehensive lifecycle thinking. However, edge AI systems actively challenge these traditional principles because critical functionality and system-quality properties emerge dynamically from complex interactions across distributed components rather than originating from isolated, static subsystems.

For instance, architectural decisions at the silicon hardware level directly and in real-time influence the feasibility, energy efficiency, inference latency, and overall system reliability of edge AI models. Concurrently, data governance policies and lifecycle management protocols for machine learning (ML) or deep learning (DL) models profoundly affect the system's trustworthiness and compliance with stringent regulatory frameworks. A robust reference architecture provides a stable, formalised conceptual structure that makes these intricate cross-layer interactions explicitly visible and analysable. This structural clarity enables systematic engineering trade-off analysis and robust system design, actively preventing brittle, ad hoc integrations.

In this context, this conceptual article proposes a foundational framework intended to guide and shape future architectural work. Because its primary purpose is to establish a theoretical blueprint for strategic design, it does not rely on empirical data or require experimental validation. Instead, the principles and structural concepts outlined herein are broadly applicable to upcoming development initiatives, providing teams with a cohesive, forward-looking vision to direct their long-term technical decisions.

The article's structure is briefly introduced below. The article reviews reference-architecture concepts from systems engineering as a foundation for standardisation and clarifies the purpose of an application-agnostic edge AI systems reference architecture and the value it enables. The article introduces the quad-optimisation paradigm to manage trade-offs across performance, resources, trust, and lifecycle evolution. It outlines a practical framework for designing the reference architecture across projects and disciplines. The following subsections present the Quality Properties View to engineer trustworthiness and dependability above the single-system level and detail the Technology Stack and Processing Continuum views to align tiers, layers, and intelligence partitioning. The article concludes by discussing value, interoperability, domain maturity, and the architecture's role as a baseline for edge AI systems designers and stakeholders

## 1.2 The Foundations of Reference Architectures in Systems Engineering

A reference architecture serves as an authoritative blueprint for a specific subject or domain. This foundational document actively guides and constrains the creation of multiple subsequent architectures and concrete solutions [19]. By providing a rigorous framework of technical standards and engineering rules, a reference architecture ensures that implementations across a complex domain remain highly repeatable, deeply interoperable, and fundamentally consistent. Reference architectures explicitly define the necessary conditions to achieve overarching domain goals and strategic objectives. Consequently, downstream solutions describe precisely how to achieve these goals as real-world implementations. These solution architectures include the concrete, specific details regarding the processes and computational resources required to deliver critical missions, system capabilities, and technological services.

Reference architectures do not exist in isolation; they are complemented by architecture frameworks. These frameworks provide structured guidance and rules for classifying and organising complex system information. They consist of an organised set of layered, hierarchical artefacts encompassing architectural descriptions, stakeholder perspectives, visualisations, and fundamental building blocks. Furthermore, these frameworks define how architectural data elements fit together and relate within the broader system. Reference models are subsequently utilised to construct these architectures, representing formalised taxonomies that provide standardised categorisation of system entities.

There is no "one-size-fits-all" approach to systems architecture as the systems must address the users' physical constrains and environmental factors as illustrated in Figure 1.2. Because every technological domain possesses unique characteristics and operational constraints, reference architectures naturally vary in scope, levels of abstraction, and overall coverage. Each proposed architecture must be stringently "fit-for-purpose," designed specifically to maximise functional value and accelerate technological development within its intended domain.

When designing a robust reference architecture, several core components must be meticulously addressed. The architecture must clearly identify its fundamental purpose, specifically outlining the goals, objectives, and engineering problems it intends to solve. It must specify its principles, establishing the high-level engineering foundations that drive technical positions

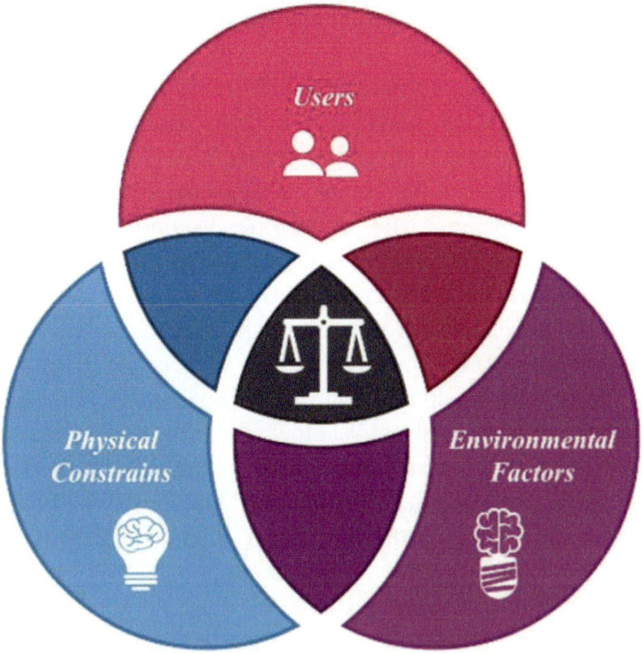


**Figure 1.2** Edge AI systems boundaries.

and structural patterns. Furthermore, it must define technical positions by integrating standards, policies, and communication protocols to constrain solutions and ensure regulatory compliance. The architecture must also provide general architectural patterns, unconstrained by specific implementation details, to guide development. Finally, establishing a standardised vocabulary through a comprehensive glossary of terms ensures consistent communication among diverse engineering teams [2].

Consequently, a complete and mature reference architecture encompasses a clearly articulated goal and problem space, detailing the recurring problem, operational context, and intended use cases. It defines strict scope and boundaries, establishing the required level of granular detail while explicitly stating what remains outside the architecture's purview. It establishes principles and guidelines for deploying specific technologies, forming a rational basis for future technical decision-making. The architecture identifies reusable components and their intricate relationships across logical, process, physical, and scenario-based views. Finally, it inherently incorporates industry best practices, integrating accepted external standards and common architectural patterns [2, 21].

Standards such as ISO 15704:2019 [11], ISO/IEC/IEEE DIS 42024 [7] and ISO/IEC/IEEE DIS 42042 [9] address structuring architectural knowledge in a clear, consistent, and reusable way and emphasise that a reference architecture should not be just a diagram, but a well-defined set of concepts, relationships, and rules that guide system design across multiple implementations. A key common element is the use of viewpoints and views. Each standard recognises that stakeholders have distinct concerns, so architectures must be described from multiple perspectives. This ensures that business, functional, information, and technical aspects are all addressed in a coordinated manner. The standards align in defining the importance of concepts, constructs, and relationships. Whether framed as enterprise constructs in ISO 15704:2019 [11] or architectural elements in the ISO/IEC/IEEE standards, the standards stress the need for a formal vocabulary and meta-model to avoid ambiguity and enable interoperability. The standards acknowledge that architectures evolve over time and must support phases such as design, implementation, operation, and evolution.

The conceptualisation of a system's architecture, as defined in ISO/IEC/IEEE 42010:2022 [5], "Systems and software engineering – Architecture," helps understand the system's essence and key properties related to its behaviour and composition. The standard specifies requirements for the structure and expression of an architecture description (AD) for various entities, including software, systems, enterprises, systems of systems, families of systems, products (goods or services), product lines, service lines, technologies, and business domains. The document distinguishes the architecture of an entity of interest from an AD that expresses that architecture and specifies requirements for the use of architectural concepts and their relationships as captured in an AD. It does not specify requirements for any entity of interest or its environment.

The concept described in the standard can support the first steps in defining an edge AI systems reference architecture, as the standard specifies in general requirements for an architecture description framework (ADF), an architecture description language (ADL), architecture viewpoints, and model kinds to usefully support the development and use of an AD. It describes the system's structure, including its entities, and the interactions between each entity and the environment.

ISO/IEC/IEEE 42010:2022 [5] considers that an architecture description expresses the architecture of a system of interest, in this case, an edge AI system. While an architecture can be abstract, consisting of concepts and properties, an AD is a work product formalising an architecture, including one or more architecture views. An architecture view addresses one or more concerns of the edge AI system's stakeholders.

An architecture view expresses the architecture of the system of interest from a given architecture viewpoint. As a result, the architecture framework (AF) contains the conventions, principles, and practices for describing architectures established within a specific domain of application and/or community of stakeholders. The AF can be described along several dimensions, establishing conventions for the construction, interpretation, and use of a system's architecture from the perspective of specific system concerns.

A graphical representation of the entities described, and their interrelationships is presented in Figure 1.3.

The lifecycle perspective ensures that reference architectures remain relevant and adaptable. Consistency and traceability are also central. Each of the ISO 15704:2019 [11], ISO/IEC/IEEE DIS 42024 [7] and ISO/IEC/IEEE DIS 42042 [9] standards requires that architectural decisions, elements, and views be logically connected, allowing stakeholders to trace requirements through implementation and assess impacts of change. All these standards promote reusability and governance. Reference architectures are intended to provide

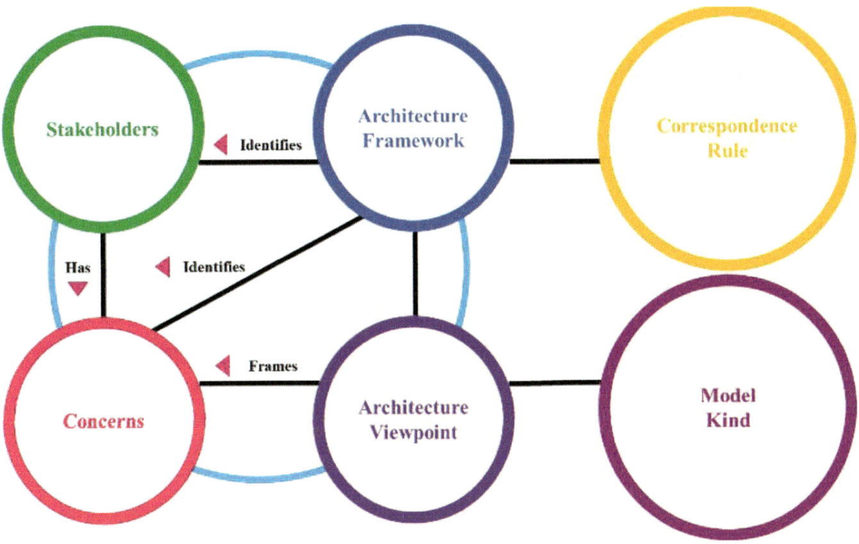


**Figure 1.3** Graphical representation of entities and their interrelationships (Adapted from ISO/IEC/IEEE 42010:2022 [5]).

reusable patterns, constraints, and best practices, while also supporting governance mechanisms that ensure compliance and alignment across systems and projects.

## 1.3 Purpose of an Edge AI Systems Reference Architecture

Systems engineering principles emphasise abstraction, separation of concerns, traceability, and lifecycle thinking. Edge AI systems challenge these principles because functionality and quality properties emerge from interactions across distributed components rather than from isolated subsystems. Decisions made at the hardware level directly influence the feasibility, energy efficiency, latency, and reliability of edge AI models, while data governance and model lifecycle management affect trustworthiness and regulatory compliance. An edge AI systems reference architecture provides a stable conceptual structure that makes these interactions explicit and analysable, enabling systematic trade-off analysis and robust design rather than ad hoc integration.

An edge AI systems reference architecture provides a shared, application-agnostic architectural baseline for engineering, integrating, and evolving edge AI systems in the presence of system heterogeneity. Edge deployments differ widely in compute and memory budgets, sensors and modalities, network connectivity, safety and security exposure, energy constraints, and lifecycle practices. Without a common architectural frame, each solution tends to develop its own terminology, assumptions, and interfaces, making cross-application communication, integration, and reuse inefficient and error prone.

This need becomes more acute as edge AI systems shift from relatively simple products to true systems-of-systems implemented in autonomous systems. Modern deployments increasingly comprise multiple edge nodes, multiple edge AI-enabled functions, multiple stakeholders, and multiple operational domains, with intelligence distributed across edge-to-cloud tiers. The resulting coupling across application boundaries and technical layers makes it difficult to maintain coherence, manage change, and reason about emergent behaviour unless there is an explicit architectural structure that can be shared and governed.

Edge AI systems-of-systems also combine multiple edge AI methods and interaction patterns within a single operational envelope. Machine learning (ML), deep learning (DL), generative AI, and agentic edge AI frequently coexist, interact, and co-adapt, often with different data requirements, safety implications, explainability needs, and runtime resource profiles. A reference architecture makes these method families key concerns, enabling consistent placement of responsibilities (for example, where generation is allowed, where agents can act, and where constraints are enforced) and supporting disciplined partitioning of intelligence across tiers.

A defining purpose is to enable co-design and optimisation across hardware, software, AI, and data as a single engineered whole. At the edge, architectural choices such as model form, quantisation strategy, scheduling, accelerators, memory hierarchy, data pipelines, and privacy/security controls are tightly interdependent. A reference architecture establishes the canonical set of architectural elements, interfaces, and viewpoints needed to jointly optimise these dimensions, rather than optimising each element in isolation and discovering conflicts late during integration or operation.

Another core purpose is to provide a common reference for comparing edge AI systems in verification, validation, testing, and benchmarking. Edge AI quality is multi-dimensional, spanning functional correctness, timing predictability, robustness, safety, security, privacy, resilience, and maintainability under continuous updates. A reference architecture supports comparable claims by standardising how systems are described, what constitutes evidence, which qualities are assessed at which level (component, subsystem, system, and SoS), and how assumptions and constraints are recorded. This directly reduces ambiguity in test scope, improves traceability from requirements to evidence, and enables fair benchmarking across heterogeneous platforms and workloads.

These purposes align with the intent of TOGAF's principles [20, 21], which frame architecture as a mechanism to translate drivers into a governed, coherent set of building blocks and implementation guidance. In TOGAF's terms, a reference architecture supports stakeholder alignment by providing a stable target architecture pattern that projects can tailor while remaining interoperable. It improves decision-making by making trade-offs explicit early, informs migration planning by clarifying what can be standardised versus what must vary, and enables reuse through a consistent catalogue of architectural building blocks, patterns, and interfaces across a portfolio of edge AI solutions [20].

They also align with ISO/IEC/IEEE 42010:2022 [5], which emphasises architecture description to address stakeholder concerns through viewpoints, views, and documented rationale. For edge AI, the reference architecture's purpose is to make concerns such as trustworthiness, dependability (including safety and security), data governance, and lifecycle evolution explicit and analysable, rather than implicit and scattered across implementations. By standardising viewpoints and terminology, it strengthens communication across disciplines, supports the analysis of alternatives and impacts, and provides a basis for consistency checking across systems and over time as systems evolve.

As a result, an edge AI systems reference architecture exists to manage heterogeneity and SoS complexity, to structure the co-design of hardware–software–AI–data under edge constraints, and to provide a standardised basis for communication, governance, comparison, and evidence-driven assurance. It is the shared starting point that makes scalable engineering, interoperability, and credible verification, validation, testing and benchmarking achievable as the edge AI domain matures.

## 1.4 The Paradigm of Quad-Optimisation

The absolute requirement for continuous, simultaneous optimisation across hardware, software, the technology stack, and data pipelines, referred to as quad-optimisation, further drives the critical need for a standardised reference edge AI systems architecture, as illustrated in Figure 1.4 [14].

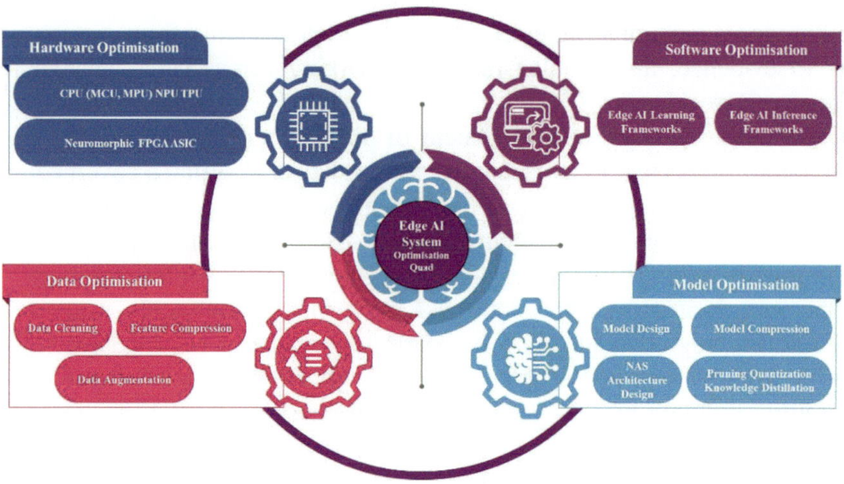


**Figure 1.4** Edge AI quad optimisation.

In constrained edge environments, systemic optimisation objectives are often in conflict with one another. Engineers must constantly navigate trade-offs such as edge AI model accuracy versus physical energy consumption, inference latency versus model explainability, or data privacy versus high availability. Crucially, these complex trade-offs cannot be resolved locally within a single architectural layer or isolated component. A comprehensive reference architecture deliberately embeds quad optimisation as a first-class architectural concern. This embedding allows system designers to logically reason about structural co-evolution and dynamic adaptation across the full system lifecycle, encompassing initial deployment, continuous operation, remote monitoring, and over-the-air updates for edge AI-driven systems.

This principle of quad-optimisation can be clearly exemplified by the engineering requirements of a battery-powered wildlife edge camera. This system imposes a significant operational trade-off between the edge AI model's detection accuracy and the underlying hardware's energy efficiency. System designers might intentionally select a heavily quantised neural network over a full-precision model, strategically accepting a minor percentage drop in animal detection accuracy. This precise trade-off enables the inference software to run on a significantly smaller, less expensive microcontroller with vastly reduced RAM requirements. This architectural decision extends the remote device's battery life from mere weeks to several months, successfully satisfying the critical sustainability quality property.

The identical engineering principle applies to a collaborative robotic arm designed to work in close physical proximity to human operators. Here, system architects must delicately balance high-resolution data fidelity with strict edge AI system latency limits. The edge AI system might be deliberately configured to process low-resolution, monochrome video data streams rather than high-definition colour streams. By intentionally reducing data richness, the edge AI algorithm becomes computationally simpler, and the software processing time decreases exponentially. This specific architectural optimisation allows the edge hardware to execute emergency safety stops in microseconds, thereby prioritising the critical quality property of human safety over unnecessary image detail.

ISO/IEC/IEEE 42010:2022 provides a foundational, conceptual framework for scientifically describing and modelling complex edge AI systems. The standard formalises the critical technical distinction between a system's physical architecture and its theoretical architectural description. Furthermore, it introduces the vital concepts of system stakeholders, engineering concerns, viewpoints, and architectural views.

In the specific context of edge AI, this standardised framework is essential. Different system stakeholders, including operational system managers, silicon hardware engineers, software developers, AI algorithm designers, embedded systems experts, data scientists, cybersecurity specialists, and domain experts, have highly distinct and often competing engineering concerns. A reference architecture structured strictly according to ISO/IEC/IEEE 42010:2022 [5] explicitly addresses these multifaceted concerns through well-defined, standardised architectural views. This formalised approach guarantees structural consistency, requirements traceability, and clear engineering communication across diverse technical disciplines and application domains.

In practice, quad-optimisation is applied by deeply integrating it into the entire development lifecycle of an edge AI system. Rather than acting as a single, isolated step, it functions as a continuous, iterative process that systematically increases performance outcomes across all phases of development. This optimisation loop begins at the very foundation with requirements engineering and system design, subsequently driving the specific architectural choices for hardware (HW), software (SW), AI models, and data pipelines. This integrated approach extends well beyond the initial design phases; the quad-optimisation framework becomes the standard metric for guiding the rigorous verification, validation, testing, and benchmarking of complex, distributed edge AI systems of systems.

## 1.5 Methodology and Framework for Edge AI Systems Reference Architecture Design

A rigorous methodology for establishing architecture principles follows a structured, cyclical process. This systematic approach begins by identifying the underlying key business requirements and architectural drivers that necessitate the formulation of specific engineering principles. These fundamental drivers provide the empirical rationale for development and ensure tight alignment with broader organisational strategy and governance objectives.

Three distinct stream activities, assess, aim, and act [3], can be effectively combined with generic system development processes. This integration is generally regarded as a practical realisation of the generalised structural lifecycle required to define complex reference architectures [1], as illustrated in Figure 1.5.

**Figure 1.5** Stream of activities used for defining a reference architecture.

The architecture principles, acting as the foundation for best practices based on this stream-of-activities approach, are further refined in subsequent stages. These sub-processes determine, specify, classify, validate, and practically apply the architecture principles. The following sub-process utilises these established principles to definitively determine whether ongoing engineering activities comply with the intended architecture [2]. The final sub-process manages architecture changes and lifecycle iterations, which may inevitably necessitate restarting the initial assessment sub-process.

The assess, aim, and act streams of activities are iterative and cyclically dependent, actively supporting the continuous improvement of the reference architecture. During assessment activities, engineers identify the precise technical motivation for the reference architecture while meticulously gathering the rigorous requirements for a possible solution. These requirements serve as direct input to the aim process, wherein a reference architecture solution is theoretically designed to meet them. The physical implementation, including the practical deployment of the architecture, is subsequently addressed by the act process. The technical requirements specify the measurable properties the reference architecture should possess, and the underlying motivations explain why diverse stakeholders require them. The final design directly reflects how an implemented reference architecture successfully meets these stringent requirements.

A comparison with the TOGAF Architecture Development Method (ADM) [20], the ADM provides a highly specific, standardised way to implement these assess, aim, and act processes. The ADM's architecture vision phase focuses intensely on understanding the essential engineering problem and generating a solution vision, effectively serving as a primary assess/aim iteration. The technology architecture phase provides further granular assess/aim iterations. Depending on the specific situational context, the engineering focus shifts between understanding the problem constraints (assess) and developing the structural solution (aim). Identifying opportunities, generating solutions, and conducting migration planning yield further vital iterations of the aim process, continuously elaborating on the actual intended reference architecture. Finally, the implementation, governance, and architecture change management phases, including the physical realisation of the envisaged architecture, directly correspond to the foundational act process.

Designing a resilient edge AI system is a demanding engineering task, as it requires continually balancing user needs, physical constraints, and environmental factors that often conflict with one another. The design process for edge AI systems invariably begins with selecting the optimal architectural style, also referred to as an architectural pattern, best suited to the system's explicit operational requirements.

An architectural style comprises a set of architectural patterns that share distinct technical characteristics, providing general engineering guidance for reliably solving a specific class of problems within a particular operational context. Each selected architecture style focuses on harmonising and optimising the interplay between hardware, software, selected AI methods, algorithms, software frameworks, operational data, and training datasets.

The comprehensive approach utilised to develop the edge AI systems reference architecture included identifying highly common engineering activities across different industrial value chains. It further involved precisely determining how these disparate functional components are seamlessly combined to create a viable edge AI solution. This was done with the core understanding that the resulting reference architecture must illustrate the logical generalisation of multiple distinct, successful solutions and implementations across different industrial sectors. Foundational reference models that support understanding the structural hierarchy of edge AI systems provide the necessary basics of these systems. These models vary in technical detail, successfully identifying the core architectural elements required for operation.

The rigorous methodology employed for constructing such a reference architecture integrates established architectural description principles with proven, concrete concepts from both edge computing [22] and 3D IoT [15] architectural paradigms as illustrated in Figure 1.6.

The relevance of this methodology is applied across diverse industrial domains, including advanced manufacturing, digital industry, energy, precision agroindustry, beverage, intelligent mobility, and broader digital society applications. In these industrial contexts, rapid, real-time data preprocessing, robust local autonomy, and fail-safe decision-making are essential. Within these domains, a reference edge AI systems architecture functions as a primary scientific and engineering instrument. It effectively structures inherent system complexity, actively supports experimental reproducibility, and enables the systematic, safe evolution of highly scalable, secure, and computationally efficient edge AI systems grounded entirely in recognised international standards.

The edge AI systems reference architecture was conceptualised and designed in accordance with the foundational engineering principles and technical definitions established in major international standards.

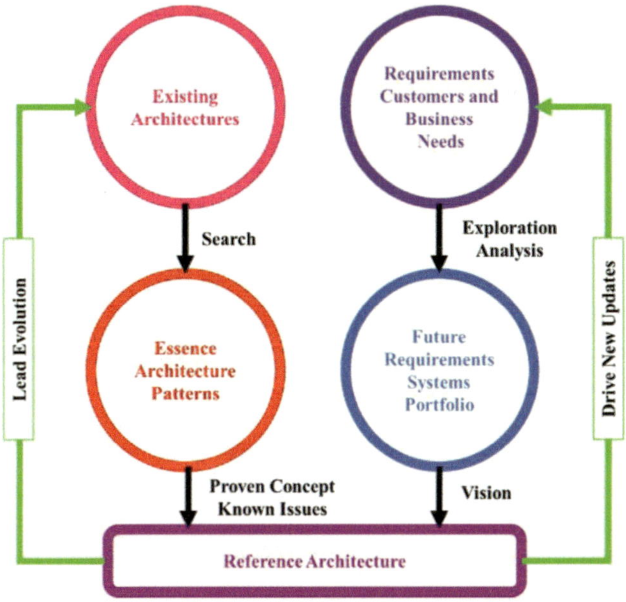


**Figure 1.6** Reference architecture methodology development.

These include ISO/IEC/IEEE 42010:2022 [5], ISO/IEC/IEEE 42020:2019 [6], ISO/IEC/IEEE DIS 42024 [7], ISO/IEC/IEEE 42030:2019 [8], ISO/IEC/IEEE DIS 42042 [9], ISO/IEC/IEEE 15288:2023 [10], ISO/IEC 25010:2023 [12], and the comprehensive TOGAF® Standard 10th edition. This alignment and adherence to standardised, globally recognised frameworks ensure that the resulting architecture provides a robust, scientifically sound foundation for edge AI system development that consistently meets modern engineering expectations.

From a pure technology perspective, the architecture dynamically synthesises proven engineering concepts by systematically mining and logically generalising prior industry experience. It draws from established frameworks such as the Industrial Internet Reference Architecture (IIRA) [4], the structured 3D IoT Layered Architecture [15], and the Reference Architecture Model for Edge Computing (RAMEC) [22].

### 1.5.1 Industrial Internet Reference Architecture (IIRA)

IIRA [4] shown in Figure 1.7 is a standards-based, open architectural framework designed to guide the design and integration of Industrial Internet of Things (IIoT) systems. It is intentionally abstract and generic, allowing it to be applied across diverse industrial domains such as manufacturing, energy, transportation, and healthcare. Rather than prescribing specific technologies or products, IIRA provides a common language and structure for describing complex systems.

At its foundation, IIRA adopts the ISO/IEC/IEEE 42010:2022 standard for architecture description. This standard defines how architectures should be expressed, including the use of viewpoints, stakeholders, and concerns. By aligning with this model, IIRA establishes a consistent ontology for describing IIoT systems, enabling architects, engineers, and stakeholders to communicate using shared concepts and conventions.

The architecture is organised around four primary viewpoints, each addressing a different set of concerns.

The business viewpoint focuses on stakeholders, their objectives, and the value the system is expected to deliver. It captures business goals, regulatory considerations, and economic drivers, ensuring that technical decisions align with organisational priorities.

The usage viewpoint describes how the system is expected to be used in practice. It models interactions as sequences of activities involving human users, automated systems, or both. This viewpoint helps clarify operational

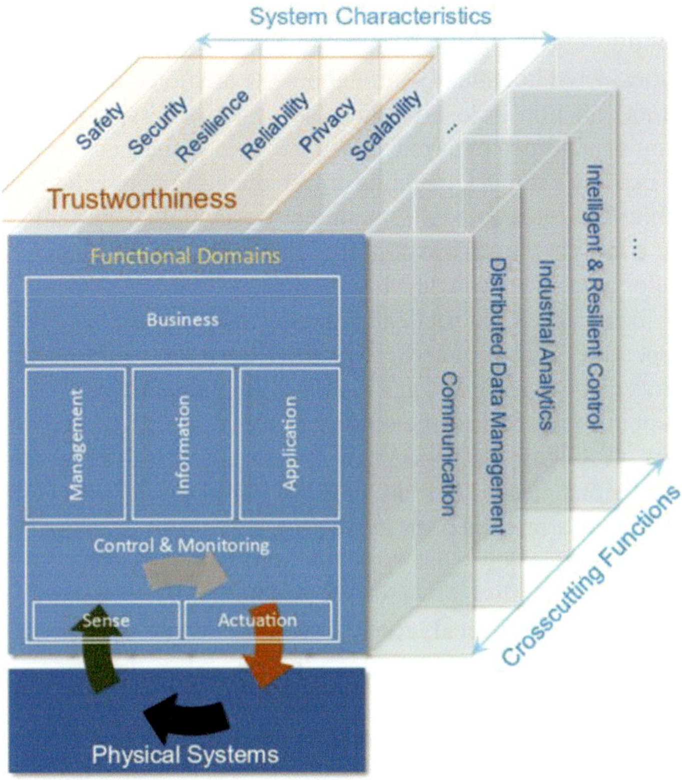


**Figure 1.7** IIRA - Functional domains, crosscutting functions and system characteristics.

scenarios, workflows, and system behaviours from an end-user or operational perspective.

The functional viewpoint provides a structural decomposition of the system into functional components and defines how these components interact. It specifies interfaces, data flows, and responsibilities without committing to specific technologies. This abstraction allows designers to reason about system capabilities independently of implementation details.

The implementation viewpoint maps the functional components to concrete technologies, platforms, and deployment configurations. It addresses concerns such as hardware, software frameworks, communication protocols, and integration mechanisms required to realise the system in practice.

In addition to these viewpoints, IIRA introduces two important dimensions that extend across the functional model. System characteristics describe emergent properties arising from component interactions, such as safety, security, reliability, and scalability. These are not tied to a single component but must be considered holistically throughout the architecture.

Crosscutting functions, closely related to system characteristics, represent supporting capabilities required across multiple functional components. Connectivity is a key example, enabling communication between distributed elements. While the terminology sometimes overlaps with system characteristics, both concepts emphasise concerns that span the entire architecture rather than belonging to a single layer or module.

IIRA provides a structured yet flexible framework that helps organisations design interoperable, scalable, and robust IIoT systems while maintaining alignment between business goals and technical implementation.

The IIRA contributes to the development of the edge AI systems reference architecture by providing the concept of system characteristic elements as part of its foundational design. The architecture introduces a "trustworthiness view" that serves as a reference for evaluating and ensuring overall system integrity. By embedding key characteristics into this view, namely safety, security, resilience, reliability, privacy, and scalability, the systems designed and implemented are functional, robust and dependable across industrial environments.

### 1.5.2 3D IoT Layered Architecture

The 3D IoT Reference Architecture [15] illustrated in Figure 1.8 extends the traditional layered IoT model by adding two extra dimensions to better capture how real-world IoT systems behave and are engineered. Instead of viewing IoT purely as a stack of functional layers, this approach frames the system as a three-dimensional structure where layers, cross-cutting functions, and system properties interact.

The first dimension consists of the traditional horizontal layers, which represent the core functional decomposition of IoT systems. These layers typically include device, connectivity, data processing, and application levels, each responsible for specific operations. This layered structure reflects how data flows from physical devices up to user-facing services and how control flows in the opposite direction.

The second dimension introduces cross-cutting functions that span multiple layers rather than belonging to a single layer. These functions address concerns such as security, privacy, identity management, and interoperability. Because these concerns must be consistently enforced across the entire

**Figure 1.8** 3D IoT layered architecture.

system, they cannot be isolated within a single layer. For example, security must be embedded at the device level, maintained during communication, and enforced in data processing and applications.

The third dimension focuses on system properties, which describe the overall qualities of the IoT system. These properties include trustworthiness, reliability, scalability, and performance. They emerge from the proper implementation and interaction of both layered functions and cross-cutting concerns. Trustworthiness is strongly influenced by how effectively security and privacy mechanisms are integrated across all layers.

Together, these three dimensions provide a more comprehensive architectural view. The model allows designers to analyse IoT systems not only in terms of functional decomposition but also in terms of system-wide qualities and transversal concerns. This multidimensional perspective supports better design decisions, ensuring that critical aspects such as security and system reliability are consistently addressed throughout the architecture rather than treated as afterthoughts.

The 3D IoT layered architecture brings important elements to the edge AI systems reference architecture by introducing the concept of cross-cutting functions that span multiple tiers rather than being confined to a single layer. This multi-dimensional approach recognises that key concerns, such as security, privacy, identity management, and interoperability, cannot be isolated within an individual layer without creating vulnerabilities; instead, they must be consistently enforced across the entire system. By providing structural input through its third dimension, the architecture adds a system properties dimension, ensuring that the overall qualities and integrity of the IoT ecosystem are maintained from edge devices to the cloud embedded into the edge AI systems reference architecture.

### 1.5.3 Reference Architecture Model for Edge Computing (RAMEC)

RAMEC [22] presented in Figure 1.9 provides a structured way to describe and analyse edge systems by organising them across three complementary viewpoints: cross-layer concerns, hierarchy levels, and technology layers.

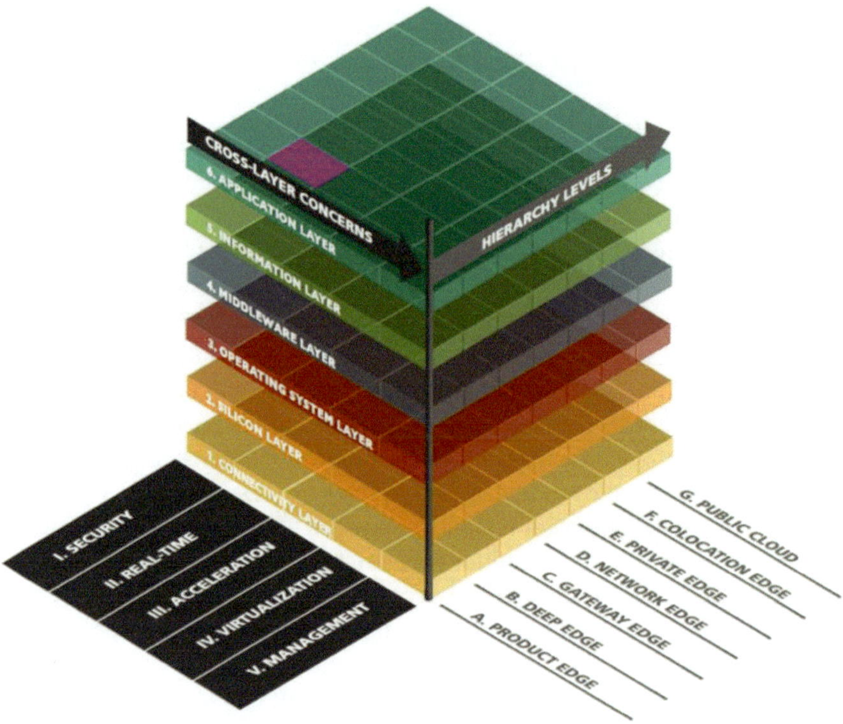


**Figure 1.9** Reference architecture model for edge computing (RAMEC).

Together, these viewpoints help clarify how diverse edge deployments can be understood within a single conceptual framework, despite wide variation in requirements and implementations.

Cross-layer concerns represent system-wide requirements that span all layers and hierarchy levels. These include security, real-time capabilities, AI acceleration, virtualisation and system management. Their characteristics are not uniform but depend heavily on where computation occurs in the topology. For example, strict real-time constraints and lightweight security mechanisms may dominate at the product or deep edge, while stronger, more resource-intensive security and orchestration mechanisms are typical at higher levels, such as the cloud. This viewpoint emphasises that these concerns must be consistently addressed but adapted to the context.

The hierarchy levels describe a continuum of processing locations from the physical device to centralised cloud infrastructure. At the lowest level, the product edge resides directly on intelligent devices, followed by the deep edge, which provides slightly more computational capability close to the source of data. The gateway edge aggregates and communicates with devices, often functioning similarly to a programmable logic controller. Above this sits the network edge, then the private edge, which may represent on-premises data centres, followed by the co-location edge or cloudlet, and finally the public cloud. Each level offers increasing computational power, storage, and abstraction, but typically at the cost of higher latency and reduced immediacy of control.

The technology layers define the stack of components required to implement edge computing systems. At the foundation is the connectivity layer, which enables communication across devices and systems. Above it lies the silicon layer, representing the hardware capabilities such as CPUs, GPUs, and specialised accelerators. The operating system layer manages hardware resources and provides basic services. Middleware adds abstraction and interoperability, enabling distributed communication and orchestration. The information layer handles data models, storage, and processing, while the application layer delivers domain-specific functionality to end users or systems.

RAMEC highlights that edge computing is not a single architectural pattern but a spectrum of possible deployments. By mapping use cases across hierarchy levels, technology layers, and cross-layer concerns, it becomes clear that different scenarios impose very different requirements on both software and hardware. As a result, no universal solution exists, and systems must be carefully designed according to their specific operational context and constraints.

Since edge AI represents a rapidly emerging, highly disruptive technology driving entirely novel applications, relying solely on historical use cases for structural validation is scientifically insufficient. Consequently, the reference architecture mandates an incremental, iterative approach to practical implementation and hardware prototyping. It utilises these practical engineering steps as important alternative evidence for continuous validation and as a necessary proof of concept.

To accurately capture both the complex system construction and its dynamic usage context, the architecture establishes three primary, interdependent views: the Computing Processing Continuum View, the Technology Stack View, and the Quality Properties View [14]. These specific views strongly facilitate detailed technical decompositions, such as successfully identifying granular functional requirements or isolating specific software building blocks within broader hardware modules.

This structured decomposition allows engineers to clearly explain the intricate relationships between these elements. Furthermore, it enables the precise allocation of specific structural building blocks to critical system functions, ensuring that optimal performance, efficient resource optimisation, and highly effective exception handling are reliably realised through the complex interaction of various distributed components.

The engineering ability to systematically generate targeted, specific views is fundamental for addressing the distinct technical concerns of various project stakeholders, ranging from low-level systems developers to high-level end users.

To actively secure and maintain stakeholder support, the architecture dynamically presents complex system information in accessible formats directly relevant to specific technical interests. This capability relies entirely on the precise, standardised distinction between an architecture view and an architecture viewpoint. A view successfully expresses the complete system architecture relative to specific stakeholder concerns, while a viewpoint rigorously establishes the formalised conventions, specific model kinds, and approved analysis techniques utilised by engineers to construct and interpret that specific view.

The reference architecture serves as a comprehensive, overarching engineering framework that encompasses the rigorous architecture definition process described by ISO/IEC/IEEE 15288:2023 [10].

The RAMEC architecture contributes to the edge AI systems reference architecture by aligning with the computing processing continuum view elements. The hierarchy levels describe the continuum of processing locations, spanning from the physical device at the edge to the centralised cloud infrastructure. By integrating this hierarchical perspective, it is possible to map and distribute computing workloads across various nodes, optimising latency, bandwidth, and resource utilisation throughout the entire network continuum.

## 1.6 Multi-Dimensional Edge AI Systems Reference Architecture

The proposed 3D representation of the edge AI systems reference architecture operationalises the foundational engineering principles by defining three distinct, complementary architectural views, as illustrated in Figure 1.10.

The proposed edge AI reference architecture is structured as a 3D model, providing a holistic view of the edge AI system.

The multi-view approach ensures that all aspects of the edge AI system, from physical data generators, to hardware, software, AI frameworks, and

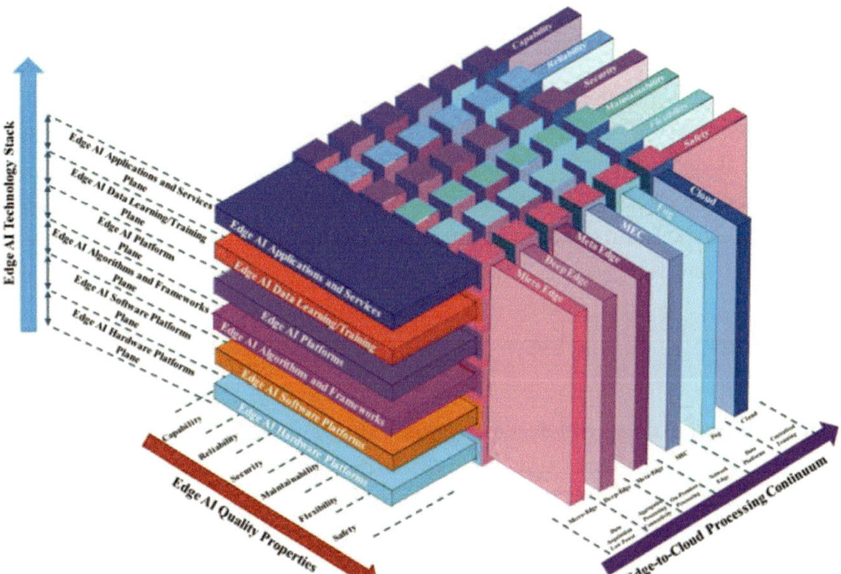


**Figure 1.10** Graphical representation of the 3D edge AI reference architecture.

data layered planes, edge AI quality properties and the edge granularity across the edge-to-cloud processing continuum are addressed simultaneously.

### 1.6.1 Quality Properties View: Engineering for Trustworthiness and Dependability

The Edge AI Quality Properties view captures the non-functional concerns that dominate edge AI systems. Grounded in ISO/IEC 25010:2023 [12], this view emphasises dependability and trustworthiness as system-wide properties rather than isolated features.

Properties such as security, reliability, explainability, transparency, and sustainability permeate every layer of the technology stack and every tier of deployment. Treating these properties as architectural planes enables systematic specification, verification, and benchmarking of edge AI systems against clearly defined quality criteria.

The Edge AI Quality Properties view captures the key non-functional requirements that inform the design and operation of edge AI systems. Grounded in ISO/IEC 25010:2023 [12] and ISO/IEC 25012:2008 [13], this view emphasises system dependability and trustworthiness as holistic, system-wide properties, rather than treating them as isolated, bolt-on software features.

Critical properties such as cybersecurity, hardware reliability, algorithmic explainability, operational transparency, and energy sustainability must actively permeate every single layer of the technology stack and every distinct tier of physical deployment. Treating these properties as intersecting architectural planes enables the systematic specification, rigorous verification, and standardised benchmarking of complex edge AI systems against clearly defined quality criteria.

### 1.6.2 Technology Stack View: Layered Composition Within Each Tier

The Edge AI Technology Stack view defines the layered technical composition within each deployment tier. By explicitly structuring the system from hardware foundations through software, middleware, orchestration, frameworks and platforms, AI frameworks, and data and application layers, the view enables separation of concerns while preserving overall architectural coherence and integration. In contrast, traditional cloud-centric architectures primarily apply separation of concerns to separate software concerns within a stable infrastructure.

Thus, the key differentiator between separation of concerns in edge AI systems and traditional AI systems lies in where complexity resides and what must be separated. This view provides a consistent basis for implementing heterogeneous edge AI platforms and supports the reuse of patterns, interfaces, and standards across application domains. This consistency is essential for reducing integration risk, improving portability, and enabling comparative evaluation of alternative implementations.

In the context of edge AI systems, it is key to understand the relationship between what is being optimised and how the system is structurally designed. The quad-optimisation framework defines the specific elements being optimised, treating data as one of its four foundational pillars. To map out these optimisations, the system utilises a 3D architectural representation composed of three distinct architectural views, which serve as a method for describing and visualising these four pillars. Within this 3D model, the data pillar is represented as a comprehensive "Data Learning/Training plane" embedded within the edge AI technology stack. As data interacts with different aspects of an edge AI system, the data plane intersects with all the other planes across the different architectural views, illustrating how data flows through and unifies the entire architectural design.

Traditional cloud-centric IT architectures primarily apply the principle of separation of concerns solely to separate distinct software concerns within a stable, uniform physical infrastructure. Therefore, the key engineering differentiator between the separation of concerns in modern edge AI systems and traditional centralised AI systems lies in where the intrinsic complexity resides and what physical and logical elements must be separated.

The structured stack view provides a consistent, reproducible basis for safely implementing heterogeneous edge AI systems. It actively supports the extensive reuse of structural patterns, APIs, and data standards across diverse application domains. Architectural consistency is essential for substantially reducing systems integration risk, improving software portability, and enabling rigorous comparative evaluation of alternative engineering implementations.

### 1.6.3 Processing Continuum View: Partitioning Intelligence Across Edge-to-Cloud Tiers

The Edge Granularity Across the Edge-to-Cloud Processing Continuum view captures the spatial and topological distribution of computing and intelligence. Edge AI systems span multiple tiers, from micro-edge devices with severe resource constraints to deep-edge and meta-edge to cloud infrastructures with virtually unlimited capacity.

The view explicitly defines how functionality, data processing, and decision-making responsibilities are partitioned and coordinated across the continuum. It also provides the architectural context needed to analyse latency, resilience, scalability, data, and AI sovereignty, which are critical in industrial, societal, mission-critical, and safety-critical applications.

This specific view defines exactly how critical functionality, data processing workloads, and autonomous decision-making responsibilities are securely partitioned and dynamically coordinated across the entire computing continuum. It provides the architectural context engineers need to accurately analyse network latency, system resilience, dynamic scalability, and strict data sovereignty requirements. These analytical factors are critical in industrial, societal, mission-critical, and highly safety-critical applications.

The specific processing characteristics, hardware targets, and latency constraints of the various components spanning from the extreme micro-edge to the centralised cloud are detailed in Table 1.1.

Together, these three tightly integrated views, as illustrated in Figure 1.11, form a coherent, sound architectural description that actively supports the full, rigorous systems engineering lifecycle.

These views enable rigorous theoretical analysis and precise specification during early conceptual design phases. They directly guide physical implementation through highly consistent patterns and standardised interfaces, providing a reference basis for formal system verification, operational validation, physical testing, and comparative benchmarking. By aligning with international standards such as ISO/IEC/IEEE 42010 and ISO/IEC 25010, the reference architecture establishes a shared vocabulary and a rigorous quality model, thereby facilitating seamless collaboration among diverse stakeholders and enabling strict comparability across competing vendor solutions.

The edge AI systems reference architecture serves as the foundational blueprint for implementing complex edge AI systems, transforming abstract, high-level requirements into a functional structure comprising physical hardware, embedded software, specialised AI algorithms, and secure data components. It fundamentally bridges the challenging gap between theoretical conceptual design and concrete technical implementation by defining exactly how distinct components within the edge AI technology stack must interact securely across the entire processing continuum, thereby ensuring the realisation of all required systemic quality properties.

**Table 1.1** Comparative Analysis of the Edge-to-Cloud Processing Continuum Tiers.

| Tier | Typical Hardware | Key Accelerators | Latency Target | Primary Function |
|---|---|---|---|---|
| **Micro-Edge** | MCUs (Cortex-M), MPUs, SoCs. | TinyML, micro-NPU, NPU. | < 1 ms | Sensing, simple inference, wake-up triggers. |
| **Deep-Edge** | Gateways, Industrial PCs | Edge GPU, TPU, VPU, NPU. | 2 - 5 ms | Aggregation, sensor fusion, local control |
| **Meta-Edge** | On-premises micro-servers, high performance embedded servers. | High-end GPU, FPGA. | < 10 ms | Local training, complex analytics, orchestration. |
| **MEC** | Telecom-Grade servers, rack servers. | GPUs for packet processing, large FPGAs for network function virtualization (NFV). | < 30 ms | Content caching, high-bandwidth processing, application offloading. |
| **Fog** | Industrial routers, servers. | TPUs, DSPs, large FPGAs. | < 50 ms | Bridging OT (Operational Technology) and IT. Focus on data processing before the cloud. |
| **Cloud** | Hyperscale Datacentres. | Tensor Core GPUs, ASIC. | > 100 ms | Global training, archiving, fleet management. |

The edge AI systems reference architecture significantly advances beyond RAMEC and 3D IoT layered architectures by introducing a unified conceptual framework that integrates the structural elements of both the 3D IoT architecture and RAMEC. What truly sets this new architecture apart is its incorporation of diverse AI method families, specifically mapping out where ML, DL, GenAI, and agentic models can optimally execute. The architectural concept elevates the edge AI system's design by including the edge AI model lifecycle and quality properties as dedicated quality planes. The edge AI systems reference architecture innovates by addressing the continuum of computational workload and the actual intelligence that spans

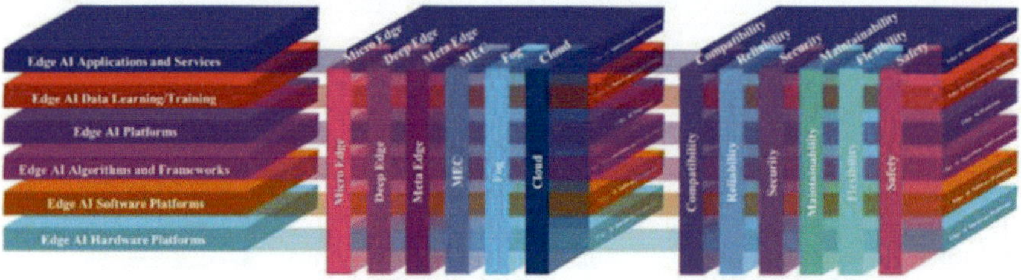


**Figure 1.11** AI systems reference architecture views unfolded.

multiple architectural tiers, enabling a dynamic, distributed, and capable edge environment for edge AI systems-of-systems implementations.

Examples of complex, real-world operational scenarios anchor the practical implementation of these edge AI architectural views. Consider a fleet of autonomous delivery vehicles operating on a tiered architecture, which illustrates the edge processing granularity architectural view considering that the onboard the vehicle specialised hardware (deep-edge) runs safety-critical pedestrian detection algorithms with millisecond latency, prioritising the quality property of safety above all else by focusing on the edge AI hardware, edge AI platforms and data learning/training planes of the edge AI technology stack architectural view. At the same time, non-critical telemetry data, such as GPS coordinates of road potholes, is compressed locally and subsequently transmitted to a centralised server cluster (the cloud). This data is used to continually update and train the highly complex route optimisation software models for the entire vehicle fleet. This dual-path process demonstrates highly complex interaction across the entire processing continuum without ever compromising the individual vehicle's immediate, safety-critical reaction time.

Another example is a highly secure, remote medical facility for elderly care. Vulnerable patients constantly wear biometric smart wristbands that directly represent the extreme micro-edge computing tier. These specialised wearable devices utilise ultra-low-power microcontrollers to continuously run lightweight, optimised anomaly-detection models directly on the local silicon hardware, enabling instant identification of potentially life-threatening heart arrhythmias. By securely processing this sensitive, regulated biometric data locally rather than continuously transmitting massive raw data streams to vulnerable cloud servers, the entire system strictly adheres to stringent privacy and cybersecurity standards while simultaneously maximising the device's critical battery life. This scenario illustrates exactly how the edge

AI technology stack view must be aggressively and continuously optimised for severely resource-constrained hardware environments.

## 1.7 Discussion: Value, Interoperability, and Domain Maturity

The primary driver for actively adopting the edge AI systems reference architecture is the extreme heterogeneity inherent in modern multi-X edge AI environments. These complex environments comprise multiple interacting edge AI systems, utilising multiple sensory modalities, and employing multiple autonomous AI agents spanning continuously from the extreme edge to the centralised cloud.

New edge AI systems developments have fundamentally transitioned from creating simple, isolated, closed systems to engineering highly complex systems-of-systems that feature distributed intelligence.

The paradigm shift requires coordinated engineering efforts spanning multiple spatial nodes and sites, diverse solution stakeholders, and varied scientific disciplines. As the physical scope and computational complexity of edge AI systems increase, so does the immense engineering difficulty of safely maintaining structural coherence and operational stability across these distributed systems.

Edge AI technologies are rapidly maturing, and a formalised reference architecture for edge AI systems is required as the sheer multiplicity of competing edge solutions reaches a critical mass in the global market. Without a shared engineering framework, successfully integrating diverse edge AI systems developed across completely different applications and distinct industries becomes massively inefficient, highly expensive, and inherently error prone.

The edge AI systems reference architecture addresses this critical bottleneck by providing a common technical lexicon and a standardised functional taxonomy. This standardisation enables diverse engineering teams to communicate precisely and effectively, and to align their development efforts toward a shared, secure edge AI architectural vision.

The widespread industrial implementation of an edge AI systems reference architecture delivers increased economic and technological value by driving and harvesting synergy across the entire edge AI domain. It allows architects to identify exactly where shared software assets and hardware standardisation can be effectively and profitably applied, and conversely, where such standardisation might be technologically counter-productive. This deep strategic insight enables rapid, efficient development of robust edge AI solutions, standardised edge AI workflows, product lines, and technological portfolios. The approach reduces the significant time and financial costs typically associated with continually reinventing complex technical solutions for problems that have already been solved in engineering.

The edge AI systems reference architecture can improve interoperability among evolving, disparate edge AI systems. By explicitly and properly modelling critical system functions and operational qualities above the localised single-system level, engineers can ensure strict backward compatibility and facilitate smoother, safer over-the-air system upgrades for edge AI-driven systems. The approach directly leads to reduced systems integration costs and improved overall dependability of deployed edge AI systems.

The edge AI systems reference architecture serves as a foundational, baseline, shared starting point that firmly anchors future technical discussions and architectural changes, thereby mitigating the risks typically associated with the evolution and deployment of complex edge AI systems.

The collaboration across the European edge AI ecosystem brought together complementary expertise from multiple projects, which significantly increased the value of the reference architecture. Instead of addressing isolated challenges, the joint effort aligned advances in hardware, software, toolchains, and applications. This created a more coherent framework that reflects real-world system complexity, making the architecture not just theoretical but directly usable by industry and research communities.

Using the edge AI systems reference architecture, interoperability can be improved by addressing technical, syntactic, and semantic interoperability issues across the stack, from low-level AI chips to high-level applications. By sharing requirements and solutions, the reference architecture supports defining common interfaces, data flows, and integration patterns. For example, a smart manufacturing system defined using the edge AI systems reference architecture can combine edge devices from different vendors with AI models developed in separate toolchains while still adhering to a unified architectural approach.

The ecosystem collaboration and cooperation accelerated the maturity of the edge AI domain. By validating ideas across multiple projects and use cases, the architecture reflects tested practices rather than isolated concepts. In energy systems, for instance, edge AI can monitor and optimise distributed energy systems and lighting luminaries with intelligent capabilities in real time, while in mobility, it supports autonomous mobile systems, software-defined vehicles (SDV), and AI-defined vehicles (AIDV) functions at the edge. These diverse validations strengthen confidence in the architecture and make it applicable across sectors.

The reference architecture is particularly valuable because it adapts to the needs of different industries.

In agrifood, it enables precision farming by combining sensor data and local AI inference. In healthcare, it supports wearable devices that process sensitive data locally to preserve privacy. In digital society applications, such as smart cities, it helps coordinate distributed intelligence across cameras, sensors, and infrastructure.

Each sector benefits from a common structure while tailoring specific components to its requirements.

Looking ahead, the architecture provides a foundation for emerging edge AI trends by offering a holistic view of how technologies fit together. It is designed to accommodate embodied AI systems, such as robots that interact with the physical world, as well as generative AI models running at the edge for real-time content creation.

The architecture also supports agentic AI, where autonomous agents make decisions locally, and immersive technologies such as augmented (AR), virtual (VR), mixed (MR), and extended (XR) reality that require low-latency intelligence close to users and integration into metaverse, omniverse and multiverse simulation platforms.

In a future smart factory, the reference architecture can support the implementation of edge AI systems-of-systems where embodied AI robots could collaborate with human workers, generative AI could assist in design and troubleshooting directly on-site, and agentic systems could autonomously manage workflows.

The reference architecture helps ensure that all these elements interoperate in real-time, providing a shared blueprint for building complex, distributed, and intelligent edge AI systems-of-systems.

## Acknowledgements

This publication has received funding through the projects Chips JU EdgeAI and HE dAIEDGE. The Chips JU EdgeAI "Edge AI Technologies for Optimised Performance Embedded Processing" project is supported by the Chips Joint Undertaking and its members, including top-up funding by Austria, Belgium, France, Greece, Italy, Latvia, the Netherlands, and Norway under grant agreement No 101097300. The HE dAIEDGE "A network of excellence for distributed, trustworthy, efficient and scalable AI at the Edge" project is supported under grant agreement No 101120726. Funded by the European Union. Views and opinions expressed are, however, those of the authors only and do not necessarily reflect those of the European Union or the Chips Joint Undertaking. Neither the European Union nor the granting authority can be held responsible for them.

## References

[1] J. Dietz, "Architecture – Building strategy into design." Netherlands Architecture Forum. Academic Service – SDU, The Hague (2008), http://www.naf.nl ISBN-13: 9789012580861.

[2] D. Greefhorst and E. Proper "Architecture Principles - The Cornerstones of Enterprise Architecture." Springer-Verlag Berlin Heidelberg 2011. ISBN 978-3-642-20278-0, e-ISBN 978-3-642-20279-7, doi: 10.1007/978-3-642-20279-7. https://sar.ac.id/stmik_ebook/prog_file_file/f7KjsxWOBJ.pdf.

[3] F. Harmsen, H. Proper, and N. Kok, "Informed Governance of Enterprise Transformations." In: Proper HA, Harmsen AF, Dietz JLG (eds) Advances in enterprise engineering II—Proceedings of the first NAF academy working conference on practice-driven research on enterprise transformations, PRET 2009. Held at CAiSE 2009, Amsterdam, The Netherlands, June 2009. Lecture notes in business information processing, vol 28. Springer, Berlin, pp 155–180. ISBN-13:9783642018589. https://www.erikproper.eu/publications/EP-2024-05-22-12-14-32.pdf.

[4] Industry IoT Consortium®(IIC®). The Industrial Internet Reference Architecture. Version 1.10. https://www.iiconsortium.org/wp-content/uploads/sites/2/2022/11/IIRA-v1.10.pdf.

[5] ISO/IEC/IEEE 42010:2022. Software, systems and enterprise - Architecture description https://www.iso.org/standard/74393.html.

[6] ISO/IEC/IEEE 42020:2019. Software, systems and enterprise - Architecture processes. https://www.iso.org/standard/68982.html.

[7] ISO/IEC/IEEE DIS 42024. Enterprise, systems and software - Architecture fundamentals. https://www.iso.org/standard/87510.html.

[8] ISO/IEC/IEEE 42030:2019. Software, systems and enterprise - Architecture evaluation framework. https://www.iso.org/standard/73436.html.

[9] ISO/IEC/IEEE DIS 42042. Enterprise, systems and software — Reference architectures. https://www.iso.org/standard/87310.html.

[10] ISO/IEC/IEEE 15288:2023. Systems and software engineering - System life cycle processes. https://www.iso.org/standard/81702.html.

[11] ISO 15704:2019. Enterprise modelling and architecture - Requirements for enterprise-referencing architectures and methodologies. https://www.iso.org/standard/71890.html.

[12] ISO/IEC 25010:2023. Systems and software engineering - Systems and software Quality Requirements and Evaluation (SQuaRE) - Product quality model. https://www.iso.org/standard/78176.html.

[13] ISO/IEC 25012:2008. Software engineering - Software product Quality Requirements and Evaluation (SQuaRE) - Data quality model. https://www.iso.org/standard/35736.html.

[14] Chips JU EdgeAI Project. Deliverable D5.07. Edge AI systems reference architecture. 2026.

[15] O. Vermesan et al., "The Next Generation Internet of Things - Hyperconnectivity and Embedded Intelligence at the Edge." In, O. Vermesan and J Bacquet, "Next Generation Internet of Things Distributed Intelligence at the Edge and Human Machine-to-Machine Cooperation". 2018. https://www.riverpublishers.com/pdf/ebook/chapter/RP_9788770220071C3.pdf.

[16] O. Vermesan, "Edge AI Reference Architecture", European Conference on EDGE AI Technologies and Applications – EEAI 2025, 22 October 2025 Naples, Italy. https://doi.org/10.5281/zenodo.17666483.

[17] O. Vermesan, "The Edge AI Systems Reference Architecture - Orchestrating Autonomous and AI-Defined Systems Through GenAI and Agentic AI in the Intelligence Mesh", HiPEAC Conference 27 January 2026, Kraków, Poland. https://doi.org/10.5281/zenodo.18816484.

[18] O. Vermesan, The strategic imperative of Edge AI systems reference architecture, INSIDE Magazine Issue 12, March 2026, pp.18-23.

[19] US Department of Defense, Office of the Assistant Secretary of Defense, Networks and Information Integration (OASD/NII), Reference Architecture Description, June 2010. https://dodcio.defense.gov/Portals/0/Documents/Ref_Archi_Description_Final_v1_18Jun10.pdf.

[20] The Open Group Architecture Framework (TOGAF) Version 10, https://www.opengroup.org/togaf.

[21] The Open Group. The TOGAF®10$^{th}$ Edition Standard. Introduction and Core Concepts. 2022. Van Haren Publishing, 's-Hertogenbosch -

NL, SBN eBook: 978 94 018 0860 6. https://www.avtechcn.com/pdf/togaf10part01.pdf.

[22] Willner and V. Gowtham, "Toward a Reference Architecture Model for Industrial Edge Computing," in *IEEE Communications Standards Magazine*, vol. 4, no. 4, pp. 42-48, December 2020, https://www.doi.org/10.1109/MCOMSTD.001.2000007.

# 2

# Towards Smart and Adaptive Agents for Active Sensing on Edge Devices

**Devendra Vyas[1], Nikola Pižurica[2,3] Nikola Milović[3], Igor Jovančević[2,3], Miguel de Prado[1], and Tim Verbelen[1]**

[1] VERSES, USA
[2] Computer Science Center, University of Montenegro, Montenegro
[3] Fain Tech, Montenegro

## Abstract

TinyML has made deploying *deep learning* models on low-power edge devices feasible, creating new opportunities for real-time perception in constrained environments. However, the adaptability of such deep learning methods remains limited to data drift adaptation, lacking broader capabilities that account for the environment's underlying dynamics and inherent uncertainty. Deep learning's scaling laws, which counterbalance this limitation by massively up-scaling data and model size, cannot be applied when deploying on the *Edge*, where deep learning limitations are further amplified as models are scaled down for deployment on resource-constrained devices.

This paper presents an innovative agentic system capable of performing on-device perception and planning, enabling active sensing on the edge. By incorporating *active inference* into our solution, our approach extends beyond the capabilities of deep learning, allowing the system to plan in dynamic environments while operating in real-time with a compact memory footprint of as little as 300 MB. We showcase our proposed system by creating and deploying a Saccade agent connected to an IoT camera with pan and tilt capabilities on an NVIDIA Jetson embedded device. The Saccade agent controls the camera's field of view following optimal policies derived from

DOI: 10.1201/9788743815211-2 

the active inference principles, simulating human-like saccadic motion for surveillance and robotics applications.

**Keywords:** smart agents, edgeAI, dynamic planning, active inference.

## 2.1 Introduction

The human visual system has a unique ability to focus on key details within complex surroundings, a process known as saccading [1]. This quick and dynamic scanning allows us to gather essential information. Saccading is part of a larger concept known as active (visual) sensing [2, 3], an innate capability that enables organisms to forage for information and dynamically adapt to an evolving environment [4].

Active sensing is critical in various applications, particularly when the information is unavailable or too vast to process. For instance, in remote sensing for Earth observation [5], or aerial search-and-rescue operations [6], the system must parse vast, detailed scenes, focusing only on critical features, such as sea ice or missing persons. Similarly, in sports events, tracking dynamic scenes requires a system to zoom in on players, capturing players' faces or gestures while not missing the play. Other areas, such as smart cities and surveillance systems [7], demand robust monitoring solutions for crowded areas to track movement, anticipate potential issues, and enhance safety. Active sensing becomes even more apparent in robotics, where the agent's actions determine the next observations for the system, driving exploration [8].

Recent advances in machine learning (ML), particularly in deep learning, have substantially improved sensing accuracy and complexity. However, state-of-the-art deep learning models exhibit limitations in their adaptability [9], specifically in the ongoing accumulation and refinement of knowledge over time. These limitations are further amplified when these models are scaled down for deployment on resource-constrained devices, where memory, computational power, and energy efficiency are limited. As a result, true active sensing—requiring both perception and planning—remains challenging to implement on embedded systems.

Active inference, an approach rooted in the first principles of physics, offers a promising alternative to address these limitations [10]. Emerging as a viable paradigm, active inference grounds learning within probabilistic principles, enabling smart systems, or agents, to model the uncertainty and variability inherent in dynamic environments, making it well-suited for continual learning and adaptive decision-making [11]. This shift represents a move beyond perception-focused AI toward adaptive systems capable of adjusting their actions based on environmental feedback. Thus, agents on the edge provide a powerful framework for real-time perception and planning, eliminating dependence on cloud resources and ensuring low-latency responses and enhanced data privacy.

This work presents an integrated system that combines deep learning and active inference to realize an adaptive, memory-efficient, real-time Saccade agent for edge devices. Our system leverages a deep learning-based object detection module for initial perception and an active inference planning module to actively sense and adapt to the environment. The Saccade agent can observe, plan, and control a camera for strategic information gathering, demonstrating adaptive decision-making and exploration. Our deployment on an Nvidia Jetson platform showcases the potential for responsive applications in robotics and smart city environments, highlighting the feasibility of edge-based adaptive systems for complex, real-world tasks.

## 2.2 Related work

We categorize the related work in three main areas as described below.

### 2.2.1 Active Sensing

Active sensing is an essential building block across various fields where efficient scanning is necessary to locate and focus on critical details. Historically, the roots of the active sensing concept can be traced back several decades, particularly in the field of computer vision. R. Bajcsy [30] defined active sensing as an intelligent data acquisition process. In this context, a passive sensor, such as a camera, is actively used by purposefully controlling its state parameters (e.g., pose, zoom, and focus) in accordance with task goals. This view emphasizes the closed-loop feedback between perception and action, and distinguishes between local models of sensor/algorithm properties and global models that coordinate sensing strategies over time. Furthermore, [31] and [32] formalized active and "animate" vision, demonstrating that an observer who can control their viewpoint and gaze (e.g., via saccading and pan–tilt camera motions) can convert ill-posed vision problems into well-posed ones and drastically reduce computational demands by aligning sensing with task constraints.

Building upon these foundational ideas, subsequent work in robotics has developed active vision systems that plan where and how to look to support manipulation, navigation, and scene understanding. Surveys on active vision in robotic systems and view-planning highlight methods that select camera poses that constrain scene interpretation and trade off coverage, accuracy, and computational cost [33]. More recent approaches explicitly formulate active sensing as an information-gain or mutual-information maximization problem, for instance, in next-best-view selection for volumetric 3D reconstruction or multi-camera surveillance [34] for public safety in smart cities. This, combined with other deep learning methods for people tracking and counting [12], enables security, crowd management, and urban analytics applications.

Other fields, such as Earth observation, employ active sensing sea ice detection by maximizing area coverage and detection through adaptive zooming, which is indispensable for safe navigation and has prompted the AutoICE Challenge benchmark [5]. Similarly, active search strategies are also explored in rescue operations [6], emphasizing techniques such as saccading to enhance search efficiency over large areas.

Most of the methods share similarities with our work, but they optimize handcrafted information-theoretic criteria rather than deriving sensing policies from a unified active inference generative model.

### 2.2.2 TinyML

TinyML has made deploying ML models on low-power edge devices feasible, bringing opportunities for real-time perception in constrained embedded devices. The edge deployment pipeline is summarized in [13], streamlining the end-to-end model deployment on embedded platforms to enhance the accessibility of edgeAI applications. A popular example of this process is YOLO [14], an efficient single-stage detector that enables object detection and tracking at the edge, thereby improving the responsiveness of embedded applications. Recent works have made progress in enabling on-device domain adaptation, adjusting deployed applications to account for data distribution shifts between training and target environments [15, 16]. However, these adaptations remain limited to addressing data drifts and lack broader capabilities for behavioral changes.

Our approach overcomes this limitation by integrating active inference on top of a deep learning module, allowing the system to plan and adapt to the environment.

### 2.2.3 Probabilistic computing

Probabilistic computing has shown promise for active sensing by optimizing information acquisition in dynamic environments. Probabilistic principles can be utilized to maximize information gain through camera adjustments [17], which is particularly valuable in applications such as surveillance, sports analysis, and patient monitoring. This is extended to maximize mutual information gain in multi-camera setups, combining objectives like exploration and tracking to enable adaptive scene monitoring [18]. Unlike these methods, our probabilistic agent is based on active inference, grounding our approach in the Free Energy Principle.

## 2.3 Methodology

To develop an effective active sensing solution, it is essential to consider the unpredictable and dynamic nature of real-world environments. Smart sensors must be able to handle uncertainty and adapt to constant changes. Therefore, any change in the observed environment must influence the policy selection for the following action. For a system to operate autonomously and intelligently, it must be able to adjust its perception and actions in real time without relying on cloud processing. This requirement for on-device adaptation supports faster decision-making and enhances data privacy.

In this work, we propose an efficient active sensing agent composed of two modules: i) a deep learning-based perception module and ii) an active inference module that enables planning and control. This architecture combines deep learning's feature extraction performance with active inference's Bayes-optimal control, presenting an adaptable and scalable solution for various resource-constrained edge applications.

### 2.3.1 Perception

Deep learning techniques have achieved remarkable success in detecting features of interest in images, audio, or textual data [19]. Convolutional neural networks (CNNs) have demonstrated exceptional performance in visual tasks like object detection and segmentation [20]. By employing deep learning for perception, active sensing agents can rapidly process high-dimensional data and identify patterns that provide relevant spatial information.

Recent advances in transformer architectures and large language models (LLMs) have further expanded the scope of deep learning. Transformers excel at capturing complex dependencies and long-range relationships in data, making them highly effective for tasks that require a deeper contextual understanding. The self-attention mechanism, a core component of transformers, enables models to focus selectively on the most relevant aspects of the data, thereby enhancing the agent's ability to perform active sensing by prioritizing critical visual cues.

However, while deep learning and LLMs offer powerful feature extraction, their static nature limits adaptability when deployed in uncertain or changing environments, which can only be counteracted by massively scaling data or model size. Thus, to address this challenge, our approach integrates deep learning for perception but relies on active inference as a much lighter, sample- and parameter-efficient higher-level module, enabling the agent to plan and dynamically adapt based on ongoing observations in real-time.

### 2.3.2 Planning

Active inference builds on the Free Energy principle, a theoretical framework that states intelligent agents minimize the discrepancy between their internal (generative) model of the environment and incoming sensory data. By reducing this discrepancy, or "free energy", the agent maintains an updated and accurate representation of its surroundings, enabling it to make predictions about its environment and actively take actions to reduce uncertainty.

Concretely, the agent's generative model is a joint probability distribution over states $s$ and observations $o$. As inferring hidden states $s$ given some observations $o$ is typically intractable, an approximate posterior $Q(s|o)$ is introduced and optimized by minimizing the free energy $F$ [10]:

$$\min_{Q(s|o)} F = \underbrace{D_{KL}[Q(s \mid o) \| P(s)]}_{\text{complexity}} - \underbrace{\mathbb{E}_{Q(s|o)}[\log P(o \mid s)]}_{\text{accuracy}} \tag{2.1}$$

Hence, the agent strives to provide the most accurate predictions $P(o| s)$ while minimizing the complexity of the model with respect to the prior $P(s)$. To select actions or policies $\pi$ for the future $\tau$, an active inference agent will evaluate and minimize the expected free energy $G$ [10]:

$$G(\pi) = \underbrace{\mathbb{E}_{Q(o_\tau|\pi)}\left[D_{KL}\left[Q\left(s_\tau \mid o_\tau, \pi\right) \| Q\left(s_\tau \mid \pi\right)\right]\right]}_{\text{(negative) information gain}} - \underbrace{\mathbb{E}_{Q(o_\tau|\pi)}\left[\log P\left(o_\tau \mid C\right)\right]}_{\text{expected utility}} \tag{2.2}$$

The agent now averages across expected future outcomes $o_{\mathcal{T}}$ and balances the expected information gain (i.e., exploration) with the expected utility (i.e., reward) encoded in prior preferences $C$. Both the observations $o$ and hidden states $s$ can be modeled as discrete variables with Categorical distributions, whereas optimizing $F$ and $G$ can be done using tractable update rules [11]. Therefore, we convert the outputs of the deep learning perception module into a discrete observation space and utilize active inference for action selection in our agent.

## 2.4 Smart edge agent

Our smart edge agent, the Saccade agent, comprises two modules, as introduced in the previous section, which combine deep learning perception capabilities with active inference planning, as shown in Figure 2.1. Specifically, we employ i) a deep-learning object detection model, offering efficient object and human detection capabilities directly at the edge, and ii) an active inference module that enables adaptive motion control (pan and tilt), allowing the agentic system to dynamically adjust its field of view or track detected entities autonomously. This adaptive behavior enhances the camera's utility as an intelligent surveillance IoT tool or for scene exploration and information foraging in robotic applications.

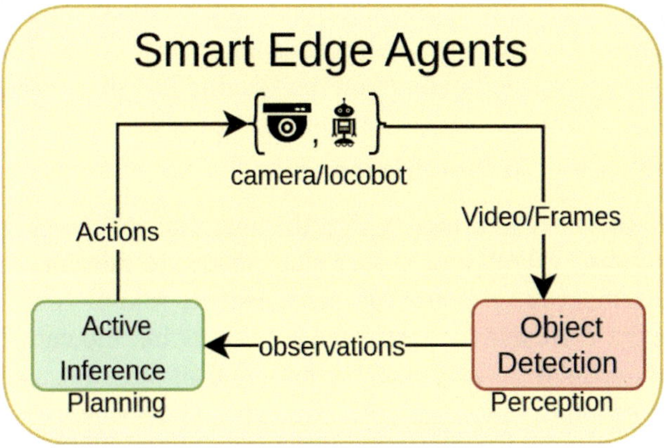


**Figure 2.1 Conceptual Framework for Smart Edge Agents**, composed of a deep-learning perception module and an active inference planning module for active (visual) sensing. The camera frames are processed by the object detector, which forwards the detected results to the active inference module. Our agent plans its next action, minimizing free energy, and dynamically adapting to the environment.

### 2.4.1 Object detection using YOLOv10

We chose *YOLOv10* [14] from the YOLO family for our perception module due to its strong balance of detection accuracy and computational efficiency. YOLO models are single-pass object detectors that predict object categories and locations, making them ideal for real-time applications. YOLOv10 consistently demonstrates state-of-the-art performance and reduced latency across various model scales (N/S/M/L/X). We employ the Nano (N) variant, with 2.3 million parameters, as it offers an efficient accuracy-speed-memory trade-off for edge deployment.

To deploy the YOLOv10n as efficiently as possible, we export it to *ONNX* [21]. ONNX has become a standard for neural network representation and exchange, and is widely supported by the software stacks of hardware vendors, including inference engines. This positions ONNX as a strong candidate for deployment in space exploration on a range of embedded devices. Thus, we create an *edge-deployment workflow* to find the most suitable deployment for YOLOv10n.

The edge-deployment workflow comprises several edge-oriented inference engines, including ONNX-runtime [22], TensorFlow Lite [23], and TensorRT [24], which can take an ONNX model as input and generate an optimized implementation for a specific target hardware platform. These frameworks apply several optimizations across the network's graph, e.g., operator fusion, quantization, on the software stack, e.g., algorithm optimization, and leverage parallel hardware acceleration, vectorization, and optimized memory scheduling. The process yields a bespoke network description and a runtime that is ready for deployment on the specified hardware platform.

### 2.4.2 Planning using Active Inference

To enable an efficient Saccade agent with active inference planning, we define a discrete action, observation, and hidden state space. To this end, we divide the full area the camera can pan and tilt into a discrete grid of $K\ x\ L$ blocks, as shown in Figure 2.2. Given a particular fixation point, the camera's field of view will only span $W\ x\ H$ blocks, highlighted in blue. For each block, at each timestep, an observation $o_{w,\ h}$ is a Categorical distribution with three bins, i.e., the block can have no object detected (0 - blue), an object detected (1 - red), or not visible (2 - gray). The confidence of the bounding box outputs of the object detection neural network provides the probability of an object being detected. As state space, we similarly have a state variable $s_{k,\ l}$ per block, which is Bernoulli, i.e., object not present (0) or present

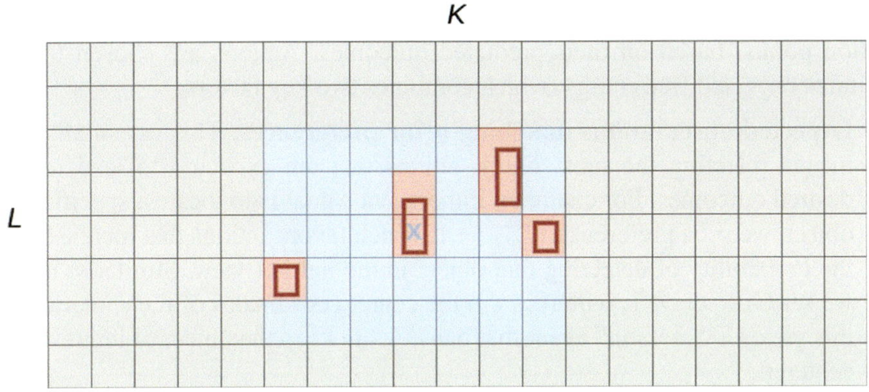


**Figure 2.2 Action space:** We discretize the action space into $K$ $x$ $L$ fixation points. Given a fixation point, the field of view of the camera spans $W$ $x$ $H$ blocks (in blue), and object detections are translated into discrete bins (in red).

(2.1). In addition, we also equip the agent with a proprioceptive state $s_p$ and observation, i.e., it observes the fixation point it is currently looking at. We specify the likelihood mapping **A**, which predicts observation $o_{w,\,h}$ given state $s_{k,\,l}$ and fixation point $s_p$:

$$A_{w,h,k,l,p} = \begin{cases} 0 & \text{if } s_{k,l} = 0, k \rightarrow_p w, l \rightarrow_p h \\ 1 & \text{if } s_{k,l} = 1, k \rightarrow_p w, l \rightarrow_p h \\ 2 & \text{otherwise} \end{cases} \tag{2.3}$$

Where $k \rightarrow_p w$ means "block $k$ maps to observation $w$ given the agent looks at the fixation point $p$". We currently also assume that objects do not move considerably between timesteps and use the previous timestep posterior as the current prior, i.e.,

$$P(s_t) = Q(s_{t-1}|o_{t-1})$$

We leave the expansion of this modeling assumption for the dynamics of the objects as future work.

The Saccade agent uses the object detections received to perform inference, updating its beliefs about the hidden states. For example, detecting a "person" with high confidence would increase the probability assigned to the hidden state "person present" corresponding to the particular block. The absence of detection, on the other hand, would decrease the probability of that object being present.

After each observation, the agent evaluates possible actions, i.e., the next fixation points, based on their predicted outcomes. Actions are chosen to minimize expected free energy, which combines two key factors:

1. **Expected observations matching prior preferences:** This essentially means selecting the most likely actions that are expected to lead to desired outcomes. For example, if the agent's goal is to locate a specific object, we set a preference $C_{w,h} = 1$, which favors actions that increase the probability of detecting that object in the field of view. Similarly, if we set $C\mathrm{c}_w, \mathrm{c}_h = 1$, with ($\mathrm{c}_w$, $\mathrm{c}_h$) the center coordinates of the camera, this yields a "tracking" agent that pans/tilts to keep the object of interest centered.
2. **Epistemic value:** The agent also aims to reduce uncertainty about the hidden states. Actions expected to provide more informative observations about the environment have higher epistemic value (i.e., information gain, as defined in Eq. (2.2)). In our model, moving the field of view to previously unobserved blocks will result in a high amount of information gain. Hence, in the absence of objects of interest, the camera will pan and tilt to cover the whole area with as few moves as possible.

We provide a qualitative demonstration of our Saccade agent here [29].

## 2.5 Experimental results

### 2.5.1 Experimental Setup

Our experimental setup comprises the following components (see Figure 2.3):

1. **Tapo Camera:** We employ an IoT Tapo camera equipped with pan and tilt capabilities, which serves as both the input for the observations, i.e., images/frames, forwarded to the object detector, and the actuator for our Saccade agent. The agent commands the camera to perform dynamic adjustments in its field of view based on optimal policies derived by minimizing free energy, simulating a human-like saccadic motion to maintain focus on areas of interest.
2. **Locobot WX250:** We also deploy our agent on the Locobot WX250, a mobile robot platform for autonomous mobility. Equipped with a 6-DOF manipulator and pan/tilt camera, the Locobot enables active exploration of the environment. This capability complements the Tapo camera's pan and tilt actions with navigation. The robot's mobility enhances the agent's capacity for active sensing in new environments, allowing it to

**Figure 2.3 Applications**: Our agentic system enables active sensing solutions for edge robotics and surveillance IoT cameras. On the left, the Tapo IoT camera [27] is used for surveillance applications. On the right, the Locobot robot WX250 [28] for information gathering and scene discovery.

reposition itself and collect additional perspectives to refine perception in complex settings.

3. **Nvidia Jetson Orin NX:** Our setup leverages the Nvidia Jetson Orin NX. Equipped with an 8-core ARM Cortex-A78 CPU and a 1024-core Ampere GPU, the Jetson Orin NX represents a powerful edge AI platform designed for accelerated machine learning tasks, offering up to 100 TOPs of processing capability and 16 GB of memory, all while operating at 25W.

A pre-trained YOLOv10n model, trained on the COCO dataset [25], is deployed on the Nvidia Jetson Orin NX for real-time detection. The active inference module receives bounding boxes as observations and returns the optimal pan and tilt actions for the IoT or robotic camera. Both the perception and planning modules utilize the edge-deployment workflow to identify the most suitable deployment engine, resulting in the highest performance.

### 2.5.2 Results

It is worth noting that this work does not aim to provide a quantitative benchmarking of behavioral performance against alternative baselines (e.g., algorithms based on other probabilistic paradigms, or simple heuristics). While such comparative evaluations are important, the primary objective of this study is to validate the feasibility of deploying an active inference agent on resource-constrained edge hardware. For this reason, our experimental focus was on system-level optimizations for latency and memory footprint, which directly determine real-world deployability. These metrics represent hard constraints in embedded and IoT settings and constitute a necessary prerequisite for any future large-scale behavioral benchmarking. A systematic comparison of task-level scores (e.g., accuracy or exploration efficiency) across alternative methods is therefore left as an important direction for future work.

Next, we summarize our deployment experimental results:

### 2.5.2.1 Perception

We optimized the YOLOv10n model, as introduced in Section 1.4, by exporting the original Torch model from the original *Ultralytics*, a training-oriented framework, to ONNX. Then, the model gets compiled with one of the various deployment inference engines. Figure 2.4 illustrates the average results of 1,000 inference runs, with one warm-up sample, when deploying each implementation on the Nvidia Jetson's CPU, single-core, and multi-core, as well as the GPU.

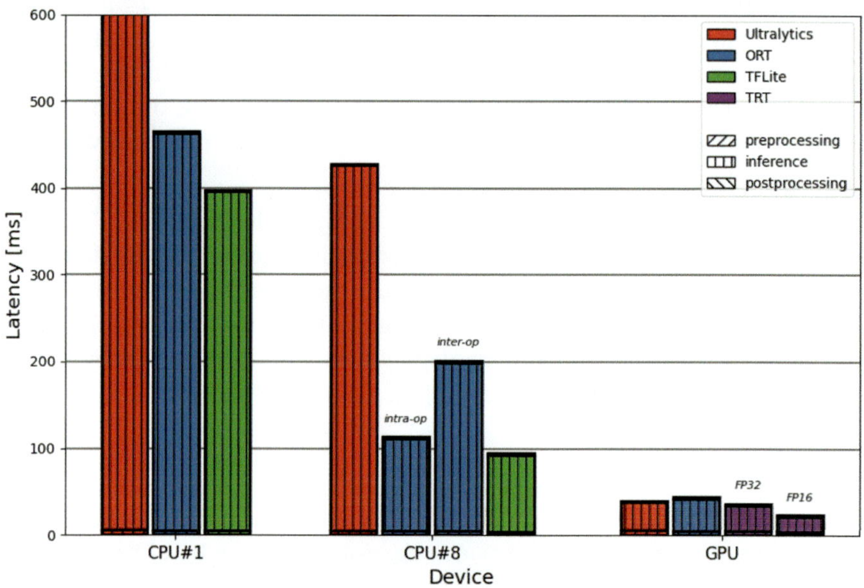


**Figure 2.4 Perception module performance**: Optimization achieved by exporting the YOLOv10n Torch model from Ultralytics to ONNX and compiling it with different deployment inference engines on the Nvidia Jetson Orin NX's CPU and GPU.

When evaluating the various inference engines using single-floating-point precision (FP32) operations on a single-core CPU, Ultralitics emerges as the slowest, with a latency of over 600 ms. When the model is exported to ONNX and compiled with ONNX-runtime (ORT) and TensorFlow Lite (TFLite), the latency decreases considerably by 23% and 35%, respectively. We achieve higher gains when parallelizing across all available 8 CPU cores, resulting in a 427 ms reduction when using Ultralytics. The performance can be notably increased if we deploy with ORT (intra-operator parallelization) and TFLite, with a 3.75x and 4.5x speed-up over Ultralytics, respectively.

Finally, when offloading inference to the GPU, we observe a performance boost for all GPU-available frameworks by leveraging the device's native parallel compute units, achieving inference times under 45 ms. When using TensorRT (TRT), which is specifically designed for Nvidia Jetson devices, we achieve optimized deployment through reduced numerical precision (FP16), with as little as 22 ms, resulting in 45 FPS.

Figure 2.5 shows the memory profile of the YOLOv10n deployments with the various inference engines. It can be observed that while TFLite provides the fastest deployment on the single-CPU setup, it also consumes the most

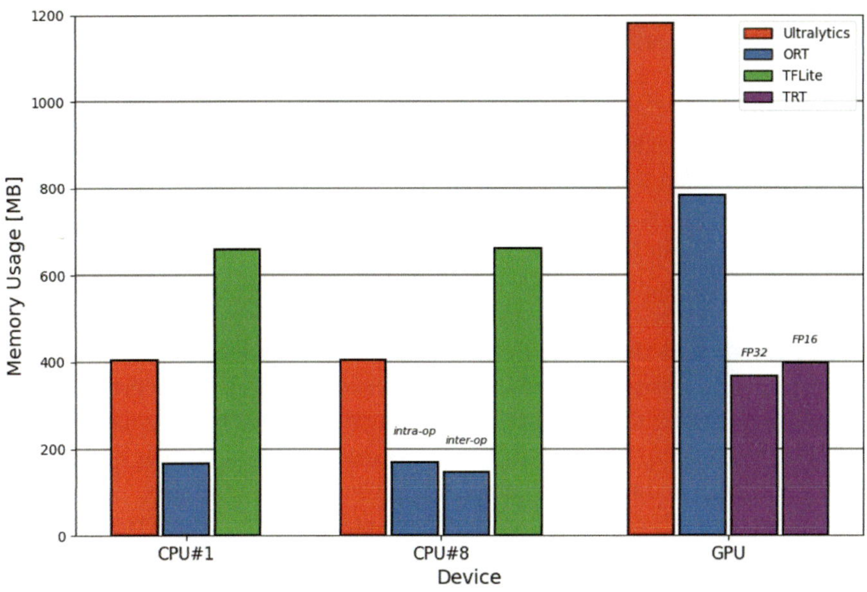


**Figure 2.5 Perception module memory profile** of the YoloV10n when executed with different deployment inference engines on the Nvidia Jetson Orin NX's CPU and GPU.

memory, with over 50% more than Ultralytics. On the other hand, ORT provides a good latency-memory balance, being slightly slower than TFLite, but achieves inference with as little as 168 MB of memory. This pattern is also repeated in the multi-CPU deployment setup. On the GPU side. Ultralytics, being training-oriented, consumes the most memory, with up to 1.2 GB. As we discussed earlier, TRT is designed explicitly for Nvidia Jetson devices. As such, it accomplishes a very performant deployment with an optimized memory usage under 400 MB.

Overall, the results demonstrate that the neural network inference stage makes the predominant contribution to overall latency. In contrast, the pre-processing phase exhibits minimal computational overhead, and the post-processing step remains negligible — a characteristic intrinsic to the YOLOv10 architecture. Moreover, the comparative analysis across inference engines and hardware configurations reveals distinct performance and memory usage behaviors. For instance, TFLite achieves favorable latency on single-core execution, although with the highest memory usage, while ORT offers an excellent performance-memory tradeoff. On the GPU side, TRT is the clear winner, offering excellent latency and memory performance. These observations highlight the importance of a flexible edge-deployment workflow that systematically identifies the most suitable software–hardware pairing for a given operational context.

#### 2.5.2.2 Planning

Next, we deploy the active inference planning module, which only contains 1.34K parameters, on the Nvidia Jetson NX. The original active inference model was designed with the *Pymdp* library [26], which contains a JAX backend. We then follow a similar workflow to that of YOLOv10n, exporting the active inference model to ONNX and deploying it with several inference engines.

Figure 2.6 depicts the latency of the active inference model when planning the following position to look at. The pre-processing step accounts for decoding and mapping the object detection bounding boxes to the generative model. The inference part involves the *infer_states* method, which updates the agent's beliefs about the hidden states given the observations, and the *infer_policies* method, which defines the set of policies from which the agent will pick the best action.

When deployed on a single CPU, the planning process executes fast, achieving 6 ms using JAX and 4 ms (250 FPS) when compiled with TFLite. The Saccade agent does not benefit from parallel processing, showing similar

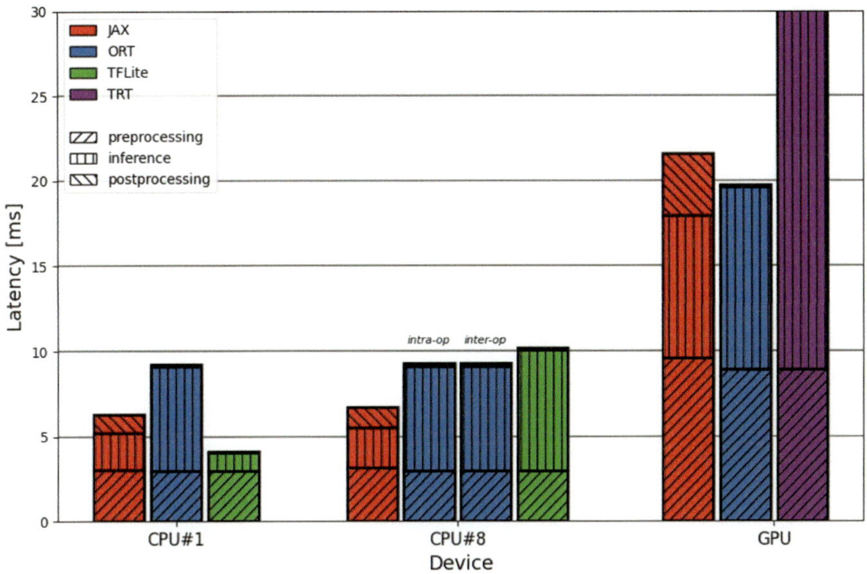


**Figure 2.6 Planning module performance**: Performance optimization by exporting the active inference model (saccade agent) from JAX to ONNX and compiling it with different deployment inference engines on the Nvidia Jetson Orin NX's CPU and GPU.

or worse performance when deployed on multiple CPUs and considerably worse when offloaded to the GPU. We argue that this is due to the small size of the agent, which incurs a high penalty for thread synchronization, thereby outweighing the benefits of parallel computation.

Figure 2.7 illustrates a trend consistent with that observed for the YOLOv10n model, revealing a trade-off between inference performance and memory consumption. For example, while TFLite delivers the fastest execution, it may consume up to four times more memory than ORT. This behavior may be related to internal optimization mechanisms in TFLite, potentially involving intermediate data caching or buffer reuse strategies to reduce computation time.

Overall, these results highlight the lightweight deployment of our active inference model, achieving real-time planning and adaptation to the environment for IoT and robotics saccading applications.

#### 2.5.2.3 System

Integrating the perception and planning modules produces a highly efficient Saccade agent capable of real-time operation with only 2.3 million

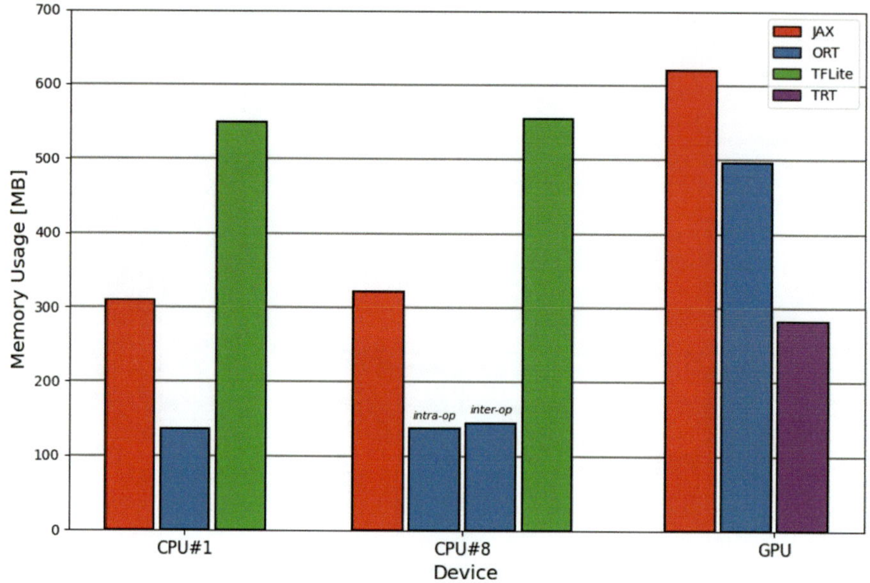


**Figure 2.7 Planning module memory profile** of the active inference model when executed with various inference engines on the Nvidia Jetson Orin NX CPU and GPU.

**Table 2.1 System parameters:** Saccade agent deployed on the Nvidia Jetson Orin NX.

| Config | # Params (M) | Memory (MB) | Perception Rate (Hz) | Decision-making Rate (Hz) |
|---|---|---|---|---|
| A | 2.3 | 947 | 45 | **250** |
| B | 2.3 | 533 | **45** | 108 |
| C | 2,3 | **304** | 9 | 108 |

parameters. Table 2.1 summarizes key configurations, illustrating the trade-offs between latency and memory consumption. For example, in configuration *A*, the perception module optimized with TensorRT-FP16 achieves a throughput of 45 FPS, enabling rapid feature extraction. In parallel, the active inference module using TFLite can perform planning and decision-making at up to 250 FPS, with a total memory footprint of under 1 GB. The decision-making rate can be reduced to 108 FPS using ORT, lowering memory usage to 533 MB, as shown in configuration *B*. Finally, configuration *C* utilizes the ORT (intra-operator parallelization) for perception, reducing the perception rate to 9 FPS while maintaining a compact memory footprint of 304 MB, which includes all required libraries and runtimes. This configuration effectively balances the latency and memory requirements of perception and decision-making, enabling dynamic adaptation and efficient operation on resource-constrained edge devices.

## 2.6 Discussion

These results highlight the effectiveness of combining deep learning for perception with active inference for planning in edge-based intelligent agents. With only 1.34K parameters, the active inference module achieves real-time planning while maintaining minimal computational and memory demands. In contrast to large-scale foundation models that rely on billions of parameters to achieve general-purpose intelligence, our domain-oriented approach demonstrates how compact, task-specific active inference models can complement deep learning perception. The adaptability of our edge-deployment workflow illustrates deployment interoperability, facilitating the exploration of diverse configurations to achieve a suitable balance between latency and resource efficiency.

This validation establishes a solid foundation for a second stage of analysis focused on quantitative behavioural benchmarking. A systematic evaluation of task-level indicators such as decision accuracy, exploration efficiency, or robustness across environments remains an important avenue for future research.

## 2.7 Conclusions and Future Work

This work has introduced a smart edge agent composed of a deep learning-based perception module and an active inference planning module for active sensing. The system demonstrates the feasibility of adaptable, on-device surveillance and robotic solutions, as well as their potential to effectively handle real-world challenges. Our study highlights the potential of active inference in edge-based systems. Active inference offers a robust framework that accounts for the environment's underlying dynamics and inherent uncertainty. It allows the agent to actively reduce ambiguity or explore the environment for new information. This approach establishes a foundation for efficient edge agents for adaptive, resource-efficient decision-making in IoT and edge computing applications.

In future work, we aim to compare the proposed system against other state-of-the-art works, showing a quantitative functional comparison on popular challenges, such as the Habitat Navigation Challenge. Finally, we envision extending this concept to other applications, which could unlock a new generation of adaptive edge devices capable of context-driven interactions in complex environments.

## Acknowledgements

This work was partly supported by Horizon Europe dAIEdge under grant No. 101120726.

## References

[1] S. Grossberg, K. Roberts, M. Aguilar, and D. Bullock, "A neural model of multimodal adaptive saccadic eye movement control by superior colliculus," J. Neurosci., vol. 17, no. 24, pp. 9706-9725, Dec. 1997.

[2] M. Ferro, D. Ognibene, G. Pezzulo, V. Pirrelli, "Reading as active sensing: a computational model of gaze planning during word recognition," Front. Neurorobot., vol. 4, p. 1262, 2010.

[3] T. Parr, N. Sajid, L. Da Costa, M. B. Mirza, K. J. Friston, "Generative models for active vision," Front. Neurorobot., vol. 15, p. 651432, 2021.

[4] M. B. Mirza, R. A. Adams, C. D. Mathys, K. J. Friston, "Scene construction, visual foraging, and active inference," Front. Comput. Neurosci., vol. 10, p. 56, 2016.

[5] A. Stokholm et al., "The autoICE challenge," Cryosphere, vol. 18, no. 8, pp. 3471-3494, 2024.

[6] S. McClanahan, "Object recognition and detection: Potential implications from vision science for wilderness searching," J. Search Rescue, vol. 5, no. 1, pp. 1-17, 2021.

[7] M. Kashef, A. Visvizi, and O. Troisi, "Smart city as a smart service system: Human-computer interaction and smart city surveillance systems," Comput. Hum. Behav., vol. 124, p. 106923, 2021.

[8] L. Da Costa, P. Lanillos, N. Sajid, K. J. Friston, S. Khan, "How active inference could help revolutionise robotics," Entropy, vol. 24, no. 3, p. 361, 2022.

[9] G. I. Parisi, R. Kemker, J. L. Part, C. Kanan, S. Wermter, "Continual lifelong learning with neural networks: A review," Neural Netw., vol. 113, pp. 54-71, 2019.

[10] T. Parr, G. Pezzulo, and K. J. Friston, Active Inference: The Free Energy Principle in Mind, Brain, and Behavior. Cambridge, MA, USA: MIT Press, 2022.

[11] K. J. Friston, T. FitzGerald, F. Rigoli, P. Schwartenbeck, J. O. Doherty, G. Pezzulo, "Active inference and learning," Neurosci. Biobehav. Rev., vol. 68, pp. 862-879, 2016.
[12] N. Krishnachaithanya et al., "People counting in public spaces using deep learning-based object detection and tracking techniques," in Proc. Int. Conf. Comput. Intell. Sustain. Eng. Solut. (CISES), 2023.
[13] M. De Prado et al., "Bonseyes ai pipeline—bringing ai to you: End-to-end integration of data, algorithms, and deployment tools," ACM Trans. Internet Things, vol. 1, no. 4, pp. 1-25, 2020.
[14] A. Wang et al., "Yolov10: Real-time end-to-end object detection," in Proc. Adv. Neural Inf. Process. Syst., vol. 37, 2024, pp. 107984-108011.
[15] Q. Zhang, R. Han, C. H. Liu, G. Wang, L. Y. Chen, "ElasticDNN: On-device neural network remodeling for adapting evolving vision domains at edge," IEEE Trans. Comput., vol. 73, no. 6, pp. 1616-1630, Jun. 2024.
[16] C. Cioflan, L. Cavigelli, M. Rusci, M. De Prado, L. Benini, "On-device domain learning for keyword spotting on low-power extreme edge embedded systems," in Proc. IEEE 6th Int. Conf. AI Circuits Syst. (AICAS), 2024.
[17] E. Sommerlade and I. Reid, "Information-theoretic active scene exploration," in Proc. IEEE Conf. Comput. Vis. Pattern Recognit., 2008.
[18] E. Sommerlade and I. Reid, "Probabilistic surveillance with multiple active cameras," in Proc. IEEE Int. Conf. Robot. Autom., 2010.
[19] Y. LeCun, Y. Bengio, and G. Hinton, "Deep learning," Nature, vol. 521, no. 7553, pp. 436-444, 2015.
[20] Z.-Q. Zhao, P. Zheng, S. Xu, X. Wu, "Object detection with deep learning: A review," IEEE Trans. Neural Netw. Learn. Syst., vol. 30, no. 11, pp. 3212-3232, Nov. 2019.
[21] "ONNX: Open Neural Network Exchange," 2019. [Online]. Available: https://github.com/onnx/onnx
[22] "ONNX Runtime," 2021. [Online]. Available: https://onnxruntime.ai
[23] R. David et al., "Tensorflow lite micro: Embedded machine learning for tinyml systems," in Proc. Mach. Learn. Syst., vol. 3, 2021, pp. 800-811.
[24] E. Jeong, J. Kim, and S. Ha, "Tensorrt-based framework and optimization methodology for deep learning inference on jetson boards," ACM Trans. Embedded Comput. Syst., vol. 21, no. 5, pp. 1-26, 2022.
[25] T.-Y. Lin et al., "Microsoft coco: Common objects in context," in Proc. Eur. Conf. Comput. Vis., 2014, pp. 740-755.
[26] C. Heins et al., "pymdp: A Python library for active inference in discrete state spaces," arXiv preprint arXiv:2201.03904, 2022.

[27] "Tapo surveillance camera," Accessed: Nov. 2024. [Online]. Available: https://www.tapo.com/us/product/smart-camera/tapo-c210i

[28] "Locobot robot," Accessed: Nov. 2024. [Online]. Available: http://www.locobot.org

[29] "Saccade demonstration." [Online]. Available: https://drive.google.com/drive/folders/1VCN8MAMnsdbj-xY5qudjn7vLFlB5mSfi?usp=sharing

[30] R. Bajcsy, "Active perception," Proceedings of the IEEE, vol. 76, no. 8, pp. 996–1005, Aug. 1988.

[31] J. Aloimonos, I. Weiss, and A. Bandyopadhyay, "Active vision," International Journal of Computer Vision, vol. 1, no. 4, pp. 333–356, 1988.

[32] D. H. Ballard, "Animate vision," Artificial Intelligence, vol. 48, no. 1, pp. 57–86, 1991.

[33] S. Chen, Y. Li, and N. M. Kwok, "Active vision in robotic systems: A survey of recent developments," The International Journal of Robotics Research, vol. 30, no. 11, pp. 1343–1377, Sept. 2011.

[34] S. Isler, R. Sabzevari, J. Delmerico, and D. Scaramuzza, "An information gain formulation for active volumetric 3D reconstruction," in Proc. IEEE Int. Conf. Robot. Automat. (ICRA), Stockholm, Sweden, 2016, pp. 3477–3484.

# 3

# Prediction of Neural Network Latency on Embedded GPU Accelerators

**Adrian Osterwind[1], Domenik Helms[1], and Verena Klös[2]**

[1]German Aerospace Center (DLR), Germany
[2]Carl von Ossietzky Universität Oldenburg, Germany

## Abstract

AI systems are transforming many application areas, but resource constraints prevent many especially time critical embedded applications. In particular, a fast prediction of expected latency and energy costs can enable the hardware-aware design of such systems. Thus, we started developing a latency model for the NVIDIA Jetson platform, which, with its GPU-based architecture is interesting in e.g. automotive vision use-cases. Using latency models in automatic optimization flows yields benefits, compared to abstract metrics like parameter count. However, it needs to be fast, for optimization algorithms to cover large search spaces. We developed a layer-wise model using the parameters of the layer (like input size) and a number of hardware measurements to produce a model of the network latency. On the Jetson platform the characterization yielded a model, that in first tests provided three key insights: Using only a few measurements we can already accurately predict upper and lower bound of the execution time. Using more information, we can, under ideal conditions, estimate latency with a mean average percentage error below 3%. Lastly, we found that sometimes a small change of input parameters can lead to up to 10% reduction in latency for that layer.

**Keywords:** embedded AI, resource modelling, AI, embedded systems.

DOI: 10.1201/9788743815211-3

## 3.1 Introduction

With the increase in competency of neural networks, they have seen deployment in more and more critical applications such as automotive. In this sector, the push for fully autonomous driving demands increasingly complex functions to be executed on the onboard computer.

To be able to execute these functions together on an embedded system while adhering to critical time boundaries, they must be optimized. These optimizations require knowledge about hardware behaviour to judge the changes in performance.

This is often obtained using either high-level metrics such as the number of floating-point operations (FLOPs) or weights in a neural network, or by conducting experiments with hardware-in-the-loop.

In this paper, we explore a latency model for a GPU-based system, such as those used in automotive use-cases, which promises an accurate model of the hardware with a minimal number of measurements. This work in progress is tested on the example of an NVIDIA Jetson development board, which is a relevant hardware platform for autonomous vehicles.

The remainder of this document is structured as follows. In Section 3.2, we discuss previous solutions to the modelling problem for AI hardware accelerators, which will inform some decisions in our approach. Based on the knowledge gained, we develop our own approach in Section 3.3, discussing the general hardware model and how to characterize it effectively. Initial results of our experimentation are shown in Section 3.4, showing the hardware behaviour under changing layer configurations and the first modelling approaches. In Section 3.5, we summarize our findings and discuss next steps.

## 3.2 Related Work

The need for performance prediction has been recognized by many researchers and embedded AI engineers in the past.

Approaches range from very high-level metrics such as number of floating-point operations (FLOPs) [1], to low-level simulations of the hardware [2]. Both are valid for certain use-cases, however, they come with some inherent issues. Using a metric such as FLOPs results in a very simple and fast model of hardware performance. However, they might not accurately account for behaviour such as overhead for memory management and hardware optimizations [3].

Low-level simulations, in contrast, capture these behaviours very well and can thus be much more accurate. The cost of accuracy is the need for in-depth knowledge of the hardware, which might not be available on proprietary systems [4]. Furthermore, the complexity of these simulations results in high simulation overheads [2, 5].

A compromise between these two extremes is a hardware-aware black box method.

For this work, we are interested in a hardware-aware black box method. Previously, we presented a model for the Neural Compute Stick 2 in [6]. To achieve this, we used a generalized model of the behaviour of neural network layers, which is tailored to the hardware by latency measurements. For this, we used a simple linear regression between points. To characterize the model, we defined a search space to interpolate within. In this search space, we selected a random set of samples, which needed to be dense, to cover most non-linearities.

The work in [7] tackled this issue by using random forest regression. However, this still requires many datapoints to characterize a hardware platform.

By trying to determine points of interest for characterization, [8] reduces this number. These points of interest are determined in a sweep of the target parameter of the neural network layer.

In this work, we will use a similar methodology, sweeping through parameter ranges to determine points of interest. However, we will use composite functions for each dimension, which promise to capture more details gained in the sweep, allowing us to reduce the number of measurements taken.

## 3.3 Approach

For our modelling approach we exploit the fact that the latency of a network can be closely approximated by summing up the latencies of all layers. This way, the prediction can be done layer by layer. Furthermore, we assume a certain regularity in the change of latency of a layer.

The prediction for a layer depends on its type, e.g., Conv2D and parameters, e.g., number of channels or filters (see Figure 3.1), as well as some hardware-specific numbers that we model as variables in the general hardware-agnostic model. By instantiating the variables with values obtained from measurements, we get a hardware-specific model, that can be used to derive predictions.

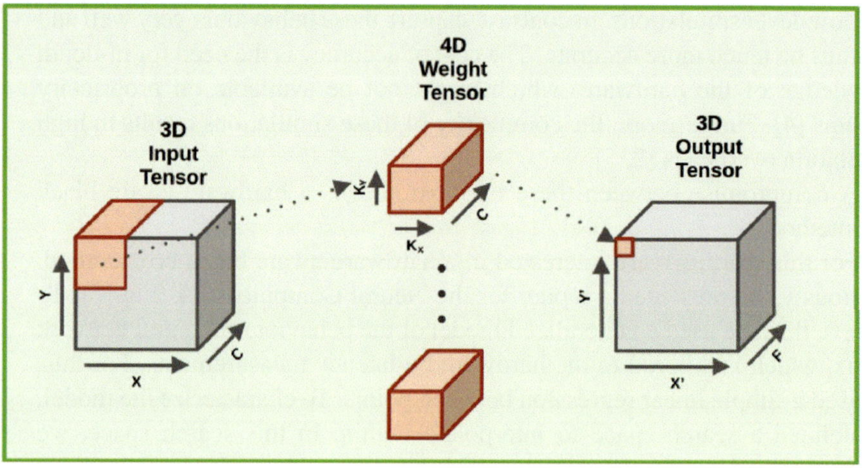


**Figure 3.1** Presentation of the primary parameters of a Convolution layer in a neural network. The network consists of an input tensor with dimensions $x, y$ and $c$ - the channels. The convolution operation itself can be described as a tensor of size $k_x$ and $k_y$ with a depth of $c$. With $F$ convolutions or filters, the output size can be described as $x'$, $y'$ and $F$, with $x'$ and $y'$ depending on stride $S_x$ and $S_y$ and the padding $p_x$ and $p_y$.

To build the latency prediction model, we must take the following steps:

Firstly, we need to create a way to profile a neural network on the layer level. Details on how to do this will be described in 3.3.1 *Profiling*.

Using this approach, we can perform some initial representative measurements to create a generalized model of the latency behaviour of a layer with regard to single parameter changes. For this, we search for repeating patterns in the measurements and determine a function describing those. The variables of this function can be divided into global variables, which should not change for a hardware class, and local variables that depend on all other parameters of the layer. A detailed description on how to do this is given in 3.3.2 *Generalized layer model.*

From this generalized model, we can then characterize, i.e. derive a hardware-specific model for a single dimension of a neural network layer such as the number of channels in a Conv2D layer by instantiating the global and local variables of the layer. How to do this, will be described in 3.3.3 *Single Dimensional Model.*

Using the single dimension model, we expect to be able to interpolate the layer parameters one at a time. As this is a work in progress, this step has not yet been achieved.

In the following, we describe our modelling approach for GPU-based systems, as well as the resulting characterization approach.

To be able to adapt the model to different hardware types easily, we want a model that fulfils the following requirements: Firstly, it should be general, meaning it should be able to cover different hardware types without recreating the model every time. Secondly, it should require as few measurements as possible, to reduce the need for extensive characterization. Thirdly, the model should not require potentially complex or proprietary hardware knowledge for characterization.

**Preliminaries** The rest of the chapters use a number of terms we define here. The primary layer being discussed is the commonly used convolution 2D (conv2D) layer. The parameters relevant to latency are shown in Figure 3.1. We refer to the measurement of hardware latency used to feed the model with hardware-specific measurements as characterization. Profiling describes the measurement of a neural network and determining the single layer latencies. A (parameter) sweep is the profiling of a neural network layer, with one parameter being changed continuously while all other parameters stay constant. Finally, the model will be described as a composite function, i.e., a function whose variable is another function.

### 3.3.1 Profiling

For the model, we have to characterize the hardware with regards to the behaviour of single layers in the neural networks. To ensure accuracy of measurements, we measure multiple times and use the resulting confidence interval until we are sure that the mean of the samples is close enough to the mean of the distribution.

As shown in [6] we need to execute the layer in a representative network, as first and last layers absorb certain initialization and deinitialization tasks, which do not occur within a neural network. Therefore, we selected a three-layer network for profiling, with the middle layer being the layer under test.

To decrease overhead of the surrounding layers, we can perform sweeps to determine how the input and output layers affect the layer under test. If these sweeps show a convergence, the smallest layer combination, which is within a margin of the convergence point, can be selected.

Once a suitable profiling network has been determined, we perform sweeps on the parameters of the layer type to determine latency behaviour in relation to those parameters. For Conv2D layers, the relevant parameters are input size (x, y, channels), and output filters. These sweeps are then analysed, and the model variables inferred.

This gives the model for just one layer parameter combination. To transfer this model to different layer combinations, it might be necessary to perform more measurements with other parameter combinations. Here, we perform a minimal set of profiles, under the assumption that some variables of the model, such as step size, stay constant. This can then be verified using targeted measurements at the presumed step-points.

### 3.3.2 Generalized layer model

To fulfil the first of our requirements, the creation of a generalized model, we first perform some sweeps along one of the parameters of a neural network layer, in this case the channel size of a Conv2D layer. We perform this with two layer configurations, varying the kernel size, to provoke a pattern change.

Based on the results shown in Figure 3.2, we can observe several trends:

Firstly, latency increases linearly with channel size. Secondly, along this linear increase the network shows a stepping behaviour with a fixed step size. Thirdly, the latency fluctuates between an upper and lower step function with a constant period.

Approximating this behaviour is possible using a nested function:

$$T(c) = \begin{cases} T_{S_U}(c), & \text{if } (c-1) \bmod r < \frac{r}{2} \\ T_{S_L}(c), & \text{else} \end{cases} \tag{3.1}$$

Here $T(c)$ is the latency of a layer based on the number of input channels $c$. $r$ is the period of fluctuation. Based on this, the function selects between the step functions $T_{S_U}(c)$ and $T_{S_L}(c)$:

$$T_{S_U}(c) = \left\lfloor \frac{c}{d} \right\rfloor * d * m_u + b_u \tag{3.2}$$

$$T_{S_L}(c) = \left\lceil \frac{c}{d} \right\rceil * d * m_l + b_l \tag{3.3}$$

In these functions $m_u$, $b_u$, $m_l$ and $b_l$ define the upper and lower bounds for the step functions, which has a depth of $d$.

From Figure 3.2, we can see that the variables $r$ and $d$ do not change with changing layer configurations, while the upper and lower bounds are locally

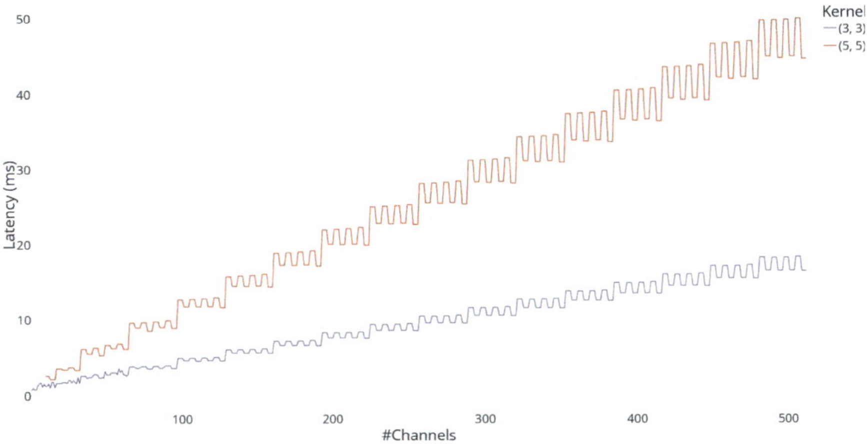


**Figure 3.2** Profiling Results of Input Channel Sweep.

determined as expected, since layers with more operations should take longer than smaller layers.

For this reason, we define $r$ and $d$ as global variables, determined once from a sweep, and the rest as local variables, which need to be determined for each layer configuration.

### 3.3.3 Single Dimensional Model

To determine the values for the variables of the model for a layer dimension, we need to follow two steps:

First, we must determine the global variables. This is based on a parameter sweep as performed in the previous section. In a manual step, we can see that, e.g., for the channel sweep in Figure 3.2, the step depth appears to be 32 with a fluctuation period of 8.

In the second step, we need to determine the upper and lower bounds. This can be done by selecting values at the start and end of the sweep, lying on the upper and lower step functions as determined by the first step. Linear interpolation between each upper and lower value results in the full definition of the model for this sweep.

If this is done for each dimension of the layer, we, in theory, should be able to interpolate any layer combination using just a few simply obtained values, satisfying requirements 2 (few characterization points) and 3 (little hardware knowledge). This will have to be validated in future work.

## 3.4 Results

To test the approach described in Section 3.3, we did some initial characterizations of the NVIDIA Jetson AGX Orin platform. These currently cover the parameters as separate dimensions.

### 3.4.1 Experimental Setup

The test-setup is comprised of a NVIDIA Jetson AGX Orin running the Jetson Linux in version 36.4.4 with CUDA version 12.6. For execution and profiling we use TensorRT in version 10.3, which is a highly performant first party neural network runtime for CUDA based devices. It was chosen, because it has shown to behave predictably, changing latency as modelled.

Profiling a datapoint consists of several steps. First, we use PyTorch to create the profiling network with the required parameters and export the resulting network to the commonly used ONNX interchange format. Afterwards, this is read and converted in TensorRT to its internal format for execution on the CUDA cores of the Jetson platform. After a warmup period, we run the neural network with the profiler enabled until a sufficient certainty is obtained.

### 3.4.2 Characterization

For our characterization, we started with the primary dimensions (input-size, output, filters) separately.

The sweep configurations used for our initial characterization can be seen in Table 3.1. For the channel sweep the range was chosen to extend to very large parameters, to investigate if the behaviour changes at higher parameters.

In the characterization results (see Figures 3.2 to 3.4) a predictable pattern can be identified. Starting with the sweep over the channels in Figure 3.2, we can see an overall linear increase in latency w.r.t. input channels. On a lower level, we see a stepping behaviour with a step size of 32, which however changes between an upper and lower step function with a stride of 4 samples each.

**Table 3.1** The sweep configurations used for the initial testing of the model hypothesis

| | Input WxH | Channels | Filters | Kernel XxY |
|---|---|---|---|---|
| **Channel Sweep** | 256x256 | 10 - 530 | 128 | 3x3 |
| **Filter Sweep** | 256x256 | 128 | 1-530 | 3x3 |
| **Input Sweep** | 10-511 | 64 | 128 | 1x1, 3x3, 5x5 |

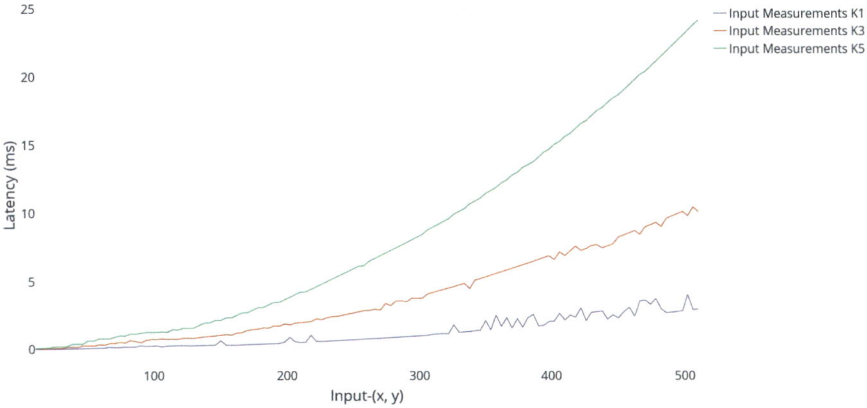


**Figure 3.3** Profiling Results of Input (x, y) Sweep

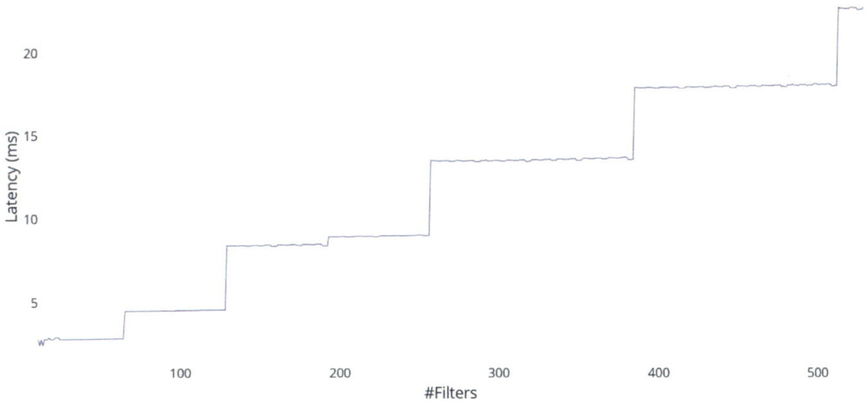


**Figure 3.4** Profiling Results of Filter Sweep.

The input sweep in Figure 3.3 shows a quadratic increase over input size in each dimension. For each input dimension this results in a strictly (within the margin of error) linear increase.

For the filter sweep in Figure 3.4, again, an overall linear increase in latency can be observed with larger step sizes of mostly 128. However, in this dimension no fluctuating behaviour can be observed.

### 3.4.3 Initial Model Results

Our model was initially only tested for the input channel dimension.

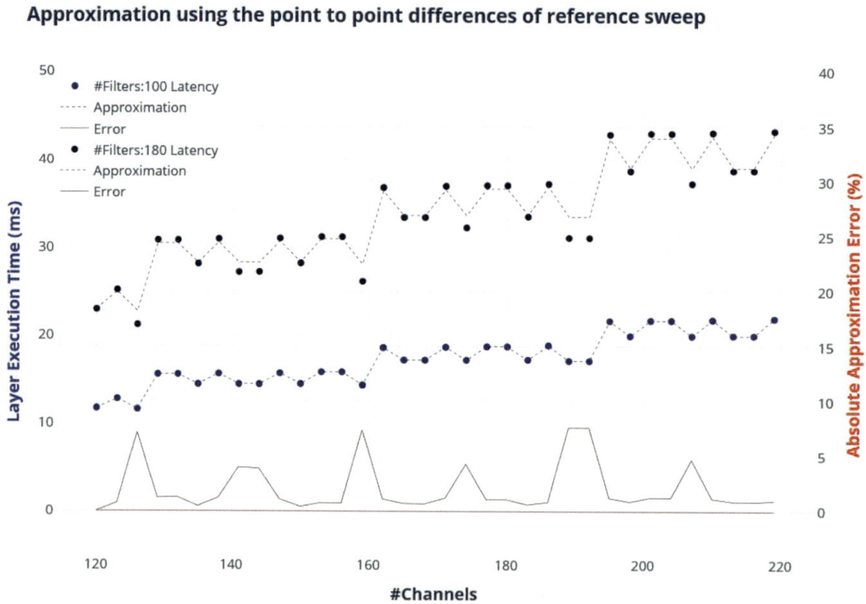


**Figure 3.5** Model Results for Channels.

For testing, we used the initial channel sweep from Figure 3.2 and collected a set of sparse channel sweeps, that we tried to approximate using knowledge from the full sweep in Figure 3.2 (such as step size) and only 4 measurements, defining the upper and lower boundaries of the function.

The channel sweeps ranged from 120 to 219 with a sampling step size of 3. This sweep was performed repeatedly, only varying the output filter from 100 to 244 in steps of 16, resulting in 9 channel sweeps.

We were able to approximate the initial channel sweep with a mean absolute percentage error (MAPE) of ca. 1.6%.

The results for the smaller sweeps can be seen in Figure 3.3. In this constellation, we see an overall MAPE of ca. 1.3%.

Our evaluation shows that our method works for a single dimension, providing very accurate predictions using just the sweep data and a small number of measurements per layer configuration.

## 3.5 Conclusion

In this paper, we have shown that GPU-based embedded systems can, in theory, be modelled using a relatively simple hardware behaviour model and few hardware measurements. Initial tests have shown prediction errors below 2% for single dimensions based on only a generalized characterization of the dimension and 4 additional measurements for the layer configuration.

In future work, we will extend this model to more dimensions, to be able to predict an arbitrary neural network layer configuration.

## Acknowledgement

This work has received funding from the Chips Joint Undertaking (Chips JU) under the European Union's Horizon Europe research and innovation programme under Grant Agreement No. 101139892.

## References

[1] D. Balemans, T. Huybrechts, J. Steckel, and S. Mercelis, "Resource-Aware Neural Network Pruning Using Graph-based Reinforcement Learning." [Online]. Available: https://arxiv.org/abs/2509.10526

[2] Q. Dariol, „Early Performance and Energy Prediction of Neural Networks Deployed on Multi-Core Platforms", Aug. 2023. doi: 10.5281/zenodo.11208197.

[3] S. Yao et al., "FastDeepIoT: Towards Understanding and Optimizing Neural Network Execution Time on Mobile and Embedded Devices," in Proceedings of the 16th ACM Conference on Embedded Networked Sensor Systems, in SenSys '18. Shenzhen, China: Association for Computing Machinery, 2018, pp. 278–291. doi: 10.1145/3274783.3274840.

[4] E. Sotiriou-Xanthopoulos, G. S. P. Delicia, P. Figuli, K. Siozios, G. Economakos, and J. Becker, "A power estimation technique for cycle-accurate higher-abstraction SystemC-based CPU models," in 2015 International Conference on Embedded Computer Systems: Architectures, Modeling and Simulation, SAMOS 2015, Greece, Institute of Electrical and Electronics Engineers (IEEE), 2015, pp. 70–77. doi: 10.1109/SAMOS.2015.7363661.

[5] R. Raj et al., "SCALE-Sim v3: A modular cycle-accurate systolic accelerator simulator for end-to-end system analysis." [Online]. Available: https://arxiv.org/abs/2504.15377

[6] A. Osterwind, J. Droste-Rehling, M.-R. Vemparala, and D. Helms, "Hardware Execution Time Prediction for Neural Network Layers," in Machine Learning and Principles and Practice of Knowledge Discovery

in Databases, I. Koprinska, Ed., Cham: Springer Nature Switzerland, 2023, pp. 582–593.

[7] M. Wess, M. Ivanov, C. Unger, A. Nookala, A. Wendt, and A. Jantsch, "ANNETTE: Accurate Neural Network Execution Time Estimation With Stacked Models," Institute of Electrical, Electronics Engineers (IEEE), 2021, pp. 3545–3556. doi: 10.1109/access.2020.3047259.

[8] A. L.-F. Jung, J. Steinmetz, J. Gietz, K. Lübeck, and O. Bringmann, "It's All About PR," in Embedded Computer Systems: Architectures, Modeling, and Simulation, L. Carro, F. Regazzoni, and C. Pilato, Eds., Cham: Springer Nature Switzerland, 2025, pp. 59–75

# 4

# Closing the Gap Between AI Models and Silicon: Application Deployment for Next-Generation Edge Accelerators

**Michal Szczepanski, Benoit Tain, Raphael Millet, Axel Farrugia, Cyril Moineau, and Sebastien Thuries**

Université Paris-Saclay, CEA-List, France

## Abstract

The deployment of deep neural networks on edge devices requires a carefully constructed pipeline flow from algorithm design to hardware execution. In this work, we present a complete application development pipeline targeting J3DAI, a low-power DNN accelerator integrated in a 3D-stacked CMOS image sensor. Starting from model training in PyTorch, we use the Aidge framework for post-training quantization and hardware-specific transformations, enabling the direct generation of binary files optimized for J3DAI execution. Our evaluation is performed using silicon-accurate simulation and gate-level netlists, providing hardware-realistic performance insights without relying on fabricated silicon. We highlight practical considerations in network design, including quantization trade-offs, tiling strategies, and the mapping of common operators to accelerator primitives. Beyond the current deployment flow, we discuss new perspectives for extending accelerator support, such as advanced operator sets, adaptive memory partitioning, and tighter hardware-software co-design. Together, these contributions demonstrate a robust pipeline that bridges machine-learning development with hardware accurate execution, offering a practical route toward real-time vision tasks directly on sensor in future silicon implementation.

**Keywords:** edge AI, low power, DNN accelerator, 3D-stacked CMOS, quantization.

DOI: 10.1201/9788743815211-4 

## 4.1 Introduction and Background

The rise of edge computing has sharply increased the need to run deep neural networks (DNNs) directly on small, resource-limited devices. Many modern applications, from real-time computer vision to autonomous systems and privacy-focused analytics depend on fast, low-latency inference while operating within strict power limits. However, bringing DNN models from development frameworks to actual silicon hardware at the far edge remains a complex and ongoing challenge.

Edge devices often operate under tight constraints: limited on-chip memory, low energy availability, and customized accelerator architectures that may only handle a fraction of common neural network operations. These accelerators tend to be optimized for specific tasks (for instance, chains of convolution layers) while processing others less efficiently (like residual connections). This imbalance can cause slowdowns due to data movement or fallback of unsupported operations. In addition, popular machine learning frameworks such as PyTorch and TensorFlow were not originally designed with hardware-aware deployment as a core priority, making the gap between model design and deployment even wider. Their abstractions often hide the underlying memory and computational costs, and do not allow the magnitude (float, int,) of intermediate values in different operators to be determined, causing a mismatch between software models and accelerator capabilities.

In this work, we present a deployment pipeline built around J3DAI, a tiny deep neural network accelerator integrated into a 3-layer 3D-stacked CMOS image sensor. The system features a dedicated AI chip in the bottom die, designed to execute quantized models under strict power and memory constraints. Our pipeline connects high-level model development to silicon execution: models trained in PyTorch are quantized and adapted using the Aidge framework, then exported into format optimized for hardware execution on J3DAI.

The main contributions of this work are as follows:

- We describe an end-to-end workflow for deploying DNNs on constrained accelerators, from PyTorch training through Aidge quantization to J3DAI execution.
- We introduce J3DAI as an ultra-compact edge AI solution, tightly integrated into a 3D-stacked image sensor for near-sensor processing.
- We provide experimental validation on both classification and segmentation tasks, demonstrating that the pipeline achieves efficient inference without significant loss of accuracy.

- We open a discussion on future perspectives, highlighting opportunities to expand operator support, improve memory utilization, and advance hardware–software co-design.

## 4.2 Related Work

### 4.2.1 Edge AI Accelerators and In-Sensor Processing

The increasing demand for low-latency vision has driven research into accelerators designed for edge inference. Conventional approaches include NPUs in mobile SoCs and external devices such as Google EdgeTPU and Intel Movidius, which provide efficient CNN acceleration but remain separated from the sensor. More recent work explores processing-in-sensor and 3D stacking techniques to bring computation closer to the pixel array. Examples include NeuroSensor [1] and 3D-stacked designs embedding convolutional logic image sensors [2–5]. These works demonstrate substantial reductions in data movement and energy consumption, though they typically support limited operator sets or shallow networks. The J3DAI architecture extends this trend by providing a programmable, quantization-aware accelerator tightly integrated into a 3-die CMOS stack [6].

### 4.2.2 Quantization and Deployment Frameworks

On the software side, multiple frameworks address model adaptation for constrained hardware. TensorFlow Lite [7], TensorRT [8] offer quantization and operator fusion for NPUs or CPUs, but they depend on backend-specific operator libraries and offer limited visibility hardware constraints. Recent surveys [9–10] highlight different strategies, advantages and the importance of post-training quantization (PTQ) for reducing the footprint of DNNs while maintaining accuracy highlighting its effectiveness as a practical deployment strategy.

Bridging ML models with accelerator execution requires careful hardware–software co-design. Compiler-based solution such as TVM [11] and Vitis AI [12] translate model to heterogeneous hardware through optimization passes for scheduling and memory management. Other efforts, such as PISA [13], integrate binarized or quantized compute into the sensor itself. Nevertheless, these approaches either target general-purpose accelerators or focus on limited model families limiting their adaptability.

The deployment tools are rarely designed for sensor-integrated accelerators. The Aidge framework fills this gap by enabling quantization and export into a hardware-ready format, ensuring that models trained in PyTorch can be directly executed directly on J3DAI. By contrast, the proposed pipeline explicitly considers operator compatibility and SRAM footprint analysis, ensuring that the deployment flow is both hardware-aware and adaptable.

## 4.3 System Overview

The experimental study was conducted on the system referenced in [6]. Below is a brief description of its key components and configuration to provide context for the experimental results.

The system is a 3D-stacked CMOS image sensor, designed for low-power on-sensor deep learning inference. The stack is composed of three dies, each implementing a distinct function:

- **Top die:** a 12-megapixel RGB pixel matrix (4096 $\times$ 3072), responsible for image capture.
- **Middle die:** analog readout and image signal processing (ISP), a lightweight RISC-V host processor, and a portion of the shared L2 memory. This die also manages communication between the sensor and external host interfaces
- **Bottom die:** the dedicated J3DAI DNN accelerator, based on PNeuro [14] which integrates Neural Compute Blocks (NCBs), a multi-bank on-chip memory hierarchy, and data-movement units such as the Direct Memory Parallel Access (DMPA) engine. The accelerator is optimized for quantized neural networks and provides high throughput under strict area and power constraints.

During deployment, the RISC-V host orchestrates execution, loading PNeuro instructions into the instruction memory and managing scheduling across compute clusters. The NCBs execute supported layers in parallel, while the DMPA unit enables efficient transfer of weights and activations, mitigating the cost of data movement—a critical bottleneck in memory-limited accelerators.

The J3DAI accelerator was implemented as the bottom die of a 3D-stacked CMOS image sensor, enabling direct execution of quantized neural networks at the sensor level. The hardware integrates multiple Neural Compute Blocks (NCBs) connected through a high-bandwidth on-chip interconnect. Each NCB supports parallel multiply–accumulate (MAC) operations, activation functions, and pooling, while memory hierarchies (L1 cluster SRAM, shared L2 SRAM, and instruction/data SRAM) ensure efficient tiling of large models. A key architectural feature is the Direct Memory Parallel Access (DMPA) engine, capable of transferring 1024 bits per cycle, which dramatically reduces the overhead of weight and activation movement compared to conventional DMA schemes.

This integration provides a streamlined path from high-level model definition to real-time hardware execution. Crucially, the workflow also includes compatibility and memory footprint checks, ensuring that the chosen model fits within the available instruction and data SRAM and does not rely on unsupported operators. As such, the system bridges the gap between software frameworks and silicon constraints, enabling practical deployment of edge vision applications directly within the sensor stack.

## 4.4 Deployment Pipeline

Deploying a deep neural network to the J3DAI accelerator requires an end-to-end flow that connects high-level model training with hardware-level constraints. The deployment pipeline is composed of four stages: model training, quantization, compatibility/memory analysis, and hardware execution.

**Model Definition and Training (PyTorch).**

Development begins in PyTorch, where models are defined, trained, and validated using conventional floating-point arithmetic (FP32). This stage benefits from the ecosystem of state-of-the-art vision architectures, datasets, and training tools. However, model design is not entirely hardware-agnostic: candidate architectures must be evaluated against the accelerator's supported operator set and memory hierarchy. In particular, operators must be structurally compatible with J3DAI execution, and activation buffers must fit within the available SRAM capacity. This consideration is especially critical for complex applications such as semantic segmentation or object detection, where diverse operators and large intermediate feature maps—driven by high input resolutions—can easily exceed hardware limits. By integrating these constraints during training, rather than postponing them to later stages as in many existing deployment flows, the pipeline establishes a hardware-aware feedback loop that reduces the risk of incompatibility and ensures that even complex models remain deployable on constrained accelerators.

**Quantization and Export (Aidge).**

The trained model is processed through the Aidge framework, which applies post-training quantization (PTQ) to reduce weights and activations to low-precision (e.g., int8). This process involves calibrating the model using a representative dataset to determine optimal scaling factors for weights and activations, ensuring minimal loss of precision during quantization. Consequently, it significantly decreases the model's memory footprint, while preserving acceptable accuracy. Model quantization requires a careful examination of both linear and non-linear operators to ensure compatibility with the accelerator's supported execution set. For instance, in dense applications such as semantic segmentation, operators like bilinear interpolation—commonly used to restore input resolution—must to be replaced or restructured to meet hardware constraints. In such cases, this stage may trigger a feedback loop to the training process so that the architecture remains both accurate and deployable. Once validated, the quantized model is exported into the 8-bit graph format, a lightweight hardware-aware representation that encodes network topology in Aidge framework.

The export will retrieve the graph in 8-bit format along with the hardware configuration of the DNN accelerator. The hardware configuration mainly includes the number of available NCBs and the size of the associated L1 and L2 memories. This configuration and the graph are essential for placing the feature maps and network parameters in the accelerator's memories. A dedicated solver explores multiple mapping solutions to find the optimal placement. Based on this mapping, the export configures each advanced function specific to PNeuro, such as automatic indexes and multidimensional address generators.

Then, the export automatically generates the assembly code and the host code. The assembly code includes the PNeuro instructions. These instructions are compiled to obtain a binary code that can be loaded into the instruction memories. The host code, written in C, consists of the main source code that calls the functions of each layer of the network with an execution routine. Each layer routine begins by loading the program into the instruction memory, then loads the kernel parameters and the input data (if first layer or use of tiling). Subsequently, the execution of the accelerator is started and synchronized via a control register. In case of tiling, the multi-pass execution continues, saving the intermediate results in the global memory at every step.

All these steps have enabled the generation of the binary that can be loaded to execute the network on the target hardware.

**Execution on J3DAI.**

As physical hardware was not available during the development phase, hardware execution of the neural network was implemented using both a high-level simulator and a post-routed netlist. The high-level simulator, based on an Instruction Set Simulator (ISS), enabled rapid and effective assessment of the model's functional performance at an early design stage. For strict cycle-accurate temporal analysis, a post-implementation netlist generated after place-and-route was employed, allowing detailed investigation of real-time circuit behavior and precise reproduction of hardware-level interactions. The combined use of these two complementary simulation methods provided robust and comprehensive validation of hardware execution despite the immediate unavailability of the physical device.

Overall, this pipeline enables a smooth transition from PyTorch training to silicon execution, while actively addressing the challenges of limited memory and selective operator support. By incorporating compatibility and memory checks into the deployment workflow, the system ensures robust and efficient operation for real-world edge applications.

## 4.5 Experimental results

To validate the proposed deployment pipeline, we conducted experiments on the J3DAI accelerator integrated within a 3D-stacked CMOS image sensor prototype. Evaluation focused on classification and segmentation tasks, emphasizing accuracy retention, inference latency, and energy efficiency under realistic operational conditions. All tests were performed with the J3DAI AI core operating at 200 MHz, processing input directly from the sensor interface to avoid off-chip data transfers.

### 4.5.1 Model Presentation

Three representative networks were selected to characterize the proposed deployment pipeline across both classification and dense-prediction tasks. The classification models: MobileNetV1 [15] and MobileNetV2 [16] were chosen for their compact structure and well-established efficiency in mobile-scale inference, while the third model implements a lightweight encoder–decoder segmentation network representative of real-time pixel-wise applications. For classification, pretrained weights provided by the torchvision library were used as the initial backbone. For segmentation, the architecture uses encoder (MobileNetV1 $\alpha = 0.5$), couple with a feature pyramid style decoder implemented as a linear combination of convolution block, trained from a scratch [17]. This configuration achieves a total integer model size below 4 MB, allowing full on-chip storage of weights and activations during inference. To ensure full compatibility with the J3DAI instruction

**Table 4.1** Key performance metric of selected models

| Model | MobileNetV1 | MobileNetV2 | Segmentation |
|---|---|---|---|
| MMACs | 557 | 289 | 877 |
| Image Input | 256x192 | 256x192 | 512x384 |
| Accuracy | 62% Top-1 | 66% Top-1 | 36.4 mIoU |
| Latency @200MHZ | 4.96 ms | 4.04 ms | 7.43 ms |
| Power @30FPS | 47.6 mW | 30.5 mW | 63.8mW |
| Power efficiency | 0.77 TOPS/W | 0.62 TOPS/W | 0.82 TOPS/W |
| MAC/Cycle efficiency | 76.8% | 46.6% | 76.5% |

set, for segmentation, bilinear interpolation layers—unsupported by the accelerator—were replaced with nearest-neighbour upsampling

Input dimensions were adjusted to fit the native 4:3 aspect ratio of the image sensor: 256 $\times$ 192 pixels for classification and 512 $\times$ 384 pixels for segmentation. This scaling preserves the natural field of view of the sensor while balancing resolution and computational load.

### 4.5.2 Experimental Validation

Under this configuration, the number of MAC operations for MobileNetV1 is 557 M, comparable to the classic 224 $\times$ 224 input format (569 M MACs). Similarly, MobileNetV2 requires 289 M MACs, close to the 300 M MACs used in the standard configuration. The MobileNetV2 architecture, however, introduces branching structures and depthwise–pointwise sequences, which increase data movement and reduce MAC-per-cycle efficiency, resulting in higher latency relative to its nominal compute cost.

Across classification tasks, quantization causes minimal degradation compared to FP32 baselines. MobileNetV1 achieved 62 % Top-1 accuracy, and MobileNetV2 reached 66 % Top-1, both within 1–2 % of their floating-point counterparts validated on ImageNet dataset. Inference latency ranged from 4.0 ms to 5.0 ms, corresponding to real-time throughput above 200 FPS, while maintaining $<$ 50 mW power consumption at 30 FPS. The resulting power efficiency to 0.77 TOPS/W demonstrates the suitability of J3DAI for always-on edge vision applications.

For the segmentation task, evaluation was performed on the Cityscapes dataset. The model archives 36.4 mIoU, below large state of art architectures, with only 877 MMACs, which other models work in orders of magnitude more parameters and are not deployable in such constrained environments. The reported performance therefore reflects an optimal balance between accuracy, memory footprint, and on-chip efficiency.

Because the input resolution of 512 × 384 differs from the Cityscapes size (1024 × 2048), we present two evaluation results in each Figure 4.1 and 4.2 below. Above is a cropped-input evaluation, in which smaller section of 512 × 384 pixels is extracted from validation images. This configuration preserved fine detail and allowed reliable detection of small elements such as traffic lights and pedestrians. Below we present full-frame resizing, where

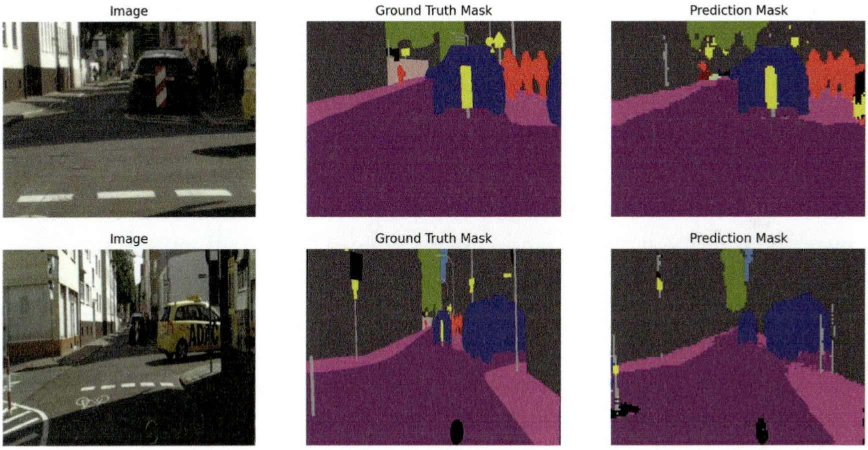


**Figure 4.1** Input Image, Ground Truth Mask and Prediction for Segmentation Network in float32.

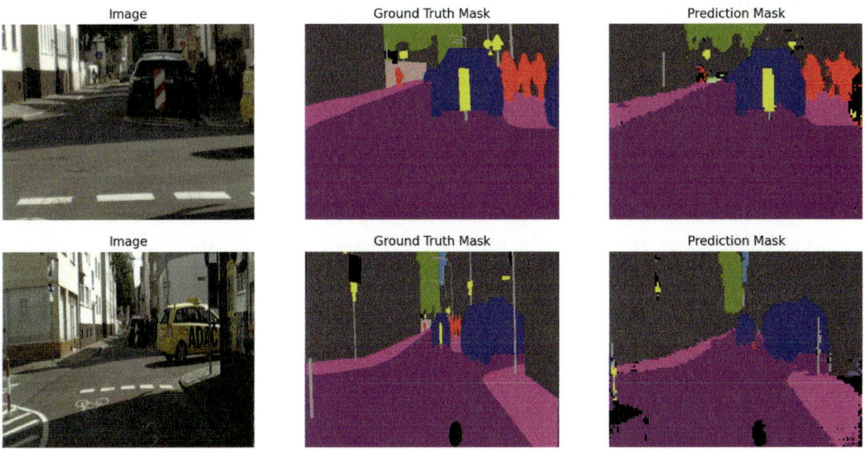


**Figure 4.2** Input Image, Ground Truth Mask and Prediction for Segmentation Network in int8.

the entire image is uniformly scaled down to 512 $\times$ 384. This approach retained global context but led to a noticeable drop in small-object accuracy and an overall lower mIoU however allows to compare our method with others. Across both methods, quantization introduced less than 1.2 % relative loss in mIoU compared with the floating-point model, which is visible on prediction Mask for both Figures 4.1 and 4.2. It confirms that the Aidge PTQ process preserves segmentation quality while meeting the accelerator's resource constraints.

## 4.6 Perspectives & Discussion

The deployment results presented above demonstrate that the proposed PyTorch–Aidge–J3DAI pipeline provides an efficient bridge between algorithmic design and silicon execution for compact convolutional networks. However, the rapidly evolving landscape of edge AI applications and model architectures opens several avenues for future development on both software and hardware fronts.

The current J3DAI instruction set and Aidge toolchain primarily target CNNs, which remain dominant in near-sensor vision tasks. Yet, emerging architectures such as the Vision Transformer models are reshaping the state of the art in visual perception. Supporting these models on edge accelerators will require extending the operator set to include primitives such as multi-head self-attention, layer normalization, and softmax. Hardware implementation of these operators must preserve efficiency while maintaining the programmability required for future algorithmic flexibility. Integrating these capabilities would enable J3DAI to process a broader range of models, including ViT-based feature extractors and lightweight transformer decoders, thereby expanding its applicability beyond classical CNN-based pipelines.

Beyond classification and semantic segmentation, future work aims to extend support toward depth estimation, object detection, and optical flow extraction. Achieving these goals will also depend on hardware evolution. Augmented on-chip memory capacity, which would relax constraints on intermediate tensor buffering and enable bigger models to be mapped with tiling strategy.

## 4.7 Conclusions

In this work, we introduced an end-to-end deployment pipeline that connects deep neural network training in PyTorch with efficient execution on the J3DAI near-sensor accelerator. The pipeline was designed to make deployment seamless, turning high-level models into hardware-ready binaries while taking into account real memory and operator constraints from the very beginning. By integrating hardware awareness directly into the training and quantization process, the approach avoids many of the late-stage compatibility issues that typically slow down deployment to edge devices.

Using the Aidge framework, models are quantized and optimized for the accelerator without sacrificing much accuracy, typically within 1–2% of the original floating-point versions. Experimental results obtained through simulation of the J3DAI hardware show that the deployed networks can achieve real-time performance with low latency and minimal power consumption, making them well-suited for embedded vision applications such as classification and segmentation directly on the sensor.

More broadly, this work demonstrates the importance of tight co-design between algorithms and hardware. Instead of treating deployment as an afterthought, the proposed flow treats it as part of the model development process, ensuring that each design decision remains compatible with hardware limits. The result is a robust and efficient system that simplifies the path from model design to silicon execution.

Looking ahead, this approach together with Aidge framework offers a strong foundation for future expansion. As AI models evolve, especially with the growing adoption of ViT architectures and more complex perception tasks, extending the J3DAI operator set and toolchain will open new opportunities for near-sensor intelligence. Overall, the proposed pipeline represents a practical and forward-looking step toward bringing high-performance, low-power AI directly to the edge.

## Acknowledgements

This work was supported by the French National Research Agency (ANR) through the "Investissement d'avenir" (investments for the future) programs: ANR 10-AIRT- 005 (IRTNANO-ELEC) and by the Neurokit2E European Project (GA101112268). Furthermore, the Aidge developers are gratefully acknowledged.

## References

[1] M. F. Amir, D. Kim, J. Kung, D. Lie, S. Yalamanchili, and S. Mukhopadhyay, 'NeuroSensor: A 3D image sensor with integrated

neural accelerator', in *2016 IEEE SOI-3D-Subthreshold Microelectronics Technology Unified Conference (S3S)*, Burlingame, CA, USA: IEEE, Oct. 2016, pp. 1–2. doi:10.1109/S3S.2016.7804406.

[2] T. Haruta *et al.*, '4.6 A 1/2.3inch 20Mpixel 3-layer stacked CMOS Image Sensor with DRAM', in *2017 IEEE International Solid-State Circuits Conference (ISSCC)*, San Francisco, CA, USA: IEEE, Feb. 2017, pp. 76–77. doi:10.1109/ISSCC.2017.7870268.

[3] K. Kiyoyama, Q. Zhengy, H. Hashimoto, H. Kino, T. Fukushima, and T. Tanaka, 'Development of a CDS Circuit for 3-D Stacked Neural Network Chip using CMOS Analog Signal Processing', in *2019 International 3D Systems Integration Conference (3DIC)*, Sendai, Japan: IEEE, Oct. 2019, pp. 1–4. doi:10.1109/3DIC48104.2019.9058856.

[4] P. Vivet *et al.*, 'Advanced 3D Technologies and Architectures for 3D Smart Image Sensors', in *2019 Design, Automation & Test in Europe Conference & Exhibition (DATE)*, Florence, Italy: IEEE, Mar. 2019, pp. 674–679. doi:10.23919/DATE.2019.8714886.

[5] P. Vivet *et al.*, 'Advanced 3d Design and Technologies for 3-Layer Smart Imager', in *2022 International Symposium on VLSI Technology, Systems and Applications (VLSI-TSA)*, Hsinchu, Taiwan: IEEE, Apr. 2022, pp. 1–2. doi:10.1109/VLSI-TSA54299.2022.9771026.

[6] B. Tain *et al.*, 'J3DAI: A tiny DNN-Based Edge AI Accelerator for 3D-Stacked CMOS Image Sensor', in *2025 IEEE/ACM International Symposium on Low Power Electronics and Design (ISLPED)*, Reykjavík, Iceland: IEEE, Aug. 2025, pp. 1–7. doi: 10.1109/ISLPED65674.2025.11261786

[7] R. David *et al.*, 'TensorFlow Lite Micro: Embedded Machine Learning on TinyML Systems', 2020, *arXiv*. doi:10.48550/ARXIV.2010.08678.

[8] E. Jeong, J. Kim, and S. Ha, 'TensorRT-Based Framework and Optimization Methodology for Deep Learning Inference on Jetson Boards', *ACM Trans. Embed. Comput. Syst.*, vol. 21, no. 5, pp. 1–26, Sep. 2022, doi:10.1145/3508391.

[9] Z. Yuan *et al.*, 'Benchmarking the Reliability of Post-training Quantization: a Particular Focus on Worst-case Performance', 2023, *arXiv*. doi:10.48550/ARXIV.2303.13003.

[10] A. Gholami, S. Kim, Z. Dong, Z. Yao, M. W. Mahoney, and K. Keutzer, 'A Survey of Quantization Methods for Efficient Neural Network Inference', 2021, *arXiv*. doi:10.48550/ARXIV.2103.13630.

[11] T. Chen *et al.*, 'TVM: An Automated End-to-End Optimizing Compiler for Deep Learning', 2018, *arXiv*. doi:10.48550/ARXIV.1802.04799.

[12] A. Ushiroyama, M. Watanabe, N. Watanabe, and A. Nagoya, 'Convolutional neural network implementations using Vitis AI', in *2022 IEEE 12th Annual Computing and Communication Workshop and Conference (CCWC)*, Las Vegas, NV, USA: IEEE, Jan. 2022, pp. 0365–0371. doi: 10.1109/CCWC54503.2022.9720794.

[13] S. Angizi, S. Tabrizchi, and A. Roohi, 'PISA: A Binary-Weight Processing-In-Sensor Accelerator for Edge Image Processing', 2022, *arXiv*. doi:10.48550/ARXIV.2202.09035.

[14] A. Carbon *et al.*, 'PNeuro: A scalable energy-efficient programmable hardware accelerator for neural networks', in *2018 Design, Automation & Test in Europe Conference & Exhibition (DATE)*, Dresden, Germany: IEEE, Mar. 2018, pp. 1039–1044. doi:10.23919/DATE.2018.8342165.

[15] A. G. Howard *et al.*, 'MobileNets: Efficient Convolutional Neural Networks for Mobile Vision Applications', 2017, *arXiv*. doi:10.48550/ARXIV.1704.04861.

[16] M. Sandler, A. Howard, M. Zhu, A. Zhmoginov, and L.-C. Chen, 'MobileNetV2: Inverted Residuals and Linear Bottlenecks', 2018, doi: 10.48550/ARXIV.1801.04381.

[17] V. T. Quyen, J. H. Lee, and M. Y. Kim, 'Enhanced-feature pyramid network for semantic segmentation', in *2023 International Conference on Artificial Intelligence in Information and Communication (ICAIIC)*, Bali, Indonesia: IEEE, Feb. 2023, pp. 782–787. doi:10.1109/ICAIIC57133.2023.10067062.

# 5

# Multichannel Speech Enhancement under Low-Latency Constraints: Balancing Quality and Computational Cost

**Zahra Benslimane[1], Fabrice Auzanneau[1], Martyna Poreba[1], Michal Szczepanski[1], Fabian Chersi[1], and Romain Serizel[2]**

[1]Université Paris-Saclay, CEA-List, France
[2]Université de Lorraine, INRIA, LORIA, France

## Abstract

Multichannel speech enhancement is essential for robust speech intelligibility in noisy environments. Although many algorithms address this challenge, their deployment in real-time or embedded settings imposes strict computational and latency constraints. This work compares three representative methods: FaSNet-TAC, an end-to-end neural network-based approach; neural MVDR, a hybrid time-frequency method; and Tango, a fully distributed framework. For our evaluation, we employ a methodology that explicitly separates the input context needed for optimal performance from the output latency. Using a common noisy-speech test set and identical evaluation protocols, we assess the enhancement quality of these methods and their computational complexity under various target algorithmic latency requirements. Our analysis shows that a one second context is sufficient to approach full-utterance performance. It also highlights distinct trade-offs across architectures: Tango exhibits the most robust behaviour under stringent latency constraints, whereas FaSNet-TAC is the most sensitive to context and hop-size reduction. We also find that mask-estimation stages constitute the dominant computational bottleneck, underscoring the importance of

DOI: 10.1201/9788743815211-5

aligning model design with the intended latency regime for practical real-time deployment.

**Keywords:** Multichannel speech enhancement, Low-latency audio processing, Computational complexity, Neural beamforming.

## 5.1 Introduction and Background

Speech Enhancement (SE) aims to improve the perceptual quality and intelligibility of audio signals by reducing the impact of background noise, interference, and reverberation. While single-channel methods rely solely on spectral and temporal cues [1, 2], multichannel SE techniques leverage the spatial information provided by microphone arrays to better distinguish between speech and noise sources for more effective source separation and noise suppression.

Recent progress in machine learning has resulted in the development of new end-to-end neural network-based algorithms for enhancing multichannel speech [3–6]. These algorithms model complex relationships within the data and can learn to map time-domain or time-frequency representations of noisy speech directly to enhanced outputs, capturing rich spatiotemporal dependencies without relying on handcrafted feature extractors. Alongside these purely data-driven approaches, hybrid frameworks that embed classical signal-processing methods into neural pipelines have been explored in an attempt to find a balance between robustness, interpretability, and computational efficiency [7]. In these systems, deep neural networks (NN) are trained to estimate statistics that are used to compute filters such as beamformers [8].

Although these developments have led to substantial improvements in enhancement quality, practical deployment imposes additional constraints that traditional metrics fail to capture. Measures such as SNR, while informative, overlook factors critical for real-time and embedded operation. Consequently, a meaningful assessment of modern SE systems must also account for latency and computational efficiency, considerations that have driven a growing body of work on model compression and low-complexity designs.

To enable on-device SE, researchers have used pruning, quantization, and compact designs to reduce model size and inference cost. Wu and Yu (2019) [9] removed redundant channels and applied weight clustering. Tan and Wang (2021) [10] used sparse regularization and iterative pruning. Fedorov et al. (2020) [11] introduced TinyLSTMs with pruning, 8-bit quantization, and state-update skipping. Stamenovic et al. (2021) [12] compared different sparsity methods. More recently, Cohen et al. (2024) [13] proposed a Fully Quantized SE model with a quantization-aware knowledge-distillation loss for negligible Signal to Distortion Ratio (SDR). However, low computational load does not necessarily correlate with a decreased latency. Recent studies have focused on minimizing algorithmic latency in SE to satisfy the stringent requirements of real-time applications. Various strategies have been proposed, including time-domain end-to-end models, Short Term Fourier Transform-domain (STFT) processing with dual windowing schemes [14], and decoupled spatial-temporal architectures [15]. Other approaches used spiking neural networks [16] or causal filter-and-sum frameworks with low-bit-rate inter-device communication for binaural setups [17].

In this paper, we explore, evaluate, and compare three deep learning-based algorithms for multichannel SE, with a focus on their performance under the stringent constraints of real-time embedded deployment. Our goal is to systematically analyse the trade-offs inherent to each of these models, focusing in particular on the relationship between input context size and output latency, as well as their computational load.

## 5.2 Methodology

### 5.2.1 Latency reduction strategy

Real-time SE presents a fundamental trade-off between using a large input context (long audio segments) and achieving low output latency. A larger context provides the model with more information (e.g., speaker characteristics, noise patterns), which generally improves enhancement quality. However, it also forces the system to wait longer before producing any output, increasing the processing delay.

We distinguish two types of delay: *algorithmic latency*, the time required to accumulate sufficient audio data before processing, and *computational latency,* the time the algorithm itself spends performing calculations, which can vary depending on the device's processing power and resources. To keep this study hardware-agnostic, we assume that computational latency is negligible.

In contrast to the traditional STFT symmetric windows (Figure 5.1-a), Wang et al. [14] proposed a low-latency STFT framework that employs asymmetric windows for both analysis and reconstruction. Building on their approach, we conducted experiments to adapt their method for processing input context under various algorithmic-latency constraints. To achieve this,

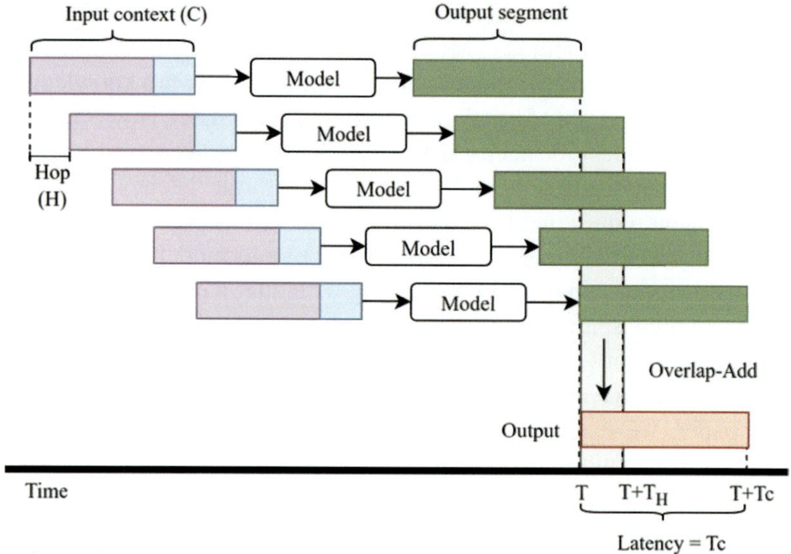


(a) Conventional overlapping inference: each input of length $T_C$ is processed giving an output of the same length. Overlap-add is used to reconstruct the continuous signal. Thereby, imposing an algorithmic delay $T_C$

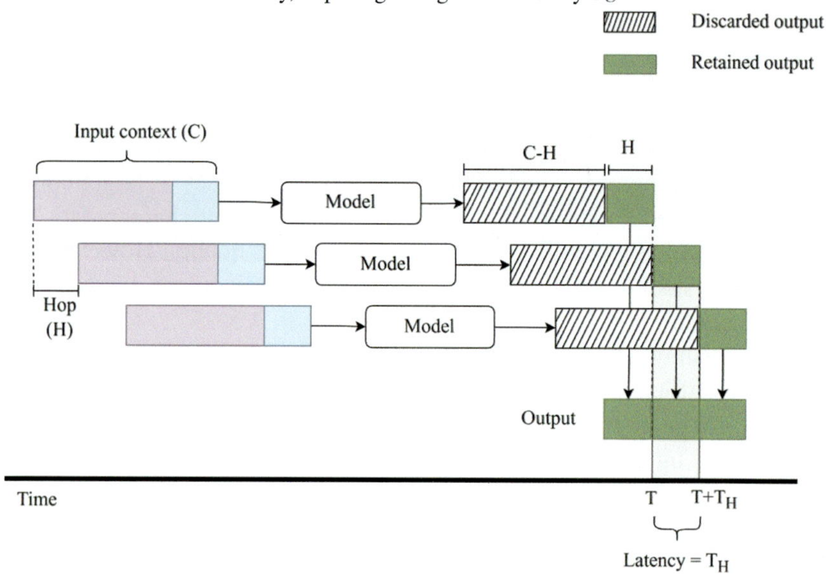


(b) Low latency inference

**Figure 5.1** Comparison of two overlapping-windows inference strategies. In (a), the model incurs an algorithmic latency of $T_C$ . In (b), by discarding overlapping outputs and retaining only the last $T_H$ seconds of each pass, the perceived latency is reduced to $T_H$.

we maintained a rolling input buffer of length C which was advanced in small hops of size H, where H < C. At each hop, the buffer window was passed through the model, producing an output window $y_k \in \mathbb{R}^C$ from which only the final H samples, yk $[C - H : C - 1]$ were retained. Here, C and H denote the sequence length and hop size in the model's internal representation. These could represent raw waveform samples, STFT frames, or any other internal representation. Their corresponding durations in seconds are denoted as $T_C$ and $T_H$. The model consistently utilized the full context C, thereby maximizing enhancement performance while producing new audio samples every $T_H$ seconds, as illustrated in Figure 5.1-b. As the hop size H was reduced, the model had to be invoked more frequently, increasing computational demand. To assess this load in a hardware-agnostic manner, we estimate the number of floating-point operations per second (FLOPs/s).

### 5.2.2 Overview of the selected algorithms

We selected three representative multichannel SE architectures (Figure 5.2), each reflecting a distinct modelling paradigm, in order to evaluate them under identical conditions. FaSNet-DPRNN-TAC [5] is a time-domain, end-to-end Neural Network operating on raw waveforms. For simplicity, we refer to it as FaSNet-TAC throughout this document. It builds upon the original FaSNet architecture [3] and incorporates dual-path RNN (DPRNN) blocks [4] to model inter-channel dependencies. Each DPRNN block incorporates a Transform Average-Concatenate (TAC) module that projects all channels features into a shared embedding space to produce an output that is invariant to both the number and ordering of microphones.

Neural MVDR [7], is a hybrid time-frequency domain architecture that integrates a neural implementation of the MVDR beamformer. Spatial filters are computed based on the Power Spectral Density (PSD) matrices of both speech and noise, which are estimated using time-frequency masks generated by an LSTM-based neural network. This allows the system to dynamically adapt the beamforming process to the acoustic scene, improving noise suppression while preserving speech integrity.

Finally, Tango [8], is a fully distributed, two-stage hybrid SE framework designed to operate on spatially unconstrained microphone arrays with multiple nodes. Each processing stage combines a CNN along with a Speech Distortion Weighted Multichannel Wiener Filter, a modified version of the traditional MWF [18], which provides an improved balance between noise suppression and speech distortion.

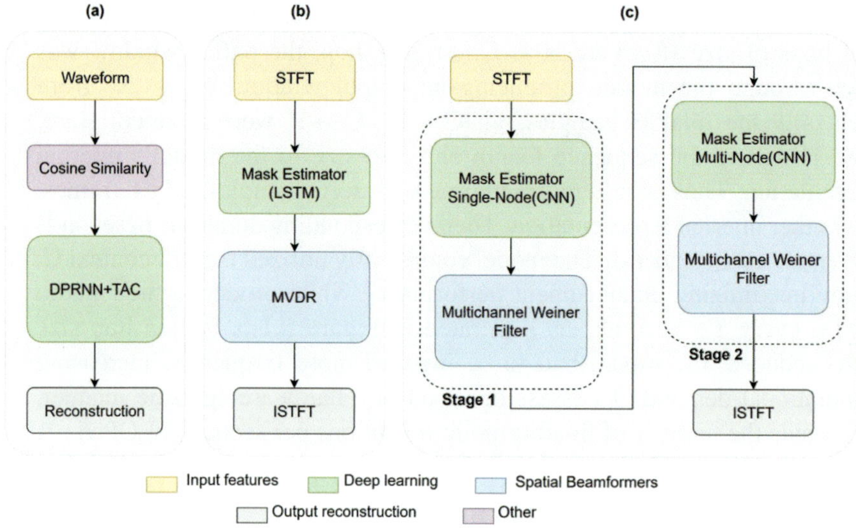


**Figure 5.2** Studied models. (a) FaSNet-TAC (b) Neural MVDR (c) Tango.

## 5.3 Experimental Setup

### 5.3.1 Testing set

The testing set was created using 1,000 utterances drawn from the LibriSpeech test-clean corpus [19], sampled at 16 kHz, with durations ranging between 3 s and 11 s. Each clean utterance was spatialized by convolution with measured binaural Room Impulse Responses (RIRs) from the Binaurec database, using a speech source positioned at 0° and noise sources at +45° and +90°. The RIRs were recorded with a dummy head in a room measuring 6.62 m × 2.57 m × 2.60 m with a reverberation time (RT60) of 0.20 s [20]. The spatialized clean and noise signals were then mixed at three different signal-to-noise ratios (SNRs) of −5 dB, 0 dB, and +5 dB. Two types of noise were considered: speech-shaped noise and white noise.

### 5.3.2 Implementation details

The three models were trained on a synthetic dataset, described in [21]. Clean speech signals were drawn from the LibriSpeech corpus and combined with two categories of noise: speech-shaped noise (30%) and environmental recordings from the Disco noise collection (70%). The speech-shaped component was created using LibriSpeech speakers excluded from the clean set to maintain spectral similarity between the speech and noise. To simulate realistic reverberant conditions, room impulse responses were generated using the *Pyroomacoustics* library [22]. The simulated rooms had lengths between 3 and 8 m, widths between 3 and 5 m, and heights between 2.5 and 3 m. Reverberation times (RT60) were randomly sampled in the range of 0.15-0.4 s to represent a variety of acoustic environments.

A four-microphone binaural array was simulated to approximate a hearing-aid configuration. For each simulated array the interaural spacing (ear-to-ear center distance) was sampled uniformly between 0.12 m and 0.18 m. Each ear included two microphones positioned with small lateral offsets of 0.01-0.02 m and vertical offsets of 0.01-0.015 m. Speech and noise sources were randomly placed within the virtual room, and mixtures were generated with signal-to-interference ratios (SIRs) uniformly distributed between $-10$ dB and $+10$ dB.

During inference, Tango is configured to produce a single enhanced signal for each ear, resulting in binaural outputs. In contrast, the FaSNet-TAC and Neural MVDR were applied twice; once with the front-left channel and once with the front-right channel as the processing reference channel, yielding corresponding left and right enhanced signals.

### 5.3.3 Evaluation metrics

Speech enhancement performance was evaluated using the scale-invariant metrics: Scale-Invariant Signal-to-Distortion Ratio (SI-SDR), Scale-Invariant Signal-to-Interference Ratio (SI-SIR), and Scale-Invariant Signal-to-Artifact Ratio (SI-SAR), which respectively assess overall distortion, interference suppression, and artifact introduction.

Along with these enhancement metrics, we used the Python libraries *torchinfo* and *ptflops* to calculate the FLOPs required to process 1 second of audio for the deep learning components of each neural architecture presented in Section 5.2.2. For the beamforming components, where automated profiling was not feasible, FLOPs were computed manually.

### 5.3.4 Context and latency trade-off

We first determined the minimal acceptable context length $C_{min}$, through a non-overlapping block segmentation experiment. Each input recording was divided into contiguous, disjoint windows of fixed length $C$, with the network processing each window independently. We tested context durations $T_C$ of

1 s, 500 ms, and 100 ms. For FaSNet-TAC, each window was fed directly into the network. For the two-hybrid mask-beamforming architectures, the same segmentation was applied to both the mask estimation and beamforming stages, enabling the entire pipeline to operate segment-wise. This setup allowed us to assess how increasing $C$ influenced enhancement quality in the absence of overlapping segments.

After identifying $C_{min}$ (the smallest context length that yields near-peak performance), we reduced the effective algorithmic latency using an overlapping-segment inference strategy, as described in Section 5.2.1 and shown in Figure 5.1-b. In this approach, the segment length is fixed at $C_{min}$, while the processing window advances by a smaller hop size $H$, such that $H < C_{min}$. We evaluated hop sizes of 500 ms, 100 ms, 50 ms, and 10 ms. For example, with $T_C = 1\ s$ and $T_H = 50\ ms$, the network processes a 1 s segment and outputs the final 50 ms of enhanced audio before shifting the input window forward by 50 ms and repeating the process.

## 5.4 Results and discussion

Note that all metrics denoted with the "out" suffix correspond to evaluations performed on the enhanced signals obtained after the speech enhancement stage. Additionally, the SI-SIR IN metric, computed on the input mixtures, is included to quantify the suppression improvement provided by each model. The "in" and "out" designations are used only in the figures for clarity. Unless explicitly stated otherwise, all mentions of SI-SIR, SI-SDR, and SI-SAR in the text refer to the output metrics.

Figure 5.3 shows SI-SIR, SI-SDR, and SI-SAR for non-overlapping segments of varying input lengths, with the leftmost blue bar indicating full-utterance evaluation: Neural MVDR exhibits a sharp interaural difference, in terms of SI-SIR, compared to the rest, which is expected given the spatial configuration of the test set. In our setup, the dominant noise sources were located at $+45°$ and $+90°$ azimuths relative to the listener's head, *i.e.*, closer to the right ear. Consequently, the right-channel mixtures inherently contain stronger interference energy and a less favourable SNR prior to enhancement, creating a more challenging separation problem on that side. In contrast, Tango demonstrates the most consistent SI-SIR between the left and right ears, indicating robust interference suppression across spatial channels. Interestingly, FaSNet-TAC achieves slightly higher SI-SIR on the right ear, suggesting that its end-to-end time-domain processing can better exploit interaural cues under asymmetric noise conditions. However, this

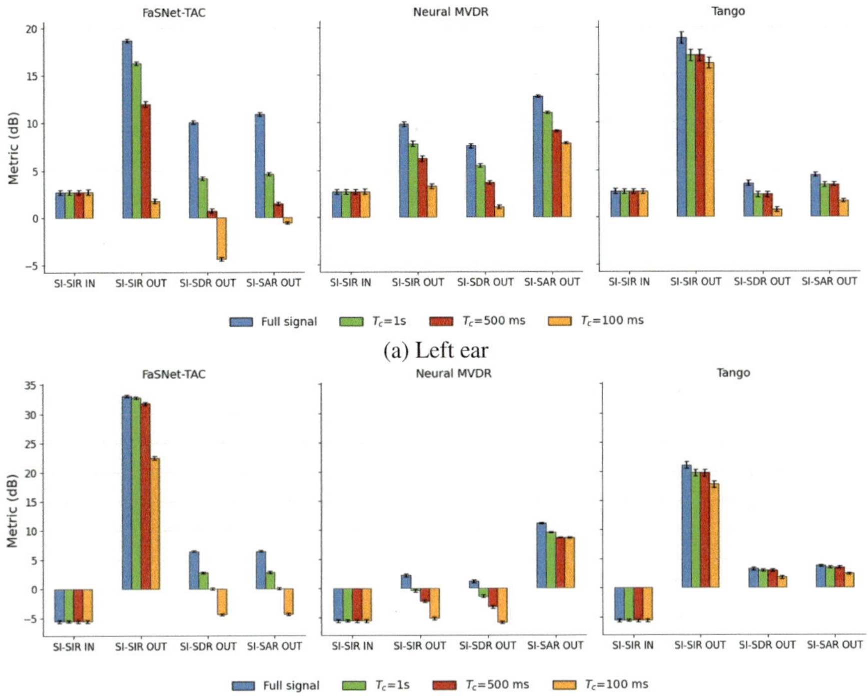


(a) Left ear

(b) Right ear

**Figure 5.3** Effect of input context length on enhancement performance on the left (a) and right (b) ear.

advantage is not reflected in the other metrics; both metrics remain lower overall, indicating that the additional SIR gain comes at the cost of higher distortion and artifact introduction.

Reducing the input context window from 1 s to 100 ms causes a steady SDR decline, highlighting the importance of temporal information. This behaviour depends on how each architecture represents or aggregates temporal context. For example, Tango's convolutional mask estimator works on fixed 128 ms segments at a time, so any window larger than 128 ms leaves its mask predictions unaffected by context reduction. Consequently, the observed degradation in Tango can be attributed primarily to the downstream PSD matrices estimation segmentation, leaving it the least affected by shorter windows among the evaluated models.

Neural MVDR's performance depends on both the LSTM-based mask estimator and the speech-and-noise covariance matrices, so errors accumulate. To isolate each component's impact under reduced context, we ran two experiments: one varying only the mask-estimator's input window (with full-utterance context for PSD matrices estimation and beamforming; Figure 5.4), and one varying only the PSD matrices input window (with full-utterance context for mask estimation; Figure 5.5). The results show that segmentation of the PSD estimation stage causes a markedly larger performance drop, even when the context is just reduced to 1s, compared to the neural-network segmentation. This indicates that accurate and temporally coherent covariance estimates are critical for maintaining spatial filtering stability.

Our preliminary experiments demonstrate that a 1s context window achieves near full-signal performance; therefore, in order to ensure optimal SE results, we set $T_c = 1s$ for all subsequent evaluations, despite the associated increase in computational cost this may entail. Extending the context beyond 1 s was not considered, as the additional temporal information would likely yield diminishing returns while substantially increasing computational demand and latency. Alternatively, other scenarios could justifiably opt for shorter context windows to reduce resource consumption, at the expense of a

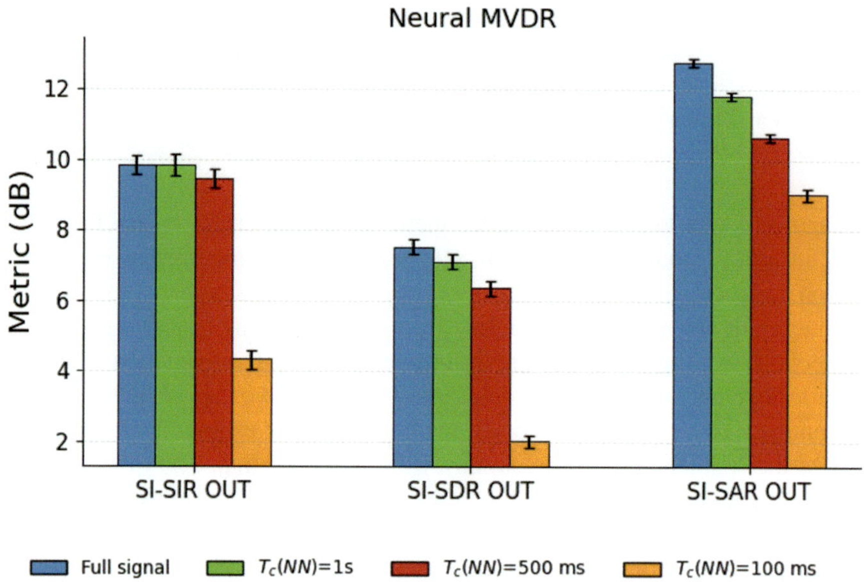


**Figure 5.4** Effect of mask estimator input context length on the neural MVDR performance (with a full-utterance PSD matrices context) on left ear.

higher drop in enhancement quality, but these cases fall outside the scope of this paper.

The next experiment (Figure 5.6) keeps constant input context, allowing us to isolate the effect of varying hop size and consequently the perceived latency, on each model's behaviour. Across both ears, Tango remains the most stable, showing only minimal degradation even at a 10 ms hop. Its consistent left-right performance reflects its binaural design, which explicitly models interaural cues. Neural MVDR exhibits moderate sensitivity to latency, with performance gradually declining, but it preserves relatively similar trends between the two ears. In contrast, FaSNet-TAC shows the steepest performance drop, particularly in SI-SDR and SI-SAR, starting from 500 ms latency. It also displays more pronounced disparities between the left and right ears, which is expected given its monaural end-to-end formulation and the noise conditions of the test set.

Table 5.1 reports the estimated floating-point operations per second (FLOPs/s) for each major processing component of our three architectures, evaluated at the four different perceived latencies. As the hop size shrinks, the model must be invoked more frequently, thus, the overall computational cost increases linearly: for example, FaSNet-TAC's DPRNN+TAC block jumps from about 2.5 GFLOPs/s at the 1 s baseline to 250 GFLOPs/s at a 10 ms hop. In both Neural MVDR and Tango, the neural mask-estimation stage incurs by far the largest share of computation. The PSD matrices estimation and beamforming steps remain in the low-mega to single-giga FLOPs/s

**Table 5.1** GFLOPs/s of different processing components at various hop sizes (perceived latencies)

| | | **Hop size / Perceived latency** | | | |
|---|---|---|---|---|---|
| **Component** | **Base** | **500ms** | **100ms** | **50ms** | **10ms** |
| | | **Neural MVDR** | | | |
| Mask estimation | 13.5 | 27.0 | 135 | 270 | 1350 |
| Speech & Noise PSD matrices | 0.009 | 0.018 | 0.094 | 0.18 | 0.94 |
| MVDR Beamformer | 0.001 | 0.002 | 0.012 | 0.024 | 0.60 |
| | | **Tango (Step 1 + Step 2)** | | | |
| Mask estimation | 3.14 | 6.28 | 31.4 | 62.8 | 310 |
| Speech & Noise PSD matrices | 0.008 | 0.017 | 0.086 | 0.17 | 0.80 |
| MCWF Beamformer | 0.002 | 0.004 | 0.02 | 0.04 | 0.50 |
| | | **FaSNet-TAC** | | | |
| DPRNN+TAC | 2.5 | 5 | 25 | 50 | 250 |

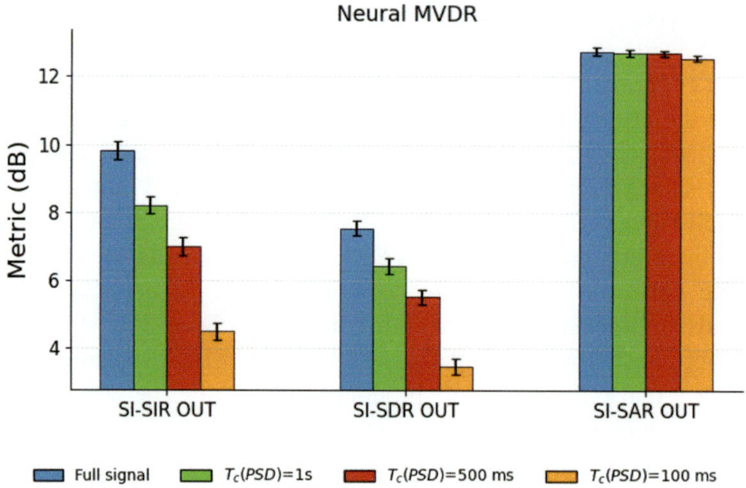


**Figure 5.5** Effect of PSD matrices input context on the neural MVDR (with a full-utterance mask estimation context) on left ear.

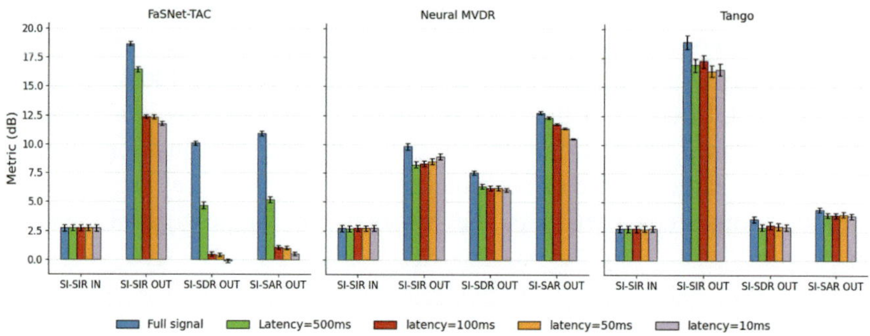


(a) Left ear

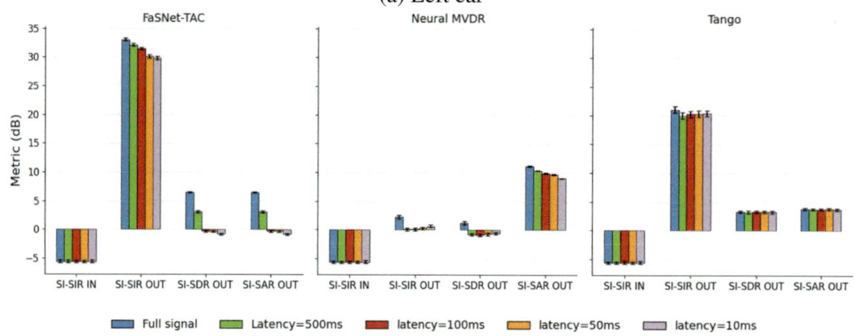


(b) Right ear

**Figure 5.6** Performance comparison of the three models at varying latency with a 1s input context of the left (a) and right (b) ear regime, even at 10 ms latency, confirming that mask estimation is the primary computational bottleneck when targeting very low latencies.

## 5.5 Conclusion

This study evaluated three multichannel SE models; FaSNet-TAC, Neural MVDR, and Tango, to examine how architectural design influences the trade-offs between enhancement quality, latency, and computational efficiency. The results highlight that different modelling paradigms exhibit distinct sensitivities to context reduction and latency constraints. End-to-end time-domain approaches show strong efficiency but higher sensitivity to reduced context, while hybrid methods demonstrate greater robustness under varying inference conditions. The overlapping-segment scheme therefore offers a flexible framework for adapting real-time SE to the latency and computational constraints of embedded hardware platforms. However, sustaining full-context performance at sub-100 ms latencies on resource-constrained devices becomes prohibitively expensive if one relies solely on brute-force windowing and frequent model inferences.

Overall, these analyses show that the overlapping-segment strategy provides a practical means to manage the trade-off between computational cost and real-time responsiveness. As the hop size decreases, all three models incur a substantial increase in FLOPs/s, driven almost entirely by the frequency of mask-estimation inference. This emphasizes the importance of aligning model design with the intended deployment scenario and latency requirements. Future work will investigate complementary approaches, such as streaming network architectures along with model-compression techniques that reduce FLOPs and end-to-end latency.

## Acknowledgements

This project has received funding from the French National Research Agency (ANR) under the project REFINED – "REal-time artiFicial INtelligence for hEaring aiDs" (ANR-21-CE19-0043).

## References

[1] C. Zheng et al., "Sixty Years of Frequency-Domain Monaural Speech Enhancement: From Traditional to Deep Learning Methods," Trends in

Hearing, vol. 27, Jan. 2023, doi: https://doi.org/10.1177/233121652312 09913.

[2] D. O'Shaughnessy, "Speech Enhancement—A Review of Modern Methods," IEEE Transactions on Human-Machine Systems, vol. 54, no. 1, pp. 110–120, Jan. 2024, doi: https://doi.org/10.1109/thms.2023.3339 663.

[3] Y. Luo, C. Han, Nima Mesgarani, Enea Ceolini, and S.-C. Liu, "FaSNet: Low-Latency Adaptive Beamforming for Multi-Microphone Audio Processing," 2019 IEEE Automatic Speech Recognition and Understanding Workshop (ASRU), Dec. 2019, doi: https://doi.org/10.1109/asru46091. 2019.9003849.

[4] Y. Luo, Z. Chen, and T. Yoshioka, "Dual-Path RNN: Efficient Long Sequence Modeling for Time-Domain Single-Channel Speech Separation," International Conference on Acoustics, Speech, and Signal Processing, May 2020, doi: https://doi.org/10.1109/icassp40776.20 20.9054266.

[5] Y. Luo, Z. Chen, Nima Mesgarani, and T. Yoshioka, "End-to-end Microphone Permutation and Number Invariant Multi-channel Speech Separation," Apr. 2020, doi: https://doi.org/10.1109/icassp40776.2020 .9054177.

[6] D. Lee, S. Kim, and J.-W. Choi, "Inter-channel Conv-TasNet for multichannel speech enhancement," arXiv.org, 2021. https://arxiv.org/abs/21 11.04312.

[7] J. Heymann, L. Drude, and Reinhold Haeb-Umbach, "Neural network based spectral mask estimation for acoustic beamforming," International Conference on Acoustics, Speech, and Signal Processing, Mar. 2016, doi: https://doi.org/10.1109/icassp.2016.7471664.

[8] N. Furnon, Romain Serizel, I. Illina, and Slim Essid, "DNN-based Distributed Multichannel Mask Estimation for Speech Enhancement in Microphone Arrays," pp. 4672–4676, Apr. 2020, doi: https://doi.org/10 .1109/icassp40776.2020.9054643.

[9] J.-Y. Wu, C. Yu, S.-W. Fu, C.-T. Liu, S.-Y. Chien, and Y. Tsao, "Increasing Compactness of Deep Learning Based Speech Enhancement Models With Parameter Pruning and Quantization Techniques," IEEE Signal Processing Letters, vol. 26, no. 12, pp. 1887–1891, Dec. 2019, doi: https://doi.org/10.1109/lsp.2019.2951950.

[10] K. Tan and D. Wang, "Towards Model Compression for Deep Learning Based Speech Enhancement," IEEE/ACM Transactions on Audio,

Speech, and Language Processing, vol. 29, pp. 1785–1794, 2021, doi: https://doi.org/10.1109/taslp.2021.3082282.

[11] I. Fedorov et al., "TinyLSTMs: Efficient Neural Speech Enhancement for Hearing Aids," Interspeech 2020, Oct. 2020, doi: https://doi.org/10.21437/interspeech.2020-1864.

[12] M. Stamenovic, Westhausen, Nils L, L.-C. Yang, C. Jensen, and A. Pawlicki, "Weight, Block or Unit? Exploring Sparsity Tradeoffs for Speech Enhancement on Tiny Neural Accelerators," arXiv.org, 2021. https://arxiv.org/abs/2111.02351.

[13] E. Cohen, Hai Victor Habi, and A. Netzer, "Towards Fully Quantized Neural Networks For Speech Enhancement," Aug. 2023, doi: https://doi.org/10.21437/interspeech.2023-883.

[14] Z.-Q. Wang, G. Wichern, S. Watanabe, and J. Le Roux, "STFT-Domain Neural Speech Enhancement With Very Low Algorithmic Latency," IEEE/ACM Transactions on Audio, Speech, and Language Processing, vol. 31, pp. 397–410, 2023, doi: https://doi.org/10.1109/taslp.2022.3224285.

[15] A. Pandey and B. Xu, "Decoupled Spatial and Temporal Processing for Resource Efficient Multichannel Speech Enhancement," pp. 12206–12210, Mar. 2024, doi: https://doi.org/10.1109/icassp48485.2024.10446087.

[16] T. Sun and S. Bohté, "DPSNN: Spiking Neural Network for Low-Latency Streaming Speech Enhancement," arXiv.org, 2024. https://arxiv.org/abs/2408.07388.

[17] N. L. Westhausen and B. T. Meyer, "Low Bit Rate Binaural Link for Improved Ultra Low-Latency Low-Complexity Multichannel Speech Enhancement in Hearing Aids," 2023 IEEE Workshop on Applications of Signal Processing to Audio and Acoustics (WASPAA), pp. 1–5, Oct. 2023, doi: https://doi.org/10.1109/waspaa58266.2023.10248154.

[18] S. Doclo, A. Spriet, J. Wouters, and M. Moonen, "Frequency-domain criterion for the speech distortion weighted multichannel Wiener filter for robust noise reduction," Speech Communication, vol. 49, no. 7–8, pp. 636–656, Jul. 2007, doi: https://doi.org/10.1016/j.specom.2007.02.001.

[19] V. Panayotov, G. Chen, D. Povey, and S. Khudanpur, "Librispeech: An ASR corpus based on public domain audio books," 2015 IEEE International Conference on Acoustics, Speech and Signal Processing (ICASSP), Apr. 2015, doi: https://doi.org/10.1109/icassp.2015.7178964.

[20] L. Delebecque and Romain Serizel, "BinauRec: A dataset to test the influence of the use of room impulse responses on binaural speech enhancement," HAL (Le Centre pour la Communication Scientifique Directe), pp. 126–130, Sep. 2023, doi: https://doi.org/10.23919/eusipco58844.2023.10289772.

[21] N.-E. Monir, P. Magron, and R. Serizel, "Frequency-Weighted Training Losses for Phoneme-Level DNN-based Speech Enhancement," arXiv.org, 2025. https://arxiv.org/abs/2506.18714

[22] R. Scheibler, E. Bezzam, and I. Dokmanić, "Pyroomacoustics: A Python Package for Audio Room Simulation and Array Processing Algorithms," IEEE Xplore, Apr. 01, 2018. https://ieeexplore.ieee.org/abstract/document/8461310?casa_token=u0fNFSqYAs4AAAAA:4-mLzpbwKd5EAOyAuEK-0OLSwxV6H7vHedb3jzkAnJsGyCqFt4i-rxzx6NBpHh2JeQrLQP4i.

# 6

# Pareto Optimal Benchmarking of AI Models on ARM Cortex Processors for Sustainable Embedded Systems

**Pranay Jain[1,2], Maximilian Kasper[1], Göran Köber[2], Oliver Amft[2,3], Axel Plinge[1], and Dominik Seuss[1,4]**

[1]Fraunhofer Institute for Integrated Circuits IIS, Germany
[2]Intelligent Embedded Systems (IES) - Lab, University of Freiburg, Germany
[3]Hahn-Schickard, Germany
[4]Center for Artificial Intelligence and Robotics - Technical University of Würzburg-Schweinfurt, Germany

## Abstract

This work presents a practical benchmarking framework for optimizing AI models on ARM Cortex processors (M0+, M4, M7), focusing on energy efficiency, accuracy, and resource utilization in embedded systems. Through the design of an automated test bench, we provide a systematic approach to evaluate across key performance indicators (KPIs) and identify optimal combinations of processor and AI model. The research highlights a near-linear correlation between floating-point operations (FLOPs) and inference time, offering a reliable metric for estimating computational demands. Using Pareto analysis, we demonstrate how to balance trade-offs between energy consumption and model accuracy, ensuring that AI applications meet performance requirements without compromising sustainability. Key findings indicate that the M7 processor is ideal for short inference cycles, while the M4 processor offers better energy efficiency for longer inference tasks. The M0+ processor, while less efficient for complex AI models, remains suitable for simpler tasks. This work provides insights for developers, guiding them

DOI: 10.1201/9788743815211-6

to design energy-efficient AI systems that deliver high performance in real-world applications.

**Keywords:** Edge AI, energy benchmarking, sustainable, deep compression.

## 6.1 Introduction

The integration of artificial intelligence (AI) into embedded systems is challenged by the need to balance model performance with energy consumption, a crucial factor for the sustainability and practicality of these systems. Edge AI provides energy efficiency, low latency, and privacy directly on the device, making them critical for applications from smart home devices to autonomous vehicles [7, 8].

As shown in Table 6.1, Edge AI platforms operate under strict resource constraints, with significantly less memory, power, and a smaller CO2 footprint compared to their cloud and mobile counterparts [1]. While considerable research has been conducted on benchmarking AI performance on single-board computers (SBCs) like Raspberry Pi, there is a gap in studies focusing on bare-metal processors. SBCs, while popular and accessible, introduce additional layers of abstraction that can obscure the true performance characteristics of the hardware. In contrast, bare-metal processors provide a more direct and granular understanding of the hardware capabilities, free from the overhead introduced by operating systems and middleware. This study addresses the need for a dedicated test bench that evaluates embedded AI systems at the bare-metal level. Key performance indicators such as accuracy, inference time, and energy consumption are measured, and Pareto front analysis is applied to identify optimal trade-offs. The results provide a solid basis for selecting AI models that achieve high efficiency even under strict resource constraints.

The rest of the paper is structured as follows. Section 2 reviews related work and highlights the need for standardized benchmarking in embedded AI. Section 3 outlines the methodology, including the design of the benchmarking framework, model selection, and experimental setup. Section 4 presents the

**Table 6.1** Cloud vs Mobile vs Edge AI systems across different parameters [1].

| Platform | Freq. | Memory | Storage | Power | | Price | CO2 Footprint |
|---|---|---|---|---|---|---|---|
| Cloud | GHz | 10+ GB | TBs-PBs | ∼1 | kW | 1000$+ | Hundreds of kgs |
| Mobile | GHz | Few GB | GBs | ∼1 | W | 100$+ | Tens of kgs |
| Edge AI | MHz | KBs | Few MB | ∼1 | mW | 10$+ | Single kgs |

benchmarking results, with a focus on trade-offs between accuracy, latency, and energy efficiency. Finally, Sections 5 and 6 suggest directions for future research and conclude the paper.

## 6.2 Related Work

This work is positioned at the intersection of sustainability in Edge AI systems and the benchmarking of AI models on embedded platforms. Existing literature provides valuable insights into these domains, yet notable gaps remain that motivate the contributions of this study.

The sustainability of Edge AI has gained attention as the growth of IoT devices contributes to rising carbon emissions and electronic waste [1]. Performing AI inference directly on resource-constrained microcontrollers offers significant reductions in energy use compared to cloud-based computation. The life cycle assessment study by [1] highlights the potential for this approach to lower emissions across diverse applications but also points out its non-trivial footprint when scaled globally. Their findings underline the need for energy-aware design principles that consider the environmental trade-offs of deploying Edge AI at scale. However fine-grained studies on bare-metal processors remain limited.

Benchmarking AI models on embedded systems has been widely studied, with challenges including restricted memory, limited energy budgets, and heterogeneous architectures [2]. MLPerf Tiny [3] provides a standardized suite for assessing the latency, accuracy, and energy efficiency of small-scale models, ensuring reproducibility across platforms. DeepEdgeBench [4] expands this scope by evaluating multiple neural networks across accelerators and processors, focusing on inference time, memory footprint, and energy use. LwHBench [5] further benchmarks lightweight models on single-board computers (SBCs), analyzing inference speed, accuracy, and power consumption to guide deployment decisions. These frameworks have advanced evaluation practices for embedded AI, but they concentrate largely on SBCs and higher-level platforms, where operating systems and middleware can obscure hardware-specific behavior.

Model compression techniques particularly structured pruning [6] and static quantization [7] are widely used to reduce model size and energy consumption for edge deployment. Meanwhile, multi-objective Bayesian optimization has emerged as a powerful tool to navigate trade-offs between accuracy, latency, and energy [8]. However, to the best of the authors knowledge these methods have not been systematically evaluated in bare-metal settings.

## 6.3 Methodology

The proposed test bench is depicted in Figure 6.1 and follows a structured workflow that systematically evaluates AI models on bare-metal processors to achieve energy-efficient embedded AI design. The workflow consists of four key stages: Model Generation, Model Deployment, System Benchmarking, and Pareto Optimal Solution, each contributing to the comprehensive assessment of AI models in resource-constrained environments.

The workflow begins in the Model Generation stage, starting with a baseline architecture for a given use case. To explore various trade-offs between performance and resource requirements, we employ an automated multi-objective optimization method to guide the application of structured pruning [6, 8]. This process generates a diverse population of pruned models. Following this, each model undergoes static 8-bit quantization to further reduce memory footprint and improve computational efficiency [7]. The final output of this stage is a collection of multiple models in the ONNX format, each representing a unique trade-off point.

The Model Deployment stage converts the ONNX models into executable binaries tailored for the target hardware. First, each ONNX model is translated into a self-contained C model library. This library is then integrated with a C++ benchmarking framework designed to control the inference execution

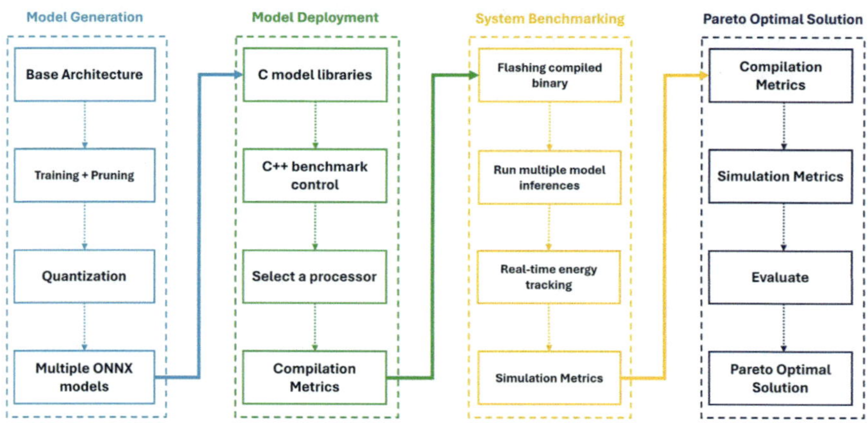


**Figure 6.1** Overview of the Test Bench Architecture and Workflow.

**Table 6.2** Overview of Benchmark AI Use-Cases.

| Use-case | Model | #Params | Dataset | Quality Target |
|---|---|---|---|---|
| Image Classification | ResNet [3], [9] | **78k** | CIFAR-10 [10] | $\geq$80% |
| Optical Digit Recognition | LeNet-5 [11] | **140k** | MNIST [11] | $\geq$95% |
| Anomaly Detection | Autoencoder [3], [12] | **269k** | ToyADMOS [13] | AUC $\geq$0.85 |
| Visual Wake Words | MobileNetV1 [14] | **3198k** | MSCOCO14 [15] | $\geq$80% |

and data collection. The test bench allows for the selection of a specific target processor (Cortex-M0+, M4, or M7), ensuring the code is compiled for the correct architecture. Finally, the C++ control code and the C model are compiled together, producing a single executable binary ready for the System Benchmarking stage.

In the System Benchmarking stage, the compiled binary is flashed onto the target processor. The benchmarking framework then executes multiple model inferences to gather stable performance data. During this execution, we use real-time energy tracking to precisely measure power consumption, while simultaneously recording key inference metrics such as execution latency.

Finally, the Pareto Optimal Solution stage processes the benchmarking results to determine the most efficient AI model configuration by analyzing compilation metrics (e.g. computational overhead) and inference metrics (e.g., latency, accuracy, and power consumption), while also considering use case and hardware specific factors such as idle time between inference cycles, since idle power consumption can significantly affect overall efficiency. Through this systematic evaluation, models are compared to identify optimal trade-offs, ensuring that the final deployed AI model achieves the best balance between energy efficiency and performance for resource-constrained embedded environments.

This structured workflow provides a systematic approach to benchmarking AI models on bare-metal processors, enabling precise evaluation and optimization for energy-efficient Edge AI applications.

### 6.3.1 Use-Cases

The selected use-cases are representing diverse application domains relevant to embedded AI benchmarking and are adopted from [3]. Optical digit recognition was additionally included and serves as a foundational computer vision task, leveraging LeNet-5 on MNIST [11]. We set a target accuracy of 95%, as MNIST is largely considered a solved task but remains a useful benchmark for assessing high-accuracy performance under edge constraints. Anomaly detection employs an Autoencoder trained on industrial sound datasets [3, 12, 13], targeting robust detection when only normal data is available. Compact image classification relies on a customized ResNet architecture [3, 9] optimized for embedded constraints, evaluated on CIFAR-10 [11]. Finally, Visual Wake Words uses MobileNetV1 [14] for binary person detection on MSCOCO [15], reflecting IoT-oriented scenarios.

### 6.3.2 Experimental Setup

The experimental setup is designed to systematically evaluate the performance and energy efficiency of AI models deployed on bare-metal processors. As illustrated in Figure 6.2, the setup consists of key hardware components, including an ATP carrier board, a Segger J-Link debugger, a Power Profiler Kit (PPK), and associated signal connections to facilitate accurate measurement of inference-related metrics.

The ATP carrier board serves as the primary hardware platform for executing AI models across different embedded processors. It supports multiple processor configurations, including M0+, M4, and M7 cores, enabling comparative benchmarking of AI models under varying computational capabilities. The deployment process involves flashing the model.hex file onto

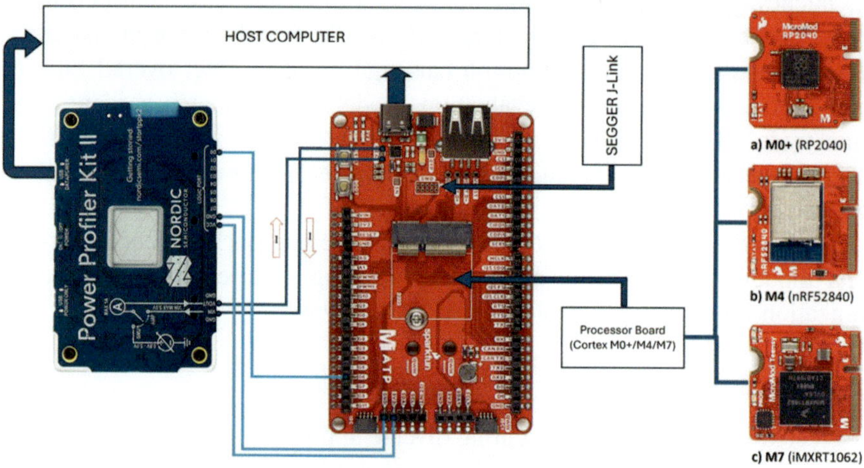


**Figure 6.2** Experimental Setup for Test Bench Evaluation.

the respective processor. For the M0+ and M4 processors, the Segger J-Link debugger is used for programming, ensuring precise execution and debugging capabilities. In contrast, the M7 processor is flashed via the USB-C interface, providing a streamlined deployment process.

To measure energy consumption during model inference, a Power Profiler Kit (PPK) is integrated into the setup. The PPK's Vin and Vout pins are connected to the MEAS pins on the ATP carrier board, enabling real-time measurement of the current flowing through the board. This configuration provides critical insights into the power and energy consumption across different AI models and hardware configurations. Additionally, to accurately mark the inference execution phases, a GPIO pin on the ATP carrier board is connected to the D0 pin of the PPK. This connection allows the PPK's state to be toggled as shown in Figure 6.3, ensuring precise synchronization of power measurements with inference execution.

The flow diagram on the left in Figure 6.3 illustrates the control sequence for toggling a GPIO pin and executing multiple inferences per active phase. The plot on the right depicts the measured current consumption (red) and inference state (blue) over time, with the dashed green line indicating the mean current during active processing. Within each cycle, repeated inference execution ensures sufficient measurement duration and enables averaging of current values across multiple runs, resulting in more reliable and representative measurements.

This experimental setup ensures a robust and reliable evaluation of AI model efficiency on embedded processors by facilitating direct power measurements and enabling comparative performance analysis across different core architectures.

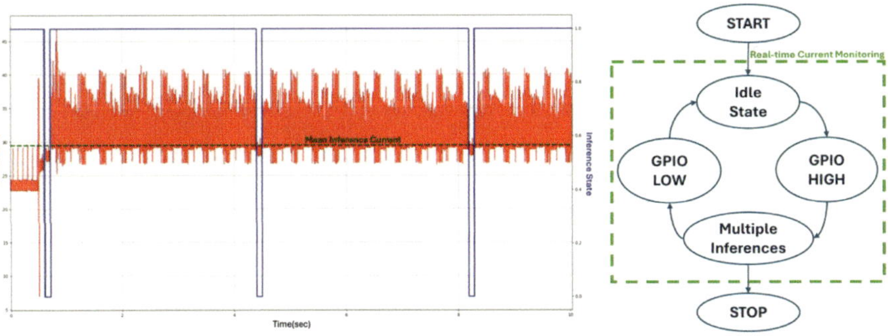


**Figure 6.3** Benchmarking flow diagram (left) and exemplary current measurement (right).

## 6.4 Results

This chapter presents the key results of the study, including test-bench reliability, model variation, the relationship between FLOPs and inference time, and a Pareto analysis of varying inference cycle times to reveal trade-offs between energy consumption and model accuracy.

### 6.4.1 Test-bench Reliability

To validate the reliability of our test bench, each AI model was benchmarked five times to assess the consistency of the measurements. The variance across key metrics like Inference Current, Time, and especially Energy was minimal. This negligible variability confirms the stability and robustness of our experimental setup, ensuring the trustworthiness of the subsequent findings.

### 6.4.2 Model Size across use-cases

Figure 6.4 shows the ROM requirements of quantized and unquantized models across the benchmarked use cases (log scale). Quantization yields a substantial reduction in model size, often to one-quarter of the original, making deployment on constrained devices feasible. Among the tasks, Optical Digit Recognition is the smallest, while Visual Wake Words is nearly 50× larger, highlighting the wide range of memory footprints. Notably, unquantized Visual Wake Words models exceeded the available memory on the target processors.

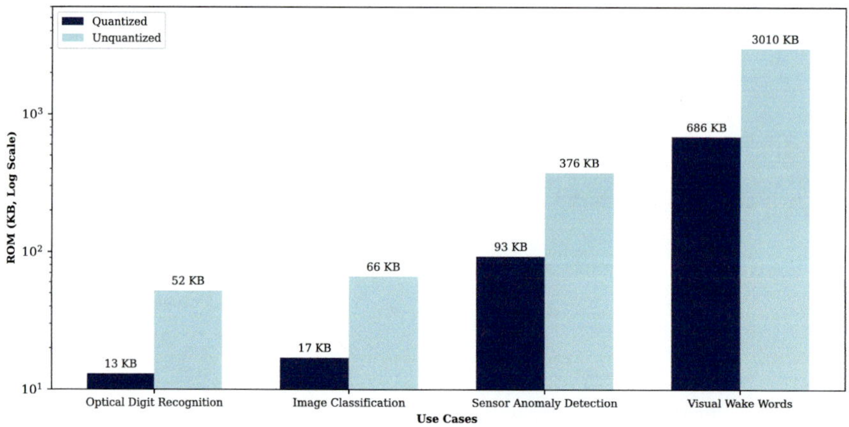


**Figure 6.4** Mean AI Model Sizes per use-case.

### 6.4.3 Correlation Between FLOPS and Inference Time

Through our experiments, RAM and ROM usage were found to be poor predictors of energy consumption and are therefore considered primarily as hardware constraints that determine whether a model can be deployed on a given device. In contrast, Figure 6.5 shows a linear relationship between FLOPS and inference time. This correlation indicates that models with higher FLOPS tend to have longer inference times, highlighting the importance of FLOPS as a critical metric in evaluating model efficiency. Understanding this relationship helps to anticipate the computational demands of the models and make informed decisions about resource allocation and optimization strategies.

The analysis of the relationship between FLOPS and inference time for the M0+, M4, and M7 processors (Figure 6.5) reveals a strong linear correlation ($R^2 \geq 0.93$). This indicates that FLOPS can serve as a reliable predictor of inference time within the evaluated range. The results from Table 6.3 highlight that while all processors exhibit strong linear scaling, their computational efficiencies differ substantially—the M0+ and M4 show a higher sensitivity, whereas the M7 achieves significantly faster inference per FLOP due to its more advanced architecture.

This established relationship supports using FLOPS as a predictive metric for inference time on embedded platforms. As illustrated in Figure 6.6, this

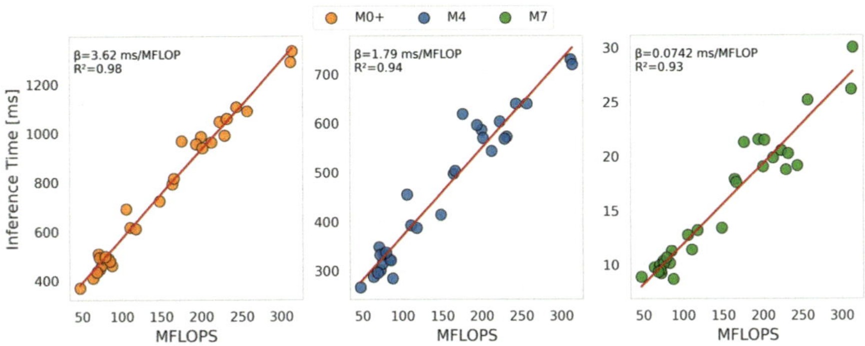


**Figure 6.5** Linear Dependency of FLOPS on Inference Time.

**Table 6.3** Linear Regression Model Fit between FLOPs and Inference Latency.

| Processor | β [ms/MFLOPs] | $R^2$ |
|---|---|---|
| M0+ | 3.620 | 0.98 |
| M4 | 1.790 | 0.94 |
| M7 | 0.074 | 0.93 |

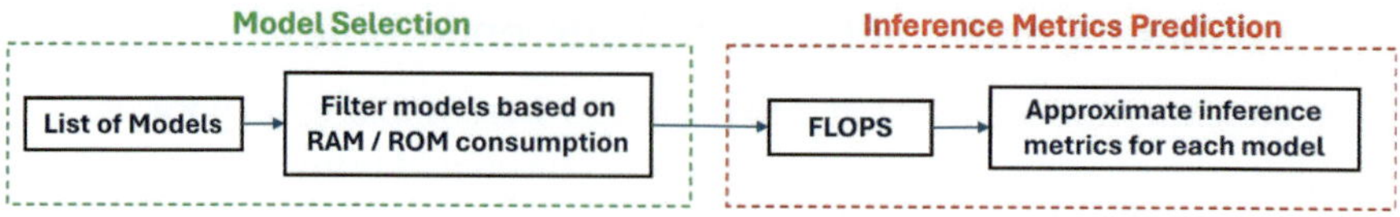


**Figure 6.6** Process Flow for Model Selection and Inference Metrics Prediction.

allows developers to estimate performance early in the design phase: once model feasibility is confirmed via RAM and ROM constraints, FLOPS can be used to approximate expected inference latency. This approach facilitates processor–model co-design, enabling more efficient benchmarking and selection in constrained environments.

For instance, if a particular processor's RAM and ROM capacity align with the requirements of a given model, its FLOPS can then be used to approximate the expected inference time and inference energy. This benchmarking analysis not only validates the use of FLOPS as a predictive metric for inference time but also highlights the potential for using it in conjunction with RAM and ROM specifications to guide the selection of the most appropriate processor for specific applications.

### 6.4.4 Analysis of Inference Cycle energy

Our energy efficiency analysis focuses on the total energy consumed per inference cycle, a metric combining both the active inference period and the subsequent idle time. The energy consumed during the idle state is especially critical in applications with infrequent events, as it can dominate the total power budget.

The processors exhibit significant differences in their datasheet deep sleep currents. The Cortex-M4 is highly optimized for low-power states with an idle current of just 0.30 mA, making it far more efficient during inactivity than the M0+ (4.20 mA) and the M7 (1.60 mA). This idle current profoundly impacts overall efficiency, as demonstrated when analysing the key performance indicators (KPIs) of the full inference cycle.

Figure 6.7 shows the total inference cycle energy for each processor over varying cycle times (0–5 s), comparing the smallest and largest models obtained from our optimization to illustrate the performance range. Because the supply voltage remains constant at 3.3 V, power trends directly reflect current measurements.

The data reveal distinct energy–performance characteristics. The M0+ processor consistently exhibits the highest energy consumption due to its

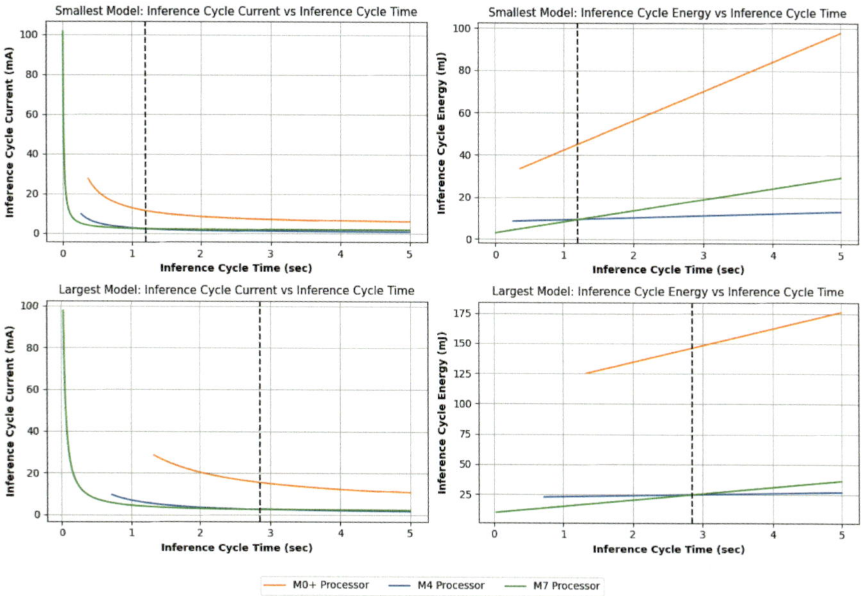


**Figure 6.7** Inference Cycle Current and Energy vs Cycle Time across processors for the smallest and largest models.

elevated inference and idle currents. In contrast, the M4 processor becomes increasingly efficient at longer cycle times, where its low idle current dominates the energy budget. The M7processor, benefiting from its high computational speed, achieves the lowest energy consumption during short inference cycles by minimizing active power-on duration.

These results emphasize the trade-offs between processor architectures: the M7 is best suited for short, frequent inference tasks, while the M4 offers superior efficiency for longer, intermittent workloads. The M0+ remains the least efficient across all scenarios.

### 6.4.5 Analysis of Energy Efficiency and Accuracy Trade-offs

Given its consistently higher inference and idle currents, the M0+ processor was excluded from further energy–accuracy analysis, as it offers no competitive advantage under the evaluated constraints. Figure 6.8 presents a Pareto front analysis comparing inference cycle energy and accuracy across varying cycle times (0.5 s, 2.5 s, 5.0 s) for the M4 and M7 processors.

The results reveal a fundamental shift in design priorities depending on how frequently inference occurs. When inference tasks are frequent—such as

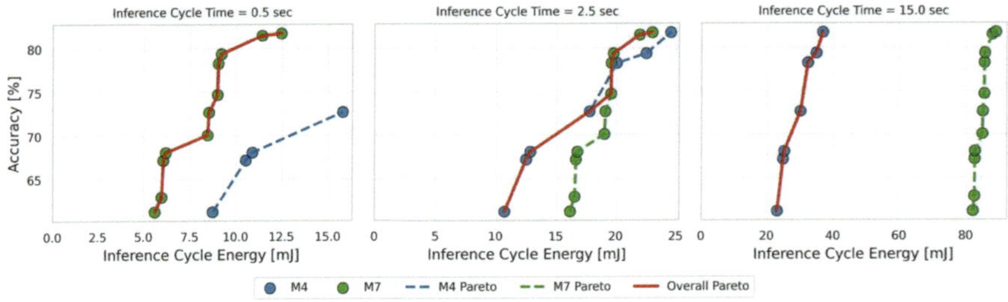


**Figure 6.8** Energy vs. accuracy trade-offs for M4 and M7 across short, medium, and long inference cycles. Pareto fronts highlight optimal choices per workload.

in applications with short cycle times (e.g., $\leq 0.5$ s)—the energy consumed during active computation dominates the total budget. In this regime, the Cortex-M7's high computational throughput allows it to complete inference significantly faster, resulting in lower total energy for a given level of accuracy. Here, model efficiency directly translates into system-level savings, and even modest reductions in inference time can yield meaningful energy benefits. Consequently, models should be optimized primarily for speed, with accuracy maintained only to the extent necessary for functional correctness.

In stark contrast, when inference is infrequent and long idle periods separate executions—as in applications with cycle times of 2.5 s or more—the energy consumed while waiting far outweighs that used during computation. Under these conditions, the Cortex-M4's ultra-low idle current becomes decisive, making it the more energy-efficient choice despite its slower inference speed. More importantly, in this idle-dominated regime, the marginal energy cost of running a slightly slower but more accurate model becomes negligible. The execution time contributes little to the total energy budget, so there is little to gain from aggressive model compression or latency optimization. Instead, designers should favour models that maximize accuracy, as the performance benefit during the rare inference event outweighs the minimal energy penalty of a longer active phase.

This duality underscores a critical principle for embedded AI deployment: the optimal balance between energy and accuracy is not fixed—it is dictated by the application's temporal behaviour. Processor and model selection must therefore be guided not only by hardware capabilities and model metrics, but also by the expected duty cycle of the target use case. The Pareto fronts in Figure 6.8 thus serve not just as performance benchmarks, but as a decision map for co-designing hardware, models, and application timing.

## 6.5 Discussion and Future Work

This study provides embedded AI developers with a practical, application-driven framework for selecting hardware and optimizing models — moving beyond simplistic "faster is better" assumptions. Instead, the optimal choice depends on how a processor's energy profile aligns with the temporal structure of the target application.

Inference cycle duration emerges as the primary determinant of architectural preference. For applications demanding frequent, low-latency inference, such as real-time industrial monitoring ($\leq$0.5 s cycles), the Cortex-M7's high computational throughput dominates energy efficiency. Its DSP-enhanced architecture minimizes active execution time, making it ideal when inference is the dominant energy sink. Conversely, for battery-powered devices with long idle intervals, such as environmental sensors ($\geq$5 s cycles), the Cortex-M4's ultra-low idle current becomes decisive. Here, minimizing power during waiting periods outweighs the benefit of faster computation. The Cortex-M0+, while unsuitable for frequent-inference AI workloads due to its high idle consumption, retains value in non-AI contexts and DIY projects, where cost, accessibility, and development simplicity are prioritized over performance.

Critically, this dichotomy informs not only processor selection, but also model optimization strategy. In short-cycle regimes, where active computation dominates energy use, reducing inference latency directly improves system efficiency favouring compact, fast models. In long-cycle regimes, however, the energy cost of inference becomes negligible compared to idle consumption. Here, developers can prioritize accuracy over latency, selecting higher-performing models without significant energy penalty.

To aid this complex decision-making process, our work establishes two practical tools. First, FLOPs serve as a reliable early-stage predictor of inference latency, allowing for hardware-aware model selection without exhaustive testing. Second, the Pareto front, which visually maps the energy–accuracy trade-offs per cycle time, guiding developers toward optimal processor-model pairings.

### 6.5.1 Limitations

Despite its practical insights, this study has several limitations. Power measurements were conducted under controlled laboratory conditions and may not fully capture variability introduced by environmental factors, peripheral usage, or long-term deployment effects. In addition, the analysis focuses on a limited set of microcontroller architectures, which may restrict the generalizability of the conclusions to newer or heterogeneous platforms. Finally, while FLOPs correlate well with inference latency in the evaluated setups, this relationship may weaken for models with complex memory-access patterns or hardware-specific accelerations.

### 6.5.2 Future Work

Future research should focus on refining power-measurement methodologies, particularly through standardized evaluations of idle current and wake-up latency to enable fair cross-processor comparisons. Furthermore, long-term, real-world deployments are required to validate the robustness of these findings under environmental variation, workload drift, and hardware aging. Extending the framework to additional architectures and accelerator-based systems would further strengthen its applicability.

## 6.6 Conclusion

This work presented a framework for benchmarking AI models on bare-metal ARM Cortex processors, revealing that the optimal system design is dictated by the application's operational cycle. The core finding is that the balance between active computation energy and passive idle energy not only determines the best processor choice but also shapes the ideal model optimization strategy.

For frequent-inference tasks, the Cortex-M7 is superior, and model efficiency is critical for minimizing energy use. For tasks with long idle periods, the Cortex-M4 is the clear winner, allowing developers to prioritize model accuracy over inference speed with minimal energy penalty. Our framework, which uses FLOPs as a latency predictor and Pareto analysis to visualize trade-offs, provides a structured basis for navigating these decisions. Ultimately, these findings guide developers toward creating embedded AI applications that are both sustainable and high performing by aligning hardware selection and model optimization with the specific demands of the real-world use case.

## Acknowledgement

This work is part of the GreenICT@FMD project and is funded by the German Federal Ministry for Research, Technology and Space (BMFTR) (grant number 16ME0491K).

## References

[1] S. Prakash *et al.*, "Is TinyML Sustainable? Assessing the Environmental Impacts of Machine Learning on Microcontrollers," *arXiv.org*, 2023. https://arxiv.org/abs/2301.11899

[2] C. R. Banbury *et al.*, "Benchmarking TinyML Systems: Challenges and Direction," *arXiv:2003.04821 [cs]*, Jan. 2021, Available: https://arxiv.org/abs/2003.04821.

[3] C. R. Banbury *et al.*, "MLPerf Tiny Benchmark," *arXiv (Cornell University)*, Jun. 2021, doi: https://doi.org/10.48550/arxiv.2106.07597.

[4] S. P. Baller, A. Jindal, M. Chadha, and M. Gerndt, "DeepEdgeBench: Benchmarking Deep Neural Networks on Edge Devices," *arXiv.org*, 2021. https://arxiv.org/abs/2108.09457.

[5] A. Garcia-Perez, R. Miñón, A. I. Torre-Bastida, and E. Zulueta-Guerrero, "Analysing Edge Computing Devices for the Deployment of Embedded AI," *Sensors (Basel, Switzerland)*, vol. 23, no. 23, p. 9495, Nov. 2023, doi: https://doi.rog/10.3390/s23239495.

[6] S. Han, H. Mao, and W. J. Dally, "Deep Compression: Compressing Deep Neural Networks with Pruning, Trained Quantization and Huffman Coding," *arXiv:1510.00149 [cs]*, Feb. 2016, Available: https://arxiv.org/abs/1510.00149.

[7] B. Jacob *et al.*, "Quantization and Training of Neural Networks for Efficient Integer-Arithmetic-Only Inference," *2018 IEEE/CVF Conference on Computer Vision and Pattern Recognition*, Jun. 2018, doi: https://doi.org/10.1109/cvpr.2018.00286.

[8] M. Deutel, G. Kontes, C. Mutschler, and J. Teich, "Combining Multi-Objective Bayesian Optimization with Reinforcement Learning for TinyML," *ACM Transactions on Evolutionary Learning and Optimization*, Jan. 2025, doi: https://doi.org/10.1145/3715012.

[9] K. He, X. Zhang, S. Ren, and J. Sun, "Deep residual learning for image recognition," *Proceedings of the IEEE conference on computer vision and pattern recognition*, Las Vegas, NV, USA, 2016, pp. 770–778, doi: https://doi.org/10.1109/CVPR.2016.90.

[10] A. Krizhevsky, V. Nair, and G. Hinton, "Cifar-10," *University of Toronto, Tech. Rep.,* 2009, https://www.cs.toronto.edu/~kriz/cifar.html.

[11] Y. Lecun, L. Bottou, Y. Bengio, and P. Haffner, "Gradient-based learning applied to document recognition," *Proceedings of the IEEE*, vol. 86, no. 11, pp. 2278–2324, 2018, doi: https://doi.org/10.1109/5.726791.

[12] G. Li and J. J. Jung, "Deep learning for anomaly detection in multivariate time series: Approaches, applications, and challenges," *Information Fusion*, vol. 91, pp. 93–102, Mar. 2023, doi: https://doi.org/10.1016/j.inffus.2022.10.008.

[13] Y. Koizumi, S. Saito, H. Uematsu, N. Harada, and K. Imoto, "ToyADMOS: A dataset of miniature-machine operating sounds for anomalous sound detection," *IEEE Workshop on Applications of Signal Processing to Audio and Acoustics (WASPAA)*, New Paltz, NY, USA, 2019, pp. 313–317, doi: https://doi.org/10.1109/WASPAA.2019.8937164.

[14] Howard *et al.*, "MobileNets: Efficient Convolutional Neural Networks for Mobile Vision Applications," *arXiv (Cornell University)*, Apr. 2017, doi: https://doi.org/10.48550/arxiv.1704.04861.

[15] T.-Y. Lin *et al.*, "Microsoft COCO: Common Objects in Context," *Computer Vision – ECCV 2014*, vol. 8693, pp. 740–755, 2014, doi: https://doi.org/10.1007/978-3-319-10602-1_48.

# 7

# Improving Classifier Latency at the Edge through ARM Helium

**Lorenzo Abate, Mario Barbareschi, and Antonio Emmanuele**

Università degli Studi di Napoli Federico II, Italy

## Abstract

The increasing diffusion of intelligent devices at the network edge has led to a growing demand for efficient on-device inference, capable of overcoming the limitations of traditional cloud-centric computing paradigms. This work investigates the acceleration of **decision tree–based inference** on **resource-constrained edge platforms** by exploiting **ARM Helium vector extensions**, which bring the **Single Instruction Multiple Data (SIMD)** paradigm to the **Cortex-M** class of processors.

A dedicated **SIMD-based kernel** was implemented and tested on the **NUCLEO-STM32N657** board across three UCI datasets (AI4I, Dry Bean, Avila). Results show up to **$\sim$15% latency reduction** over the **non-SIMD baseline**, confirming that **ARM Helium** effectively exploits data-level parallelism to enhance inference efficiency on lightweight microcontrollers.

Overall, this study provides experimental evidence that **vector extensions represent a key enabler** for bringing advanced machine learning capabilities to low-power embedded systems, bridging the gap between traditional microcontroller efficiency and modern AI acceleration at the edge.

**Keywords:** Edge AI, SIMD, Classification, Random Forest.

## 7.1 Introduction

A **cloud-centric computing paradigm** has traditionally been adopted for Edge devices, where data collected by end nodes are transmitted to large-scale

DOI: 10.1201/9788743815211-7

data centers for processing [1]. This model has largely been driven by the intrinsic constraints of those devices, which are typically characterized by limited memory resources, stringent power-consumption requirements, and modest computational capabilities [2, 3, 4]. However, the exponential growth in the number of connected devices [5, 6]—and the resulting increase in network bandwidth demand—combined with modern requirements for low-latency processing, has rendered an alternative paradigm increasingly appealing: **executing inference directly on the device** [7].

One of the most widely adopted model families at the edge is that based on **binary decision trees**, such as **Random Forests**. These models are highly valued for their ability to handle both **classification** and **regression** tasks while remaining **lightweight**, **interpretable**, and suitable for deployment on resource-constrained platforms [8].

In the literature, several approaches have been proposed to enhance the performance of tree ensembles on edge devices. However, recent **advancements in semiconductor manufacturing** and **processor design** have introduced new opportunities, notably through the integration of **vector extensions**. These technologies make it possible to further improve execution efficiency by exploiting **data-level parallelism**, thereby pushing the boundaries of machine learning performance on embedded and edge platforms.

In particular, this work focuses on the **newly introduced ARM Helium vector extensions**, specifically designed for **edge computing**. Through a **latency analysis** of the inference process, it will be shown how these technologies can **further enhance performance**, demonstrating their potential to significantly accelerate machine learning workloads on resource-constrained devices.

## 7.2 Vectorial Extensions and ARM Helium

The electronics industry is continuously driving technological advancements, enabling the integration of increasingly sophisticated features even at the edge, such as **vector extensions** [9]. This technology implements the **Single Instruction Multiple Data (SIMD)** paradigm, allowing a single instruction to be executed in parallel on multiple data elements, thereby effectively enabling **data-level parallelism**. Vector extensions **extend the standard processor instruction set** with specialized vector registers and operations capable of processing multiple operands simultaneously. Instead of performing the same arithmetic or logical operation repeatedly on individual data points, the processor can apply it once to an entire vector of values.

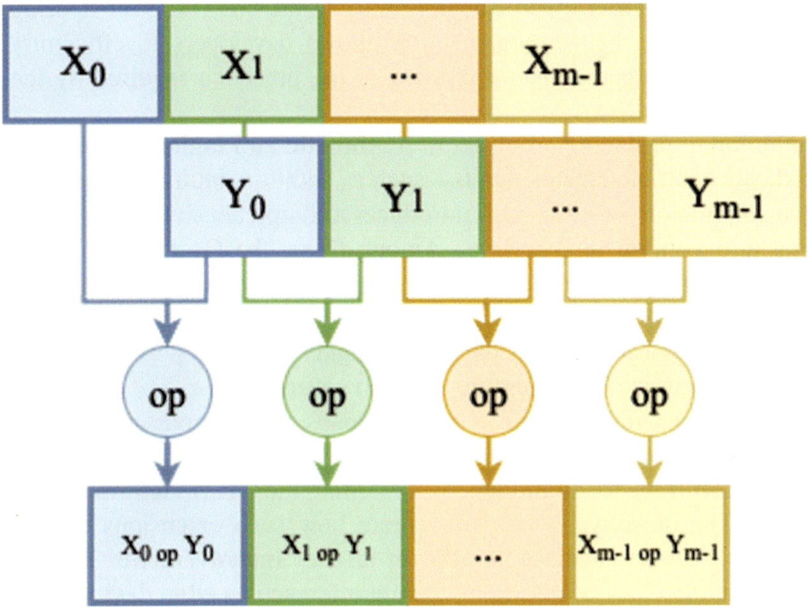


**Figure 7.1** SIMD Execution

This approach significantly **improves throughput** in workloads characterized by regular, repetitive computations — such as signal processing, image analysis, and machine learning inference — by exploiting the inherent parallelism in data streams while maintaining a compact code structure and reducing execution time.

**Figure 7.1** illustrates SIMD execution that leverages wide vector registers that are divided into multiple **lanes**. Each lane holds one data element, and the same instruction is applied simultaneously across all lanes, producing multiple results in parallel. The number of lanes depends on how the register width is partitioned according to the data type.

Over the years, numerous types of **vector extensions** have been introduced [9], each characterized by distinct design choices and architectural trade-offs. Among these, the **ARM Helium extensions** [10] are particularly relevant for this work, as they bring the **SIMD paradigm** to the **Cortex-M** family of processors, thereby enabling efficient parallel execution on resource-constrained **edge devices**.

Helium features **eight 128-bit vector registers**, which can be partitioned into a variable number of **lanes** depending on the data type being processed, supporting element sizes up to **32 bits** (8/16/32-bit int, 16/32-bit floating point). This flexible register organization allows developers to efficiently exploit the available parallelism according to the precision required by the application.

In addition to providing a rich set of **arithmetic and logical operations** extended over multiple data elements—such as addition, multiplication, and bitwise manipulation—Helium also introduces a comprehensive suite of **data handling and control instructions**. Among these, the **Gather** and **Scatter** operations are particularly noteworthy, as they enable non-contiguous memory access patterns by allowing data to be loaded from or stored to arbitrary memory locations. This capability greatly enhances performance in workloads characterized by **irregular data structures**.

It is precisely within this class of workloads that the present work is positioned, providing an analysis of **latency reduction** in the **inference of binary decision tree–based models** by exploiting the **ARM Helium vector extensions**. The objective is to demonstrate how such extensions can be effectively leveraged to achieve **significant latency improvements**, thereby enhancing the efficiency of machine learning inference on **edge devices**.

## 7.3 Experimental Results

### 7.3.1 Experimental Setup

Inference on a **decision tree** can be regarded as a **tree traversal**, where, starting from the **root node**, the computation proceeds toward a **leaf node**, at which the final prediction is produced. The specific path followed during traversal is determined by the outcome of a **comparison** between an **input feature** and a **threshold value** stored at each node [3].

Consequently, the form of **parallelization** that can be exploited lies in the ability to process **multiple nodes simultaneously**, thereby performing several comparisons within a single instruction.

In particular, this section presents a **latency comparison** between two approaches: a **SIMD-based method**, implemented using **ARM Helium**, where multiple nodes are traversed in parallel through a technique inspired by the work of **Kim et al.** [11], and a **Classic tree visiting** approach, which processes one node at a time.

The **SIMD technique** is based on reorganizing the nodes of the tree into **hierarchical blocks**, which can be visualized as **triangular sub-structures** grouping together a fixed number of nodes. The purpose of these blocks is

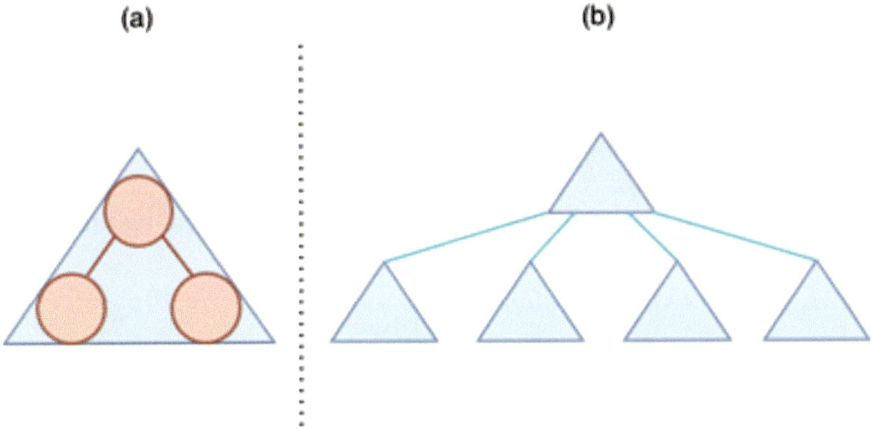


**Figure 7.2** (a) example of a block with 4 lanes. (b) example of the resultant tree structure.

to align the tree layout with the **SIMD parallelism level**. For instance, as illustrated in **Figure 7.2 (a)**, a SIMD unit with **four lanes** can accommodate a **block of three** nodes, enabling three comparisons to be executed in parallel. **Figure 7.2 (b)** then shows the structure of the resulting tree.

The experiments were conducted on the **NUCLEO-STM32N657** development board, featuring an **ARM Cortex-M55** processor equipped with **ARM Helium vector extensions**. The core was configured to operate at a frequency of **600 MHz**.

The evaluation employed **Random Forest models** trained on three datasets from the **UCI Machine Learning Repository—AI4I** [12], **Dry Bean** [13], and **Avila** [14]—selected to provide a **heterogeneous benchmarking suite** encompassing diverse data characteristics and complexity levels.

The following table summarizes the main characteristics of the three datasets.

**Table 7.1** Summary of the datasets used in the experiments.

| **Dataset** | **Samples** | **Features** | **Classes** |
|---|---|---|---|
| AI4I | 1000 | 6 | 2 |
| Dry Bean | 13610 | 16 | 7 |
| Avila | 20866 | 10 | 12 |

A **quantization process** was also applied to reduce the model size and make it more suitable for an **edge deployment scenario**. In particular,

**quantization-aware training (QAT)** [3] was adopted, in which quantization is applied to the input data already during the training phase. As a result, the trained model becomes inherently adapted to the **reduced-precision representation**, maintaining high predictive accuracy while significantly lowering memory and computational requirements. In this work, the data were represented as **int16**.

In particular, the process relies on the computation of a **scaling factor** defined as

$$scale = \frac{2^{bits-1}}{|\max\_val|}$$

where **bits** represent the target bit-width of the new representation and **max_val** is the maximum absolute value within the considered set. Each element is then multiplied by this scaling factor and rounded to the nearest integer, obtaining the new quantized representation. This process is applied **separately** to each feature in the dataset.

The following table provides detailed information on the **models** used for the analysis.

**Table 7.2** Summary of the models used in the experiments.

| Dataset | Depth | Trees | Nodes | Accuracy |
|---|---|---|---|---|
| AI4I | 10 | 100 | 23320 | 0.985 |
| Dry Bean | 10 | 100 | 50804 | 0.922 |
| Avila | 10 | 100 | 61768 | 0.878 |

### 7.3.2 Timing Analysis

At this stage, the **results of the analysis** are presented. The evaluation was carried out on **1,000 test samples**. The SIMD-based approach was evaluated using a **parallelism level of seven nodes**. With **16-bit** quantized data, each block can accommodate **seven nodes**, as **eight SIMD lanes are available**.

**Figure 7.3** illustrates a comparison between the performance of the **SIMD** and **non-SIMD** approaches across the three models introduced in **Table 7.2**. The performance metric is expressed in terms of the **number of clock cycles** required to complete the inference, with the **median value** over the **1,000 test samples** shown as the height of each bar.

The results clearly highlight that the use of **vector extensions** enables a **significant reduction in inference latency**, demonstrating the effectiveness of SIMD parallelism for accelerating decision tree–based workloads on edge devices.

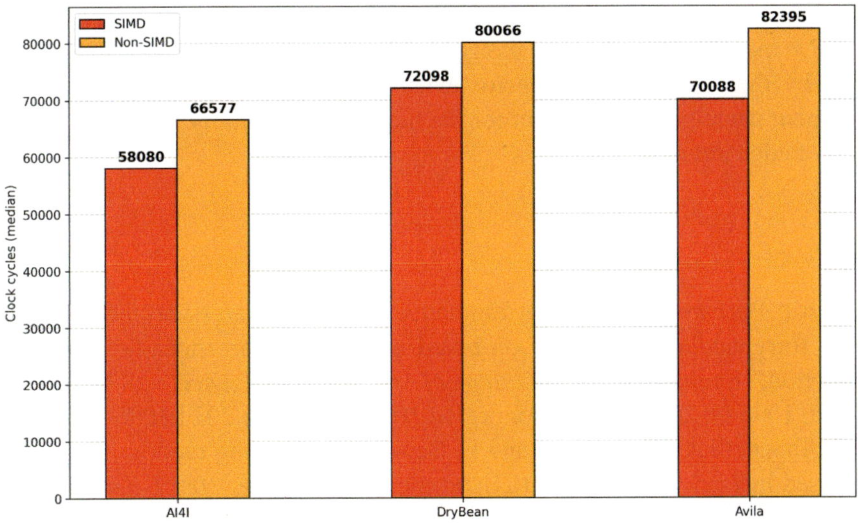


**Figure 7.3** Barplot showing the summary of the performance for each model.

Specifically, the results show a **latency reduction** of approximately:

- **13.8%** for the *AI4I* dataset;
- **10%** for the *Dry Bean* dataset;
- **15%** for the *Avila* dataset.

## 7.4 Conclusion

In conclusion, the results obtained in this study demonstrate the tangible benefits of leveraging **ARM Helium vector extensions** to accelerate **decision tree–based inference** on **edge devices**. By exploiting data-level parallelism, SIMD-based approach achieves a consistent **reduction in latency** across heterogeneous models and datasets, confirming its effectiveness in enhancing computational performance under constrained hardware conditions.

These findings highlight the growing potential of **modern embedded architectures** to support increasingly demanding **machine learning workloads** directly on the device, without relying on cloud offloading. In this context, vector extensions such as **ARM Helium** represent a fundamental step toward **bridging the gap** between high-performance computing and low-power embedded systems, paving the way for more **efficient, autonomous, and intelligent edge computing solutions**.

In future work, we aim to further investigate optimizations based on alternative memory layouts, with the goal of better exploiting the parallelism offered by the **ARM Helium** vector extensions. We also plan to explore deployment strategies that account for the hierarchical memory architectures typical of edge devices.

## References

[1] Mario Barbareschi, Antonio Emmanuele, Nicola Mazzocca and F. R. di Torrepadula, "Designing on-board explainable passenger flow prediction," *Engineering Applications of Artificial Intelligence*, vol. 139, p. Art. 109648, 2025. https://doi.org/10.1016/j.engappai.2024.109648.

[2] E. Tabanelli, G. Tagliavini, and L. Benini, "Optimizing random forest-based inference on risc-v MCUs at the extreme edge," *IEEE Transactions on Computer-Aided Design of Integrated Circuits and Systems*, vol. 41, pp. 4516–4526, Nov. 2022. https://doi.org/10.1109/TCAD.2022.3199903

[3] F. Daghero, A. Burrello, E. Macii, P. Montuschi, M. Poncino, and D. J. Pagliari, "Dynamic decision tree ensembles for energy-efficient inference on iot edge nodes," *IEEE Internet of Things Journal*, vol. 11, no. 1, pp. 742–757, 2024. https://doi.org/10.1109/JIOT.2023.3286276

[4] M. Barbareschi, A. Emmanuele, "A margin based early-stopping approach for random forest classifiers," in: 2025 55th *Annual IEEE/IFIP International Conference on Dependable Systems and Networks Workshops (DSN-W)*, pp. 123–126, IEEE, 2025. https://doi.org/10.1109/DSN-W65791.2025.00050

[5] M. Barbareschi, S. Barone, A. Emmanuele, and N. Mazzocca, "Exploiting Functional Approximation on Decision-Tree Based Multiple Classifier Systems," *in 2024 IFIP/IEEE 32nd International Conference on Very Large Scale Integration (VLSI-SoC),* Oct. 2024, pp. 1–4, iSSN: 2324-8440. https://ieeexplore.ieee.org/document/10767841/?arnumber=10767841

[6] I. Cvitić, D. Peraković, M. Periša, M. Krstić, and B. Gupta, "Analysis of IoT Concept Applications: Smart Home Perspective," in *Future Access Enablers for Ubiquitous and Intelligent Infrastructures*, D. Perakovic and L. Knapcikova, Eds., Cham: Springer International Publishing, 2021, pp. 167–180. https://doi.org/10.1007/978-3-030-78459-1_12

[7] W. Shi, J.Cao,Q. Zhang,Y. Li, andL.Xu, "Edge computing: Vision and challenges," *IEEE Internet of Things Journal,* vol. 3, pp.637–646, Oct. 2016. https://doi.org/10.1109/JIOT.2016.2579198

[8] E.Tabanelli, G.Tagliavini, and L.Benini, "Dnn is not all you need: Parallelizing non-neural ML algorithms on ultra-low-power IoT processors," *arXiv preprint arXiv:2107.09448*, 2021. https://arxiv.org/abs/2107.09448

[9] H. Amiri and A. Shahbahrami, "SIMD programming using intel vector extensions," *Journal of Parallel and Distributed Computing*, vol.135, pp.83–100, 2020. https://www.sciencedirect.com/science/article/pii/S074373151830813X

[10] J.Marsh, *Arm® Helium™ Technology: M-Profile Vector Extension (MVE) for Arm® Cortex®-MProcessors*. Cambridge, UK: Arm Education Media, 2020. https://www.arm.com/resources/education/books/mve-reference-book

[11] C.Kim, J.Chhugani, N. Satish, et al., "FAST: Fast architecture sensitive tree search on modern CPUs and GPUs," *in Proceedings of the 2010 ACM SIGMOD International Conference on Manage ment of Data (SIGMOD'10)*, NewYork, NY, USA: Association for Computing Machinery, June 2010, pp. 339–350. https://doi.org/10.1145/1807167.1807206

[12] UCI Machine Learning Repository, "Ai4i 2020 predictive maintenance dataset [dataset]," 2020. https://doi.org/10.24432/C5HS5C

[13] UCI Machine Learning Repository, "Drybean [dataset]," 2020. https://doi.org/10.24432/C50S4B

[14] C. Stefano, F. Fontanella, M. Maniaci, and A. Freca, "Avila [dataset]," 2018. https://doi.org/10.24432/C5K02X

# 8

# Structural Sensitive-Attribute Leakage in Face Recognition Embeddings for Edge AI Deployments

**Erica Liu, Enrique Orozco Olivares, Gijs Dubbelman, and Jean-Paul Linnartz**

Eindhoven University of Technology, Netherlands

## Abstract

Face recognition systems, increasingly deployed on edge devices and servers, store high-dimensional embeddings from models like ArcFace for identity verification and search. While prior work shows such embeddings can reveal sensitive attributes, most target a single attribute at the per-user level in the same-dataset settings. We present a unified study of both per-user and population level demographic leakage, quantifying whether an adversary can predict attributes for individuals and recover aggregate demographic distributions of entire databases. We evaluate both within-dataset and cross-dataset transfer settings. In the within-dataset case, classifiers are trained and tested on the same dataset, while in the cross-dataset case, models trained on one dataset are applied to another, simulating realistic adversaries without access to the target model. Using FairFace and a pretrained ArcFace extractor, we measure leakage of gender, age range, and race, with per-user AUCs exceeding 90% for gender and age range, and over 60% for race (obtained with basic MLP classifiers, making these estimates conservative). Population level estimates recover demographic proportions with low error. We further assess common blurring defences, highlighting recognition–privacy trade-offs. Results indicate demographic leakage is structural, persisting from individual users to entire databases, and across different datasets, underscoring the need for

DOI: 10.1201/9788743815211-8

stronger privacy safeguards in deployed face recognition systems, particularly in edge AI environments.

**Keywords:** face recognition, privacy risk, population level, cross-dataset transfer.

## 8.1 Introduction

Edge AI face recognition systems have been increasingly applied in real-world scenarios. The systems normally perform identity verification directly on edge devices by computing high-dimensional embeddings instead of transmitting raw images. These embeddings are typically produced by convolutional neural networks such as ArcFace and are stored on edge devices to efficiently compare and match with the data on central servers. This architecture is often assumed to improve privacy because raw images never leave the device. However, prior work found that embeddings themselves can unintentionally reveal sensitive personal information, making the systems not entirely privacy-preserving as expected. [1, 2].

Previous research has demonstrated that face embeddings can encode attributes such as gender, age, or race [3, 4]. Most analyses focus on inferring a single sensitive attribute at the per-user level within a single dataset or the same model setting, leaving open questions about the generality and structure of such leakage. Recent studies on fairness and privacy risks in biometrics have also emphasized that these representations may encode demographic information even when the original data are anonymized [5, 6].

In this work, we present a systematic framework that unifies per-user level and population level analyses of sensitive attributes leakage of high-dimensional CNN face embeddings. Our approach quantifies not only whether an adversary can infer sensitive attributes for an individual (per-user leakage), but also whether aggregate demographic distributions of an entire embedding database can be reconstructed (population level leakage), enabling large-scale profiling even without certainty at the individual level.

We evaluate leakage under two complementary settings: (i) within-dataset, where attribute probes are trained and tested on the same dataset to measure direct predictability, and (ii) cross-dataset, where probes trained on one dataset (FairFace) are applied to another (UTKFace) to model realistic transfer by adversaries lacking access to the target data. This models an attacker who exploits differences in data distribution—such as varying demographics or image conditions—while still using the same embedding model.

Using the FairFace and UTKFace datasets and a pretrained ArcFace feature extractor, we measure leakage of gender, age range, and race under varying degrees of Gaussian blurring. Our results demonstrate strong per-user leakage (AUC values larger than 0.9 for gender and age, and larger than 0.6 for race). The low mean absolute error (MAE) between the true proportion and the predicted proportion of one class reveals that population level demographic proportions can still be accurately recovered with low aggregate error. These findings suggest that information leakage in face embeddings is structural, persisting across datasets, aggregation levels, and image preprocessing. This persistence represents an underexplored privacy risk for deployed Edge AI face recognition systems and underscores the need for stronger privacy safeguards in such deployments.

## 8.2 Related Work

### 8.2.1 Face Embeddings and Edge AI Deployment

Face recognition models such as FaceNet, CosFace, and ArcFace map facial images to high dimensional embeddings that support efficient matching and storage [7-9]. These embeddings are attractive for the deployments on the edge due to latency and bandwidth constraints, and because raw images can be avoided. However, prior work shows that embeddings and biometric templates may encode more information than only identity.

### 8.2.2 Sensitive-Attribute Leakage and Template Inversion

A large body of research demonstrates that demographic attributes can be inferred from facial representations, raising fairness and privacy concerns [10]. Beyond attribute inference, template inversion attacks reconstruct faces directly from deep templates, showing that embeddings are not inherently safe [11, 12]. These findings motivate systematic evaluations of what non-identity information is exposed by embeddings under realistic conditions.

### 8.2.3 Datasets for Attribute Analysis and Bias Measurement

Balanced or demographically annotated datasets such as FairFace and UTK-Face support studying leakage, bias, and generalization [13, 14]. FairFace improves balance across seven race groups and is widely used for bias measurement, while UTKFace covers a broad age span with age/gender/ethnicity annotations.

### 8.2.4 Privacy–Utility Trade-offs and Obfuscation

Obfuscation (e.g., blurring, adversarial perturbations) can reduce recognizability, but often exhibits an asymmetric trade-off where utility degrades faster than privacy risk [15]. System-level work further frames obfuscation as a tuneable privacy–utility mechanism across sensing modalities [16]. Our study explicitly quantifies this trade-off by measuring per-user leakage versus recognition utility under Gaussian blurring.

Beyond simple image-space blurring, a rich line of work proposes privacy-enhancing techniques at the image-, template-, and feature levels. Differential-privacy-based protocols perturb face templates or intermediate features, such as PEEP and learnable frequency-domain DP mechanisms for face recognition [17, 18]. Other approaches use adversarial learning to construct privacy-preserving templates: Wang et al. generate adversarial facial features (AdvFace) that defend against feature-to-image reconstruction while preserving recognition accuracy [19]. GAN-based de-identification methods such as Privacy-Protective-GAN [20] and later anonymization frameworks learn to synthesise or modify faces such that identity is removed but task-relevant information is preserved [21, 22].

Recent surveys on privacy-enhancing face biometrics and privacy-preserving face recognition (PPFR) provide a broader taxonomy of such defences across data generation, representation learning, and template storage [6, 23, 24]. Closer to our focus on sensitive attributes in embeddings, template-level regularisation and attribute unlearning methods seek to suppress specific attributes (e.g., gender) while retaining identity. Rezgui et al. enforce angular constraints in the embedding space to reduce gender separability without significantly harming recognition performance [25]. More generally, Guo et al. formalise attribute unlearning as selectively removing information about designated attributes from feature representations via mutual-information-guided detachment losses [26]. These works highlight that attribute factors are geometrically structured within modern embedding spaces and can be actively manipulated.

Our work is complementary to these defences. Instead of proposing a new protection mechanism, we study structural sensitive-attribute leakage that persists in off-the-shelf ArcFace embeddings under a simple and widely deployed obfuscation technique (Gaussian blurring). By jointly analysing per-user and population level leakage, and by evaluating cross-dataset transfer, we show that demographic information remains recoverable in the embedding space even when (i) per-user inference becomes harder and (ii) image-level utility is severely degraded. This suggests that the leakage quantified in our framework constitutes a baseline risk that privacy-preserving representation learning and attribute unlearning methods must overcome.

### 8.2.5 Generalization and Threat Modelling

Most prior leakage studies focus on single-attribute, single-dataset, or same-model settings, leaving open how leakage generalizes across data distributions. We contribute a cross-dataset transfer evaluation (train on one dataset, test on another) to model distribution shift in realistic deployments. In parallel, the security community has examined attacks beyond attribute inference, including membership inference on representation-learning systems (e.g., Re-ID) [27], underscoring the need to evaluate embeddings under broader adversarial goals.

### 8.2.6 Positioning

In contrast to prior work that treats attribute inference or obfuscation in isolation, we provide a unified view that (i) measures per-user leakage and extends to population level aggregates, (ii) evaluates cross-dataset generalization under blur preprocessing, and (iii) ties these findings to a concrete privacy–utility analysis for edge deployments.

## 8.3 Methodology

We propose a unified framework to quantify sensitive-attribute leakage in deep face embeddings at both the per-user level and population levels.

Given a pretrained face recognition model that maps an input image $x$ to an embedding vector $\mathbf{z} \in R^d$ (in our case $d$ is 512), our goal is to evaluate to what extent $\mathbf{z}$ reveals sensitive attributes such as gender, age, or race.

The evaluation pipeline consists of three stages:

- Embedding extraction: Obtain embeddings $\mathbf{z}$ using a pretrained model (ArcFace) for all face images under varying blurring levels.
- Leakage estimation: Train simple classifiers (MLPs) to predict sensitive attributes from embeddings.

- Privacy quantification: Measure privacy leakage using per-user level and population level metrics, and analyse the trade-off between privacy and utility.

### 8.3.1 Embedding Extraction and Gaussian Blurring

Let $f_\theta(\cdot)$ denote the feature extractor (We use ArcFace backbone specifically) producing embeddings

$$\mathbf{z} = f_\theta(x) \in R^{512}. \tag{8.1}$$

To simulate privacy-preserving preprocessing, we apply Gaussian blurring to the input images before feature extraction. This technique aims to obscure fine facial details that could aid attribute inference while retaining coarse structure necessary for recognition.

The blurred image $\tilde{x}$ is obtained by convolving the original image $x$ with a Gaussian kernel $G_\sigma$:

$$\tilde{x}(u,v) = (x*G_\sigma)(u,v) = \sum_{i=-r}^{r}\sum_{j=-r}^{r} x(u-i, v-j)\, G_\sigma(i,j), \tag{8.2}$$

where

$$G_\sigma(i,j) = \frac{1}{2\pi\sigma^2}\exp\left(-\frac{i^2+j^2}{2\sigma^2}\right). \tag{8.3}$$

The kernel radius $r$ is chosen as

$$r \approx 3\sigma, \tag{8.4}$$

which ensures that 99.7% of the Gaussian's total energy is contained within the kernel.

This practical rule balances accuracy and efficiency by cutting off the kernel without significant loss of smoothing effect.

We vary the blur radius $r \in \{0, 1, 2, 3, 5, 8, 10, 12, 15, 20\}$ to analyse how increasing blurring affects both recognition utility and privacy leakage.

The resulting embeddings are then computed as

$$\mathbf{z}_r = f_\theta(\widetilde{x_r}) \tag{8.5}$$

and serve as inputs to the leakage analysis.

### 8.3.2 Leakage Classifiers

For each sensitive attribute $a \in \{\text{gender, age, race}\}$, we train a multilayer perceptron (MLP) $g_{\phi_a}$ to predict the attribute label from embeddings:

$$(\hat{y})_a = g_{\phi_a}(\mathbf{z}) \tag{8.6}$$

Each MLP consists of an input layer of size 512, two hidden layers (256 and 128 units) with ReLU activations, and a Softmax output layer.

Training minimizes the cross-entropy loss:

$$\mathcal{L}_a = -\frac{1}{N}\sum_{i=1}^{N}\sum_{c=1}^{C_a} y_{i,c}^{(a)} \log\left((\hat{y})_{i,c}^{(a)}\right), \tag{8.7}$$

Where $C_a$ is the number of attribute classes for $a$.

### 8.3.3 Metrics for Privacy Leakage

**Per-User Leakage:** For individual-level leakage, we compute the test accuracy and test area under the ROC curve (AUC) to quantify the classifier's ability to infer sensitive attributes from embeddings.

Higher ACC and AUC indicate stronger attribute predictability and thus higher privacy leakage.

Formally, for classifier scores $s_i$ and ground-truth labels $y_i$, AUC is defined as:

$$\text{AUC} = \int_0^1 \text{TPR}\left(\text{FPR}^{-1}(t)\right) dt, \tag{8.8}$$

where $TPR$ and $FPR$ denote the true positive and false positive rates.

**Population Level Leakage:** To evaluate aggregate demographic inference, we compute the mean absolute error (MAE) between the true and predicted demographic distributions.

Let $\mathbf{p} = [p_1, \ldots, p_K]$ denote the true proportions of $K$ demographic categories, and $\widehat{\mathbf{p}}$ the predicted proportions from classifier outputs:

$$\text{MAE} = \frac{1}{K}\sum_{k=1}^{K} |p_k - \widehat{p_k}|. \tag{8.9}$$

Lower MAE indicates that the adversary can more accurately reconstruct the population distribution.

For convenience, we report (1 − MAE) as a proxy privacy-leakage score for comparison with utility.

### 8.3.4 Cross-Dataset Transfer Evaluation

To assess the generalization of leakage across data domains, we perform a cross-dataset evaluation. A classifier trained on embeddings from one dataset, specifically FairFace, is tested on embeddings from another dataset UTKFace. This simulates a realistic adversary who leverages distributional similarities without having access to the exact target-domain data.

### 8.3.5 Recognition Utility Estimation

Recognition accuracy of the underlying embedding model is used as a measure of system utility. However, datasets such as FairFace and UTKFace lack consistent identity labels, making direct identity verification or retrieval evaluation infeasible. Given this limitation and the fact that ArcFace verifies embeddings using cosine similarity, we estimate proxy utility as the average cosine similarity between embeddings of original (non-blurred) and blurred images:

$$\cos\left(\mathbf{z}_0, \mathbf{z}_r\right) = \frac{\mathbf{z}_0 \cdot \mathbf{z}_r}{||\mathbf{z}_0||\ ||\mathbf{z}_r||} \tag{8.10}$$

As cosine similarity serves as the standard metric in ArcFace-based recognition systems and reflects representational separability, the trade-off between privacy and utility is analysed by comparing ACC, AUC and (1 − MAE) against the average cosine similarity across blur levels.

## 8.4 Experiments

### 8.4.1 Experimental Setup

All experiments are conducted using Python 3.8 and PyTorch 2.1 on an NVIDIA RTX 4060 GPU. Face embeddings are extracted using the pretrained ArcFace model (ResNet50 backbone) from the InsightFace repository. For each experiment, we use the same embedding extractor without fine-tuning to ensure that observed leakage arises from representational properties rather than retraining.

**Classifier Training:** For each sensitive attribute (gender, age, race), an MLP classifier $g_{\phi_a}$ is trained on top of the fixed embeddings as described in methodology. We use a 70/15/15 split for training, validation and testing, and repeat experiments with five random seeds to report mean results. Training employs the Adam optimizer with learning rate $10^{-3}$, batch size $128$, and early stopping based on validation loss.

**Blur Levels:** Gaussian blur radius $r \in \{0, 1, 2, 3, 5, 8, 10, 12, 15, 20\}$ are applied to each image. A radius of $r = 0$ corresponds to the unblurred baseline. The corresponding standard deviation follows $\sigma \approx r/3$. Each blur level generates a new embedding set, allowing us to jointly evaluate privacy leakage and recognition utility across multiple privacy intensities.

### 8.4.2 Datasets

We use two publicly available face datasets with balanced demographic annotations:

- **FairFace:** contains $108,501$ face images labelled for gender, age range, and race across seven demographic groups. It is designed to provide balanced representation across races and age ranges, making it ideal for measuring leakage in unbiased embeddings.
- **UTKFace:** includes approximately $23,700$ cropped faces annotated with age, gender, and ethnicity. It features diverse lighting, pose, and background conditions, supporting generalization evaluation.

We conduct both within-dataset and cross-dataset evaluations:

- **Within-dataset:** classifiers are trained and tested on the same dataset.
- **Cross-dataset:** classifiers are trained on FairFace and evaluated on UTKFace, simulating an adversary trained on a different but related data distribution.

Additionally, for consistency across datasets, we harmonize race categories by mapping FairFace's seven race labels to the five used in UTKFace. For age prediction, we convert the continuous or multi-class age labels into binary groups using cutoffs at 18, 30, and 50, which simplifies the task.

### 8.4.3 Evaluation Protocols

**Per-User Leakage:** For each attribute, the MLP predicts probabilities $\widehat{y_a}$ over attribute classes. The per-user privacy leakage is quantified by the AUC between predicted scores and true labels. We report the mean and standard deviation of AUC across five runs for each blur level. Higher AUC indicates stronger attribute inference capability and therefore higher leakage.

**Population Level Leakage:** To quantify aggregate demographic inference, we compute the predicted demographic proportions $\widehat{\mathbf{p}}$ from classifier outputs and compare them with ground-truth proportions $\mathbf{p}$ using the MAE defined in equation (8.9).

**Recognition Utility:** Recognition utility is estimated via the average cosine similarity between embeddings at different blur levels, as defined in equation (8.10). Cosine similarity serves as a proxy measure of representational quality: a higher average cosine similarity implies that embeddings preserve more discriminative structure. We analyse the privacy–utility trade-off by jointly examining ACC, AUC (per-user leakage), $(1 - \text{MAE})$ (population leakage), and cosine similarity (utility) across blur levels.

### 8.4.4 Results and Analysis

#### 8.4.4.1 Per-User Leakage Results

Figure 8.1 shows test ACC values for gender, age, and race inference across blur levels. Even with moderate blurring ($r = 5$), classifiers achieve ACC $> 0.85$ for gender and most age ranges, and around 0.6 for race. The test AUC results for age range and gender are shown in Figure 8.2. Similarly, the classifier can achieve AUC $> 0.80$ even at higher blur ($r = 8$). These

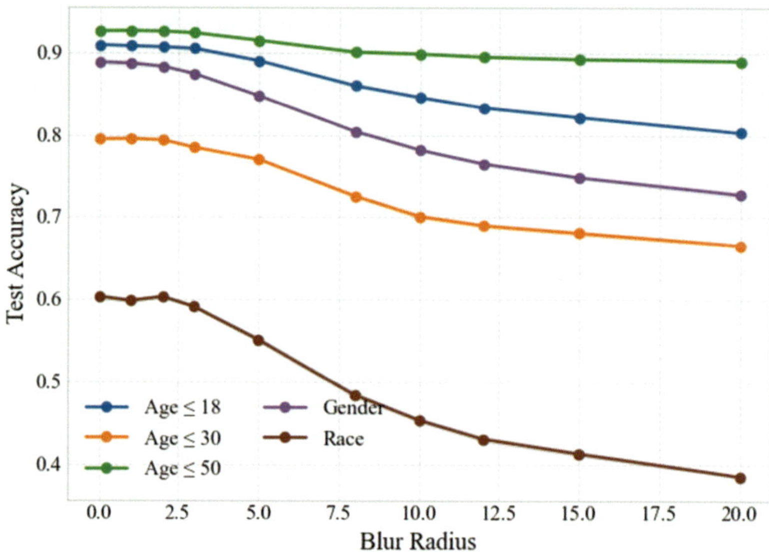


**Figure 8.1** Test ACC across blur levels by age, gender, and race on FairFace.

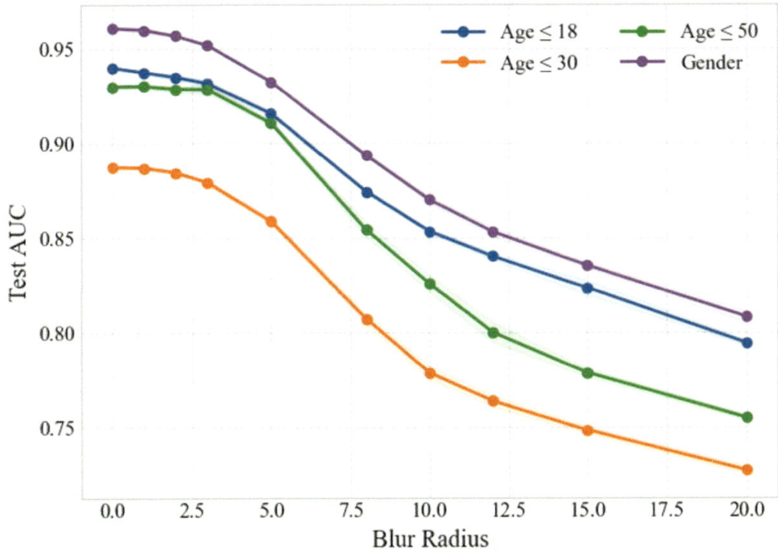


**Figure 8.2** Test AUC across blur levels by age, gender on FairFace.

indicate that sensitive attributes remain highly predictable even when visual details are suppressed. The reduction in ACC and AUC with stronger blurring is modest, suggesting that demographic information is embedded structurally in the feature space.

#### 8.4.4.2 Population Level Leakage

Table 8.1 presents the MAE scores measuring population level reconstruction accuracy, in which the lower MAE means higher leakage. Although the MAE values fluctuate without a clear monotonic trend, this variation is likely due to the overall small magnitude of errors. Results reveal that aggregate demographic distributions can be recovered with extremely low error (MAE $< 30\times 10^{-3}$) even when blur level $r = 20$, where per-user sensitive attribute leakage has already dropped substantially. This implies that an adversary can estimate the demographic composition of an entire embedding database even without confidently predicting each individual's attributes.

#### 8.4.4.3 Cross-Dataset Generalization

In the cross-dataset setting, attribute classifiers retain substantial predictive power, achieving ACC$\approx 0.8$ for gender and age range on unseen domains as shown in Figure 8.3. Blurring provides limited privacy protection in this

**Table 8.1** Population level privacy leakage based on FairFace embeddings (MAE $\times$ $10^3$; mean $\pm$ std) across blur levels for age, gender, and race.

| **Target Label** | **Blur Radius ($r$)** | | | | | | | | | |
|---|---|---|---|---|---|---|---|---|---|---|
| | **0** | **1** | **2** | **3** | **5** | **8** | **10** | **12** | **15** | **20** |
| **Age 18 cutoff** | 7.4±1.0 | 6.4±5.7 | 4.0±2.2 | 6.7±3.3 | 3.9±2.8 | 3.0±2.0 | 33.1±12.0 | 10.4±12.8 | 23.8±4.3 | 16.2±4.4 |
| **Age 30 cutoff** | 7.2±4.4 | 17.2±4.9 | 14.4±9.4 | 10.9±7.5 | 14.4±10.4 | 9.2±4.9 | 8.3±8.9 | 8.1±6.8 | 8.0±3.7 | 11.1±10.9 |
| **Age 50 cutoff** | 11.2±1.5 | 19.8±7.6 | 23.3±5.9 | 18.5±10.5 | 19.0±10.3 | 11.8±12.7 | 14.6±12.6 | 24.3±6.5 | 14.8±17.1 | 7.4±8.9 |
| **Gender** | 5.3±4.6 | 9.4±4.4 | 14.7±6.2 | 14.9±2.6 | 9.3±9.7 | 14.6±8.6 | 6.9±4.2 | 16.9±3.0 | 18.7±13.1 | 11.0±8.2 |
| **Race** | 5.6±0.9 | 5.7±1.2 | 8.6±3.5 | 8.3±2.5 | 7.7±3.4 | 6.5±1.3 | 6.6±1.8 | 8.7±2.5 | 7.8±0.9 | 5.8±1.9 |

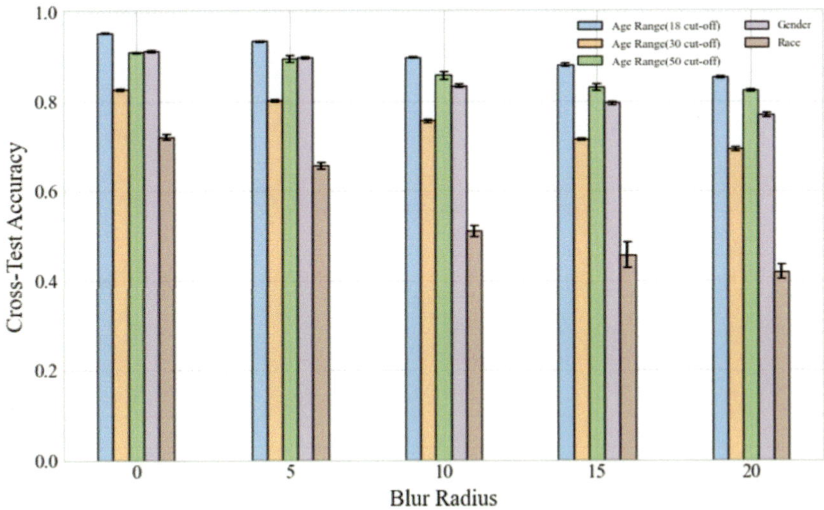


**Figure 8.3** Test accuracy across blur levels by age, gender, and race on UTKFace.

**Table 8.2** Population level privacy leakage based on UTKFace embeddings (MAE $\times 10^3$; mean $\pm$ std) across blur levels for age, gender, and race.

| Target Label | Blur Radius ($r$) | | | | |
|---|---|---|---|---|---|
| | **0** | **5** | **10** | **15** | **20** |
| **Age 18 cutoff** | 36.3±6.4 | 34.6±7.4 | 39.3±22.8 | 29.1±4.2 | 40.7±4.4 |
| **Age 30 cutoff** | 16.4±5.3 | 14.5±7.3 | 15.8±8.6 | 34.9±7.8 | 45.0±17.3 |
| **Age 50 cutoff** | 24.7±14.7 | 45.9±19.5 | 67.1±17.5 | 88.1±2.1 | 79.1±11.5 |
| **Gender** | 12.7±9.1 | 11.2±11.1 | 28.7±7.3 | 30.6±11.5 | 35.6±10.5 |
| **Race** | 61.8±6.3 | 80.8±5.1 | 110.5±6.7 | 119.5±7.3 | 123.9±6.9 |

setting. Although race test accuracy is lower, this is reasonable given the larger number of classes. This demonstrates that sensitive-attribute leakage generalizes across datasets and is not purely dataset-specific. In addition, the results of population level leakage in the cross-dataset setting are shown in table II. The highest MAE is only around $120 \times 10^{-3}$, indicating that even in cross-dataset scenarios with high blur levels, a considerable amount of demographic population level information remains recoverable.

#### 8.4.4.4 Privacy–Utility Trade-Off

Figure 8.4 and Figure 8.5 illustrate the privacy–utility trade-off on UTKFace embeddings, showing how recognition utility (cosine similarity) relates to

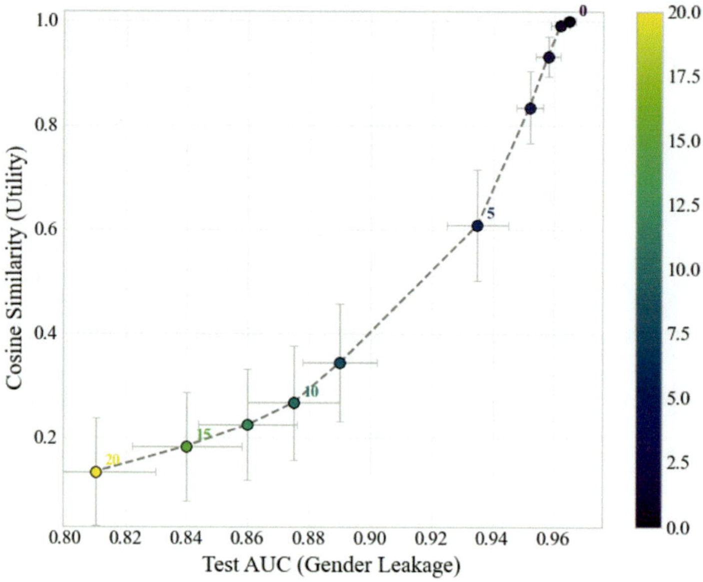


**Figure 8.4** The trade-off between utility and per-user level privacy leakage for gender on UTKFace.

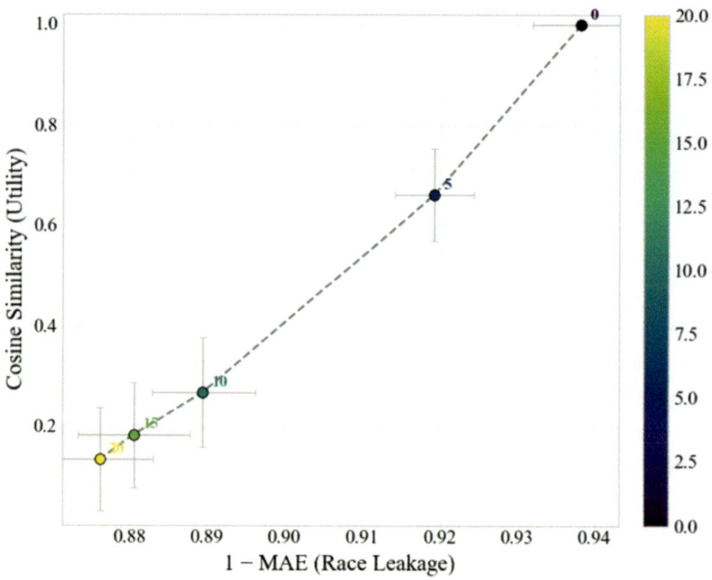


**Figure 8.5** The trade-off between utility and population level privacy leakage for race on UTKFace.

privacy leakage metrics (AUC for gender and 1 – MAE for race) across different blur levels. As the blur radius increases, cosine similarity steadily decreases, indicating a degradation in recognition quality. Meanwhile, both gender AUC and 1 – MAE for race show only modest declines, suggesting that blurring provides limited reduction in privacy leakage. Overall, the reduction in leakage is relatively minor compared to the significant loss in utility, revealing an asymmetric trade-off: blurring rapidly impairs recognition performance before achieving meaningful suppression of demographic attribute leakage.

### 8.4.5 Discussion

To highlight the robustness of structural leakage, we compare per-user and population level metrics at the strongest blur setting ($r = 20$). As expected, heavy Gaussian blurring reduces per-user attribute inference: gender and age AUCs drop noticeably, and race prediction becomes less reliable.

However, population level leakage remains largely unaffected. The MAE between predicted and true demographic proportions stays within a low range, indicating that aggregate demographic structure is still preserved even when individual predictions become uncertain. This suggests that blur disrupts fine-grained cues required for per-user inference but does not eliminate the global geometric patterns in the embedding space that reflect demographic composition.

This asymmetry has important privacy implications: while blurring may appear to protect individuals, it does not prevent reliable profiling of entire embedding databases. Combined with the strong impact of blur on recognition utility, these findings show that image-space obfuscation is insufficient and highlight the need for embedding-level privacy mechanisms.

## 8.5 Conclusion

This work presented a systematic analysis of sensitive-attribute leakage in deep face embeddings, focusing on Edge AI recognition systems that operate without transmitting raw images. We developed a unified framework to evaluate privacy leakage at both the per-user and population levels, and extended it to cross-dataset settings to assess generalization under distribution shifts.

Experiments on FairFace and UTKFace show that sensitive demographic information remains highly inferable from embeddings even under moderate Gaussian blurring. Per-user inference achieves AUC values above 0.9 for gender and age and around 0.6 for race, while population level demographic distributions can still be reconstructed with low error (MAE $< 50\times\ 10^{-3}$). Notably, population level leakage is often more persistent than individual leakage, as aggregate demographic proportions remain accurately recoverable even when per-user predictability declines. This indicates that demographic leakage is a structural property of modern face embeddings rather than an artifact of overfitting or dataset bias.

The privacy–utility analysis further reveals an asymmetric trade-off: blurring severely degrades recognition utility while offering only limited privacy gains. These results underscore the insufficiency of image-space obfuscation and the need for embedding-level privacy mechanisms.

Overall, our findings demonstrate that privacy vulnerabilities in face embeddings persist across individuals, populations, and datasets, with population level leakage emerging as a particularly robust and underappreciated threat. While our study provides a unified analysis of per-user and population level leakage under blur-based obfuscation, it also has several limitations. In particular, our evaluation is restricted to a single embedding model (ArcFace) and a single image-space defence (Gaussian blurring), which, although widely used in practice, do not cover the full spectrum of modern recognition architectures or privacy-preserving mechanisms. These limitations suggest that structural demographic leakage may vary across models or be mitigated differently by embedding-level defences such as adversarial unlearning or differential privacy. Extending the framework to additional architectures and protection strategies therefore remains a valuable direction for future work.

Future work should explore privacy-preserving embedding transformations that jointly suppress per-user and population level leakage without sacrificing recognition accuracy, including differential privacy, adversarial training, and attribute disentanglement directly in the embedding space.

## Acknowledgements

This project has received funding from the European Union's Horizon Europe research and innovation programme under grant agreement No. 101097300.

## References

[1] P. Terhörst, D. Fährmann, N. Damer, F. Kirchbuchner, and A. Kuijper, "Beyond Identity: What Information Is Stored in Biometric Face Templates?" in Proc. IEEE Int. Joint Conf. Biometrics (IJCB), 2020, pp. 1–10.

[2] C. Song and A. Raghunathan, "Information Leakage in Embedding Models," in Proc. ACM Conf. Computer and Communications Security (CCS), 2020, pp. 377–390.

[3] H. J. Ryu, H. Adam, and M. Mitchell, "InclusiveFaceNet: Improving Face Attribute Detection With Race and Gender Diversity," in Proc. ICML Workshop on Fairness, Accountability, and Transparency, 2018.

[4] H. Rosenberg, B. Tang, K. Fawaz, and S. Jha, "Fairness Properties of Face Recognition and Obfuscation Systems," in Proc. USENIX Security Symp., 2023, pp. 731–748.

[5] I. Fábián, "A Comparative Study on the Privacy Risks of Face Recognition Libraries," Acta Cybernetica, vol. 25, no. 3, pp. 233–256, 2021.

[6] L. Laishram et al., "Toward a Privacy-Preserving Face Recognition System," ACM Comput. Surv., 2025, to be published.

[7] F. Schroff, D. Kalenichenko, and J. Philbin, "FaceNet: A Unified Embedding for Face Recognition and Clustering," in Proc. IEEE Conf. Comput. Vis. Pattern Recognit. (CVPR), 2015, pp. 815–823.

[8] H. Wang et al., "CosFace: Large Margin Cosine Loss for Deep Face Recognition," in Proc. IEEE/CVF Conf. Comput. Vis. Pattern Recognit. (CVPR), 2018, pp. 5265–5274.

[9] J. Deng, J. Guo, N. Xue, and S. Zafeiriou, "ArcFace: Additive Angular Margin Loss for Deep Face Recognition," in Proc. IEEE/CVF Conf. Comput. Vis. Pattern Recognit. (CVPR), 2019, pp. 4690–4699.

[10] S. Gong, X. Zhu, and S. Gong, "Jointly De-biasing Face Recognition and Demographic Attribute Estimation," in Proc. Eur. Conf. Comput. Vis. (ECCV), 2020, pp. 330–347.

[11] K. Kärkkäinen and J. Joo, "FairFace: Face Attribute Dataset for Balanced Race, Gender, and Age for Bias Measurement and Mitigation," in Proc. IEEE/CVF Winter Conf. Appl. Comput. Vis. (WACV), 2021, pp. 1548–1558.

[12] Z. Zhang, "UTKFace: Large-Scale Face Dataset," 2017. [Online]. Available: https://susanqq.github.io/UTKFace/

[13] V. Chandrasekaran et al., “Face-Off: Adversarial Face Obfuscation,” Proc. Privacy Enhancing Technol. (PoPETs), vol. 2021, no. 3, pp. 356–375, 2021.

[14] N. Raval et al., “Olympus: Sensor Privacy Through Utility-Aware Obfuscation,” Proc. Privacy Enhancing Technol. (PoPETs), vol. 2019, no. 1, pp. 5–25, 2019.

[15] M. A. P. Chamikara, P. Bertók, I. Khalil, D. Liu, and S. Camtepe, “Privacy Preserving Face Recognition Utilizing Differential Privacy,” Comput. Secur., vol. 97, p. 101951, 2020.

[16] J. Ji et al., “Privacy-Preserving Face Recognition With Learnable Privacy Budgets in Frequency Domain,” in Proc. Eur. Conf. Comput. Vis. (ECCV), 2022, pp. 475–491.

[17] Z. Wang et al., “Privacy-Preserving Adversarial Facial Features,” in Proc. IEEE/CVF Conf. Comput. Vis. Pattern Recognit. (CVPR), 2023, pp. 8009–8018.

[18] Y. Wu, F. Yang, Y. Xu, and H. Ling, “Privacy-Protective-GAN for Privacy Preserving Face De-Identification,” J. Comput. Sci. Technol., vol. 34, no. 1, pp. 47–60, 2019.

[19] Z. Ren, Y. J. Lee, and M. S. Ryoo, “Learning to Anonymize Faces for Privacy Preserving Action Detection,” in Proc. Eur. Conf. Comput. Vis. (ECCV), 2018, pp. 620–636.

[20] H. Tian, T. Zhu, and W. Zhou, “Fairness and Privacy Preservation for Facial Images: GAN-Based Methods,” Comput. Secur., vol. 122, p. 102902, 2022.

[21] B. Meden et al., “Privacy-Enhancing Face Biometrics: A Comprehensive Survey,” IEEE Trans. Inf. Forensics Secur., vol. 16, pp. 4147–4183, 2021.

[22] Z. Sun and Z. Liu, “Ensuring Privacy in Face Recognition: A Survey on Data Generation, Inference and Storage,” SN Appl. Sci., vol. 7, no. 441, 2025.

[23] Z. Rezgui, N. Strisciuglio, and R. N. J. Veldhuis, “Gender Privacy Angular Constraints for Face Recognition,” IEEE Trans. Biometrics Behav. Identity Sci., vol. 6, no. 3, pp. 352–363, 2024.

[24] T. Guo, S. Guo, J. Zhang, W. Xu, and J. Wang, “Efficient Attribute Unlearning: Towards Selective Removal of Input Attributes from Feature Representations,” in Proc. ACM Int. Conf. Multimedia (MM), 2022.

[25] J. Gao et al., "Similarity Distribution Based Membership Inference Attack Against Person Re-Identification," in Proc. AAAI Conf. Artif. Intell. (AAAI), 2023, pp. 436–444.
[26] G. Mai, K. Cao, P. C. Yuen, and A. K. Jain, "On the Reconstruction of Face Images From Deep Face Templates," IEEE Trans. Pattern Anal. Mach. Intell., vol. 41, no. 5, pp. 1188–1202, 2019.
[27] H. O. Shahreza, M. Rabiee, and H. K. Ekenel, "Face Reconstruction From Facial Templates by Learning Latent Space Mapping," in Proc. Adv. Neural Inf. Process. Syst. (NeurIPS), 2023.

# 9

# TinyHLS, a Python-based Hardware Compiler for 1D and 2D Convolutional Neural Networks

**Raphael Gaede[1], Ingo Hoyer[1], Holger Kappert[1], Filippo Milazzo[2], Matteo Cardinali[2], Mauro Roscini[2], Carsten Rolfes[1], and Karsten Seidl[1,3]**

[1]Fraunhofer IMS, Germany
[2]AGRICOLUS, Italy
[3]University of Duisburg-Essen, Germany

## Abstract

TinyHLS is a Python-based hardware compiler that automatically generates hardware accelerators in the form of hardware description language (HDL) code for Convolutional Neural Networks (CNNs). The description of the CNN architecture as well as the training is done in advance using Python TensorFlow Keras. TinyHLS reduces the development effort to implement inference calculations in digital hardware regarding cost and time. Furthermore, tinyHLS offers a platform independent alternative to commercial high-level synthesis tools like AMD Vivado HLS™ [1]. Each hardware accelerator generated by tinyHLS is a full hardware implementation of its CNN, allowing low-latency and low-power inference. In this work, the concept of this hardware compiler is presented. The workflow of tinyHLS is demonstrated based on a smart farming use case. For this use case a CNN to detect oranges in images is developed in TensorFlow Keras, translated using tinyHLS and implemented on a field programmable gate array (FPGA). The results in terms of accuracy, latency, energy consumption and hardware requirements are then discussed based on the implementation of the use case

DOI: 10.1201/9788743815211-9

CNN. Finally, a brief outlook on the improvement of tinyHLS is given to meet requirements of edge artificial intelligence (AI) computing in the future.

**Keywords:** HLS, AI, FPGA, Accelerators.

## 9.1 Introduction

With AI playing a continuously more important role in today's technological world, the demand for resource-limited devices tailored for AI applications increases as well [2]. Hardware-based AI implementations offer greater opportunities for improvement in terms of latency and energy consumption compared to pure software-based implementation approaches [3]. Optimized for individual applications, application specific integrated circuit (ASIC) designs offer high efficiency. However, the development of ASICs is only feasible if the high non-recurring engineering costs (NRE) can be amortized by a large production volume. FPGA-based implementations, however, provide more flexibility at the expense of reduced efficiency [4, 5].

This work introduces tinyHLS, a hardware compiler designed to automatically generate hardware accelerators for CNN models. The primary objective of tinyHLS is the efficient implementation of a given CNN in digital hardware. To achieve this, tinyHLS automatically generates a hardware accelerator in the form of HDL code. A secondary objective is to mitigate NRE by automating the process of hardware accelerator development and verification. Hardware accelerators generated by tinyHLS can be used for both ASIC designs and FPGA programming. Because tinyHLS is platform independent, it provides an alternative to commercial high-level synthesis tools like AMD Vivado HLS™, that is free from vendor lock-ins.

## 9.2 Concept

TinyHLS is based on three fundamental conceptual principles. First, a template-based approach is employed to ensure the modularity of the generated designs. Second, intra-layer pipelining is implemented to enhance efficiency. Finally, to optimize resource utilization and energy consumption, tinyHLS incorporates an 8-bit fixed-point quantization.

### 9.2.1 Template Based Design

As demonstrated by Chao Qian et al. [6], template-based hardware compilers provide substantial advantages. Consequently, this work adopts a template-based approach. Initially introduced for one-dimensional (1D) CNNs [7], tinyHLS is extended by two-dimensional (2D) convolution, 2D global max pooling (GMP) and dense layer templates in this work. Each layer template is designed as a module in Verilog utilizing the parameters shown in Figure 9.6. The rectified linear unit (ReLU) is employed as the activation function.

The template-based approach introduces a critical design requirement: The input and output signals of each layer template must maintain a consistent structure. This consistency is essential for the convolution and dense layers as it facilitates the sequential connection of multiple instances of these layer types. However, an exception exists for layer types implemented between convolution and dense layers, as these types of layers are instantiated only once.

### 9.2.2 Intra-Layer-Pipelining

As illustrated in Figure 9.9, the primary computational effort for CNN inference calculations lays within the convolution layers. Consequently, intra-layer pipelining is implemented among the convolution layers and between the final convolution layer and the GMP layer. Intra-Layer-Pipelining is critical for the hardware accelerator's efficiency for several reasons. First, it enables the execution of multiple operations in parallel, leading to faster calculations, albeit at the expense of larger designs. Second, intermediate results from each layer are directly processed by the subsequent layer, eliminating the need to store complete layer results in registers. Third, intra-layer pipelining allows the inference calculation to start during the data transmission process. This saves time and resources as there is no need to save the entire input signal within the hardware accelerator.

The intra-layer-pipelining also introduces an essential design necessity: The templates for convolution and GMP layer must process their input signals within the same time frame. This synchronization ensures that, after a predetermined number of clock cycles, each layer instance receives its input from the preceding layer instance while passing its output on to the subsequent layer instance at the same time. To pass input signals to the first convolution instance, tinyHLS provides an advanced eXtensible interface4-Lite (AXI4-Lite) [8] to transmit data in a synchronized manner.

### 9.2.3 Quantization

To implement the inference calculation efficiently in digital hardware, quantization is essential. Compared to a 32-bit multiplication, an 8-bit multiplication for example consumes approximately 15 times less energy and requires roughly 12 times less area [9]. With more aggressive quantization however, the classification performance of the CNN decreases [10]. Therefore, a trade-off between efficiency and performance needs to be established. Given that 8-bit fixed-point quantization is widely employed in embedded AI applications [9, 11] and 8-bit values align well with 32- and 64-bit processors and memories, tinyHLS adopts an 8-bit fixed-point representation for all values, including the weights and bias of the CNN as well as all intermediate results computed by the hardware accelerator.

Images are typically represented with 8 bits per pixel. However, tinyHLS incorporates data preprocessing to quantize input images from 8 bits per pixel down to 4 bits per pixel. This quantization reduces the number of gradations of each colour channel from 256 to 16, while preserving the essential information contained in the image. Utilizing 4 bits per pixel instead of 8 bits reduces the effort required for data transmission and processing. More importantly, with 4 bits per pixel, intermediate results are less likely to overflow, as all intermediate results are constrained to 8 bits. In case of overflow, intermediate results are saturated. To further decrease the computational effort, input images are sampled down to a resolution of 28x28 pixels with 3 colour channels during preprocessing. The effect of the preprocessing is illustrated in Figure 9.2.

The distribution of the weights and bias is analysed for each CNN to determine the most suitable split of 8 bits into integer and fractional bits (Figure 9.4).

To identify the optimal split between integer and fractional bits for all intermediate results, tinyHLS evaluates the CNN performance concerning various 8-bit-fixpoint representations (Figure 9.5). It is important to note that the quantization of the input image, which serves as the input to the first layer, is always configured with 4 integer bits and no fractional bits. In contrast, the output of all layers - and consequently the inputs to all subsequent layers - utilizes 8 bits with a supposedly different distribution of integer and fractional bits. This distinction must be taken into account when initializing the individual layer templates.

### 9.2.4 Software Model

The evaluation of the CNN performance concerning different 8-bit-fixpoint representations is not executed in hardware simulation. Instead, the hardware accelerator's functionality is modelled in software. Although in software all operations are performed sequentially, the quantization applied is consistent with that of the hardware accelerator. The key advantage of the software model is its flexibility, allowing for the adjustment of the number of bits allocated for intermediate results, as well as their distribution in integer and fractional bits. This makes the software model a powerful tool for the evaluation of the CNN performance with respect to quantization. Additionally, the software model is used for verification purposes, as described in 1.2.6.

### 9.2.5 Translation

During the translation process, all values for weights and bias are quantized to 8-bit fixed-point representation and stored in Verilog header files. These Verilog header files are provided to the top module generated by tinyHLS. With the most suitable split into integer and fractional bits for the intermediate results determined prior to translation, the layer templates are instantiated and interconnected in the top module. When instantiating the layer templates, all available parameters according to the CNN architecture must be considered (Figure 9.6).

### 9.2.6 Verification

For verification purposes, tinyHLS also generates a testbench. That testbench reads an image and passes it on to the top module. Additionally, the outputs from each layer instance are collected within the testbench, allowing for the complete layer results to be stored at the end of the simulation. After the simulation has completed the layer results are written to designated files and imported into Python for verification. Since TensorFlow Keras employs 32-bit floating-point representation for intermediate results [12], while the hardware accelerator utilizes 8-bit fixed-point representation, deviations between the results are anticipated. Consequently, direct comparison of the results from TensorFlow Keras and those from the hardware accelerator is not feasible. Instead, the software model serves as an intermediate verification step, which aims to trace back any discrepancies between the TensorFlow Keras results and those obtained from the hardware accelerator solely to quantization effects. In the first step of the verification process, the results from the hardware accelerator are compared to those from the software model, which is configured for 8-bit quantization with the same distribution of integer and fractional bits as the hardware accelerator. In the second step, the results from TensorFlow Keras are compared to the software model,

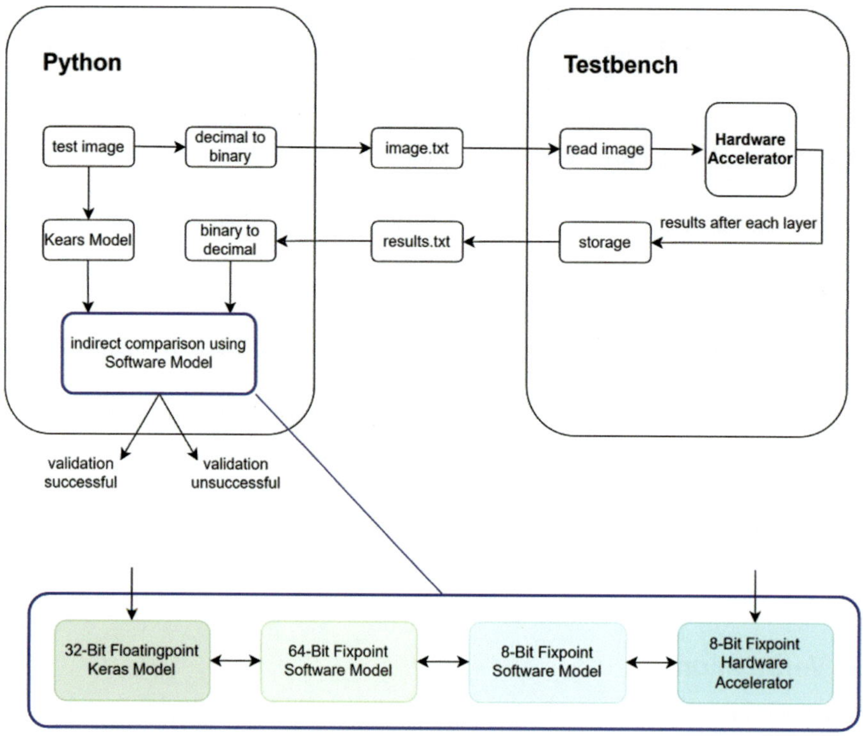


**Figure 9.1** Verification Process.

which is set to a total quantization of 64 bits, comprising 32 integer and 32 fractional bits. Each partial verification step is deemed successful only if all results after each layer match. The verification process is illustrated in Figure 9.1.

## 9.3 TinyHLS Workflow

The tinyHLS workflow is demonstrated based on a use case CNN to detect citrus fruit in images. In the context of smart farming, image classification can facilitate the detection of pests or diseases, allowing for the estimation of crop quality and quantity. In many cases only images containing fruit are relevant to these assessments. To pre-select all images containing fruit, a simple CNN can be trained using TensorFlow Keras, translated using tinyHLS and ultimately executed on an edge device.

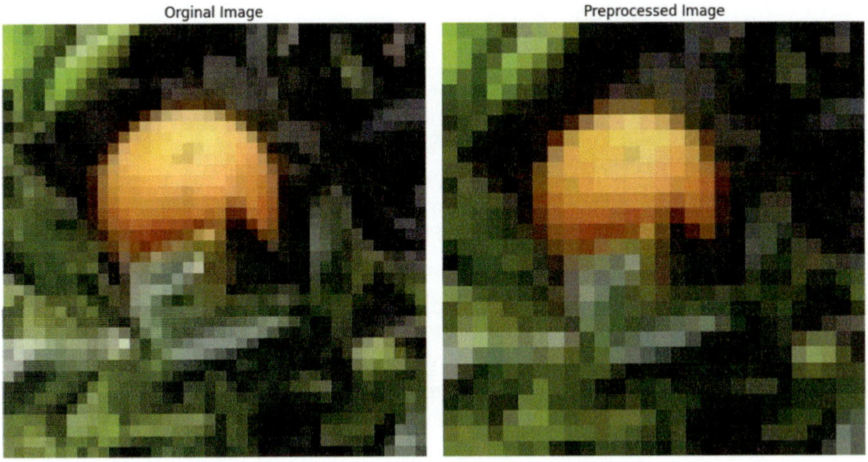


**Figure 9.2** Preprocessing of Use Case Dataset.

### 9.3.1 Preprocessing

For this use case, a dataset comprising 310 images containing at least one orange and 1,220 images without any oranges is utilized. Before training, all images undergo preprocessing which includes rescaling to 28x28 pixels and quantizing each pixel from 8 bit to 4 bit. As shown in Figure 9.2, preprocessing does not discard the information of the image significantly.

### 9.3.2 Training

With 70 % of the preprocessed dataset serving as training data and the remaining 30 % as test data, the use case CNN, utilizing the architecture described in Table 9.1, is trained over 50 epochs. As illustrated in Figure 9.3, this small CNN architecture, which employs only 864 parameters, is sufficient for this image classification task.

### 9.3.3 Evaluation

Before translating the trained CNN into HDL code, its performance is evaluated concerning 8-bit quantization. First, the distribution of the weights and bias is analysed to determine the most suitable split into integer and fractional bits. Given that most of the values range from -1 to 1 (Figure 9.4), the 8-bits are divided into 1 integer and 7 fractional bits.

**Table 9.1** Use Case CNN Architecture

| *Layer* | *Type* | *Parameter* | *UC CNN* |
|---|---|---|---|
| 1 | Conv | In. Shape<br>No. Kernels<br>Kernel Shape | [28,28,3]<br>4<br>[5,5] |
| 2 | Conv | In. Shape<br>No. Kernels<br>Kernel Shape | [24,24,4]<br>6<br>[3,3] |
| 3 | GMP | In. Shape<br>Out. Shape | [22,22,6]<br>6 |
| 4 | Dense | In. Neurons<br>Out. Neurons | 6<br>18 |
| 5 | Dense | In. Neurons<br>Out. Neurons | 18<br>10 |
| 6 | Dense | In. Neurons<br>Out. Neurons | 10<br>2 |

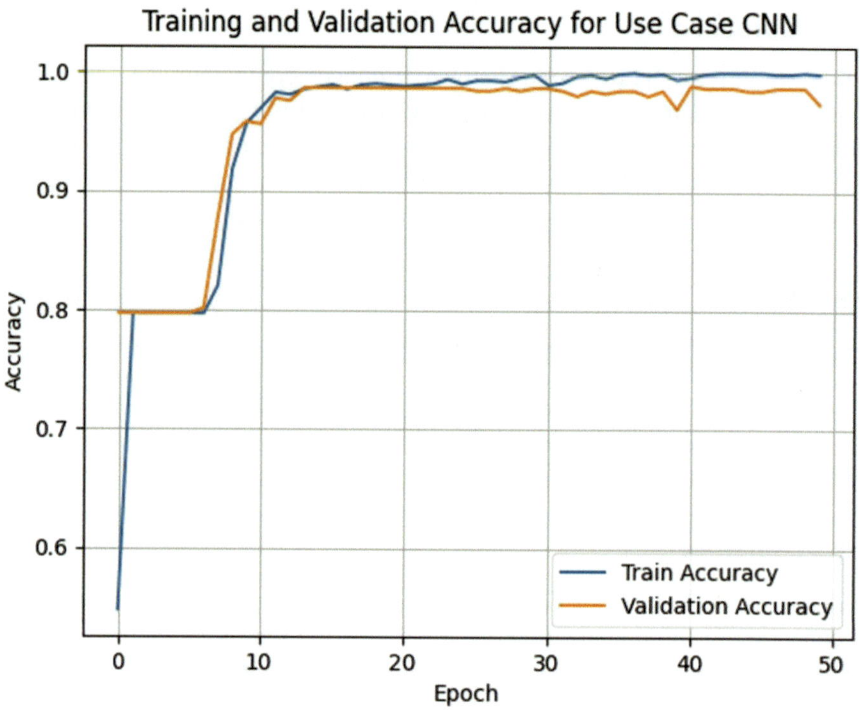


**Figure 9.3** Training of Use Case CNN.

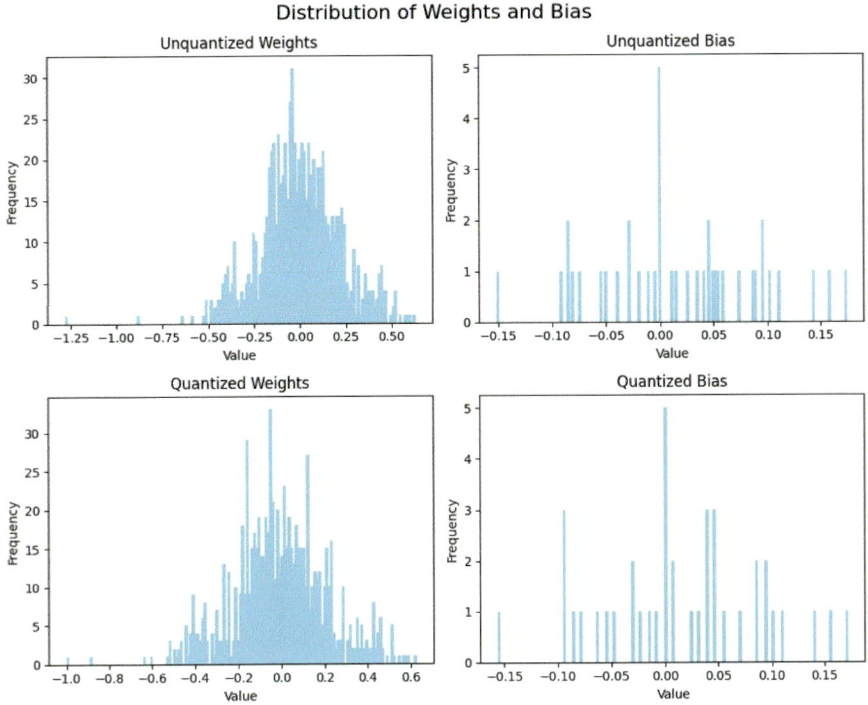


**Figure 9.4** Distribution of Weights and Bias of Use Case CNN.

To determine the most suitable split into integer and fractional bits for all intermediate results, the software model is employed to calculate the inference for all 459 test images using various 8-bit fixed-point representations. As illustrated in Figure 9.5, a split into 5 integer and 3 fractional bits is found to be optimal. With an accuracy of 97.59 % the loss in performance due to quantization amounts to only 1.75 percentage points compared to the performance achieved in TensorFlow Keras.

### 9.3.4 Translation

With the most suitable split for intermediate results determined to 5 integer and 3 fractional bits during the evaluation step of the tinyHLS workflow, the layer templates are instantiated and interconnected in the top module during the translation process of the tinyHLS workflow. These layer templates are instantiated with all respective parameters taken into account. (Figure 9.6). The values for all weights and bias are provided to the top module via Verilog header files.

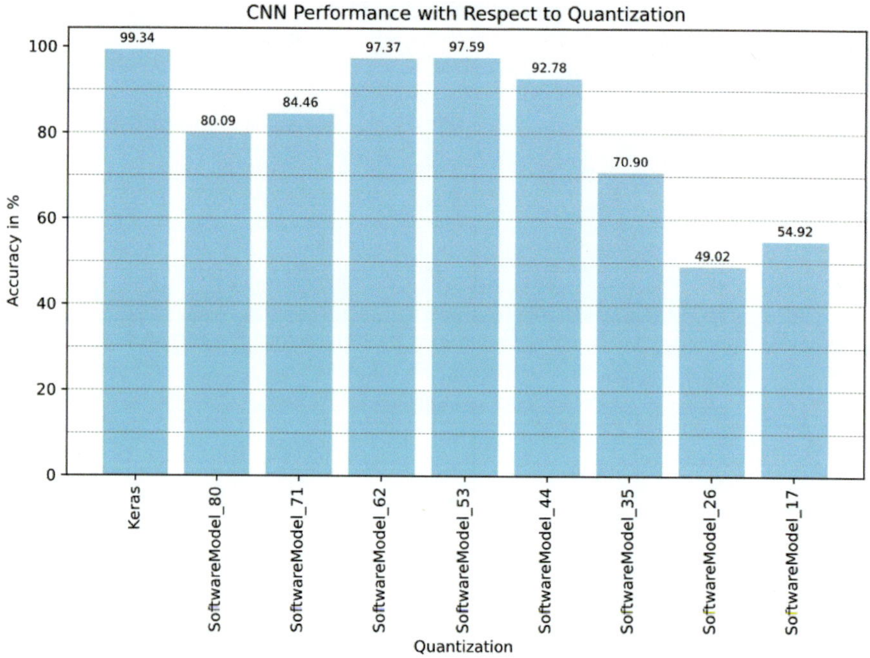


**Figure 9.5** Evaluation of Performance of Use Case CNN with Respect to 8-Bit Fixed-Point Quantization.

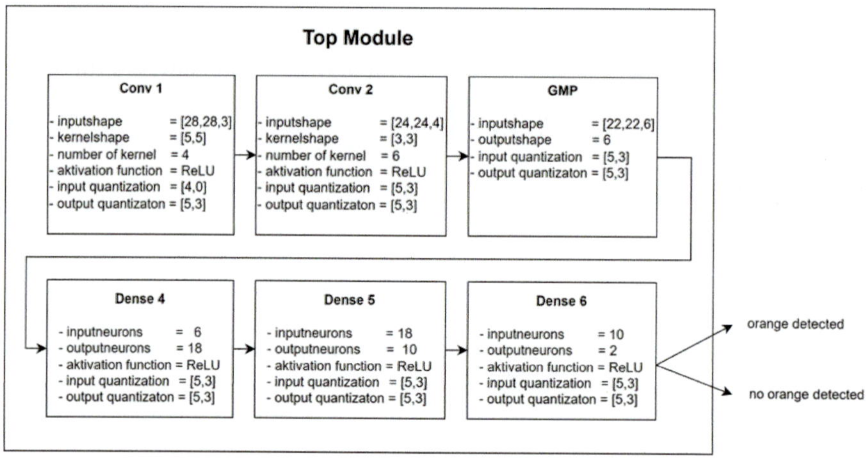


**Figure 9.6** Top Module for Use Case CNN.

**Table 9.2** Verification Results for Use Case CNN

| *Image* | *Inference Keras* | *Inference SW 64* | *Inference SW 8* | *Inference HWA* | *Verification Successful* |
|---|---|---|---|---|---|
|  | 1.000000 | 1.000000 | 0.999981 | 0.999981 | True |
|  | 0.000158 | 0.000158 | 0.017986 | 0.017986 | True |
|  | 1.000000 | 1.000000 | 0.999997 | 0.999997 | True |
|  | 0.000009 | 0.000009 | 0.014064 | 0.014064 | True |
|  | 0.000016 | 0.000016 | 0.009708 | 0.009708 | True |

### 9.3.5 Validation

The generated hardware accelerator is verified based on 5 test images as described in 1.2.6. As shown in Table 9.2, all 5 test images are verified successfully. Although the inference results of the hardware accelerator are not as confident as the results obtained from TensorFlow Keras, the hardware accelerator classifies all 5 test images correctly.

## 9.4 Implementation

Due to platform independency, the hardware accelerator generated by tinyHLS can be used for ASIC designs as well as vendor independent FPGA programming. In this work, the hardware accelerator for the introduced use case CNN is implemented on the Kria KR260 Robotics Starter Kit [13] using AMD Vivado$^{TM}$. As illustrated in Figure 9.7, the Kria FPGA Board comprises a processing system (PS) containing a quad-core Arm Cortex-A53 processor and a programmable logic (PL), where custom logic is located. To

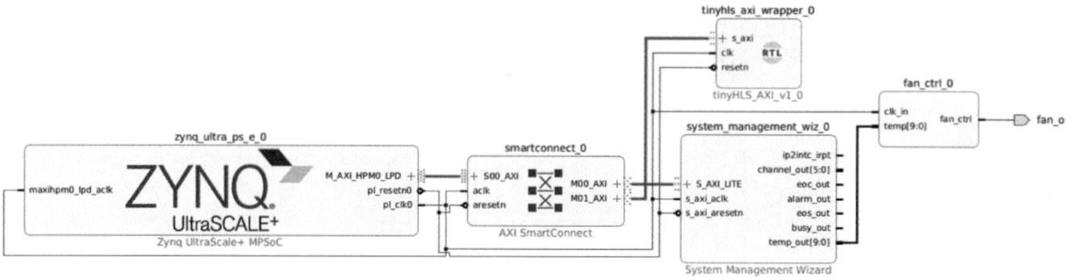


**Figure 9.7** Setup on Kria Board.

connect master and slaves via AXI4-Lite bus, the smartconnect intellectual property (IP) block is included in the PL of the board. Besides the processor, which serves as a master, the hardware accelerator and a fan controller are connected to the AXI4-Lite bus as slaves. In this work, both, the fan controller and the hardware accelerator run on a 100 MHz frequency, even though the hardware accelerator can be clocked as fast as 180 MHz.

## 9.5 Results

The efficiency of the hardware accelerator in terms of hardware requirements as well as latency and energy consumption per inference is assessed based on the implementation of the use case CNN on the Kria board. The results are discussed in the following sections.

### 9.5.1 Hardware Requirements

Although the CNN utilizes only 864 parameters, its hardware accelerator requires 65,805 look up tables (LUTs) utilizing 56.19 % of the available LUTs on the PL of the Kria board and 27,380 Flip Flops (FFs) utilizing 11.69 % of the available FFs on the PL of the Kria board (Figure 9.8). This large design is a result of extensive parallel computing. Despite the Kria board comprising 1248 digital signal processing (DSP) tiles and 144 block random access memory (BRAM) tiles, none of these specialized resources are utilized in the design. Therefore, the primary reasons for the large design footprint are parallelization and the lack of utilization of specialized tiles.

### 9.5.2 Latency

For latency considerations, the hardware accelerator is first analysed as a stand-alone implementation meaning that the input image is provided directly to the hardware accelerator without accounting for data transmission via

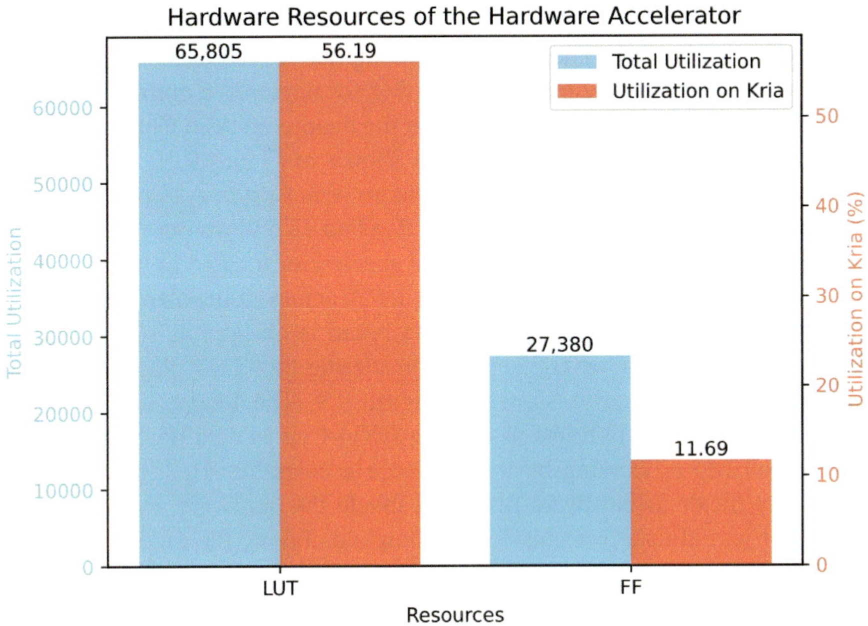


**Figure 9.8** Resource Utilization.

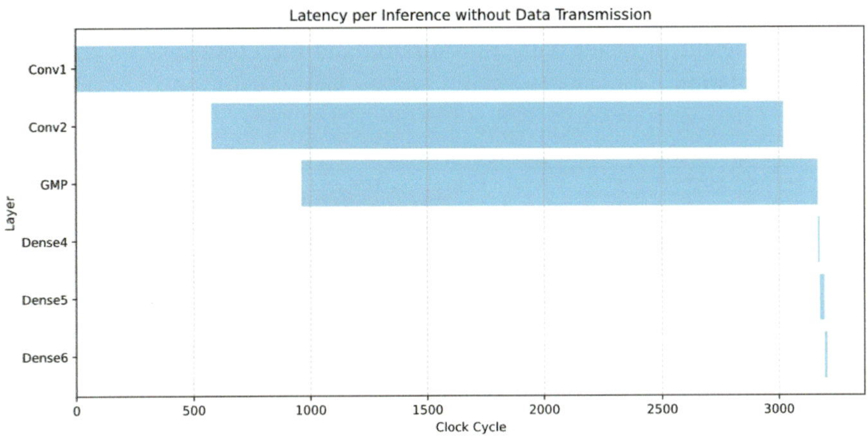


**Figure 9.9** Latency per Inference Without Data Transmission.

AXI4-Lite. As shown in Figure 9.9, intra-layer pipelining has a significant impact on latency leading to a total number of 3211 clock cycles per inference calculation.

For benchmarking purposes, the use case CNN is implemented in C code using keras2C [14]. The C code is compiled using GCC compiler with -O0 flag for no optimization and -O3 flag for aggressive optimization. After compilation, the C code is executed on the quad-core Arm Cortex-A53 processor in the PS of the Kria board. As shown in Figure 9.10 the pure software-based implementation on the quad-core Arm Cortex-A53 processor requires 48.563 ms per inference using -O0 flag and 48.538 ms per inference using -O3 flag. With 0.063 ms the hardware accelerator located in the PL of the Kria board requires only 0.13 % of the latency achieved in software.

As the hardware accelerator on the Kria board is clocked at 100 MHz, the latency is expected to be 0.03211 ms considering that 3211 clock cycles are required per inference as shown in Figure 9.9. The longer latency is primarily attributed to data transmission via AXI4-Lite as data transmission is slower than data processing by the hardware accelerator. This leads to a lower activity factor as hardware resources inside the hardware accelerator must wait for partial data transmission to complete. Taking the time for data transmission into consideration, the latency per inference doubled compared to latency without data transmission. As no interrupt has been implemented in the current design, polling is one reason for long data transmission times. Also note that low power domain (LPD) is utilized for the interactions between PS and PL part of the Kria board. Using full power domain (FPD) instead might result in faster data transmission and therefore faster overall inference calculation.

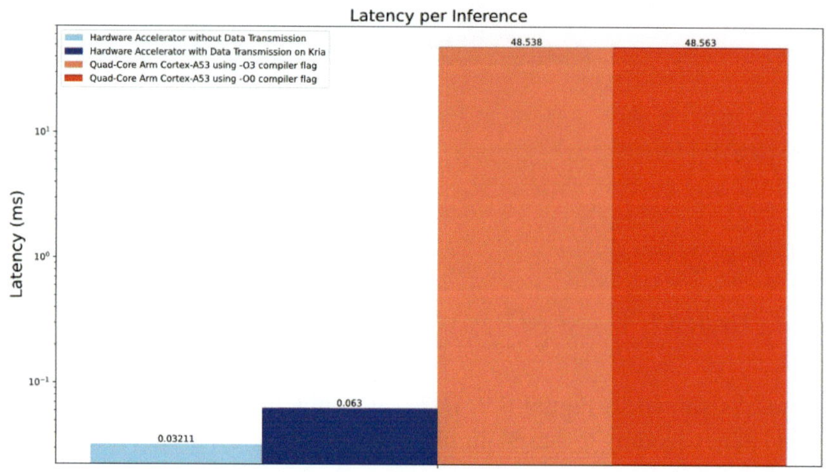


**Figure 9.10** Benchmarking Regarding Latency.

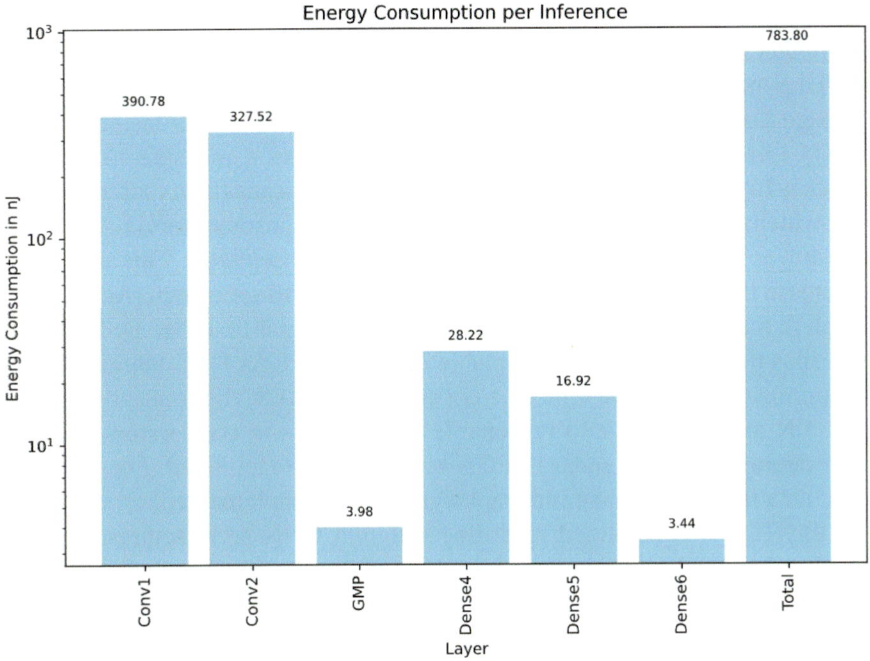


**Figure 9.11** Energy per Inference.

### 9.5.3 Energy

To estimate the energy for one inference calculation required by the hardware accelerator the toggle activity of the design is estimated using Cadence xCelium$^{TM}$. Furthermore, the design is synthesized using Cadence Genus$^{TM}$. Based on the toggle activity and the results from place and routing using Cadence Innovus$^{TM}$, the overall power consumption per inference can be estimated. The energy consumption can then be determined considering the latency information provided in 1.5.2. With more than 91 % of the overall energy consumed, the convolution layers make up for most of the computational effort of the inference. Note that the energy observations in Figure 9.11 do not take data transmission into account.

## 9.6 Conclusion and Outlook

As demonstrated in previous sections, the hardware accelerator generated for the use case CNN executes inference calculations efficiently regarding latency and energy consumption albeit at the expense of resource utilization.

Considering that more complex image classification tasks require larger CNN architectures [15], the designs of the hardware accelerators generated by tinyHLS need to be minimized in order to meet requirements of complex image classification tasks in the future. As tinyHLS works faster than the AXI4-Lite data transmission, a rational optimization measure to save resources is to execute less operations in parallel. This leads to an increase of latency which remains imperceptible as long as data transmission via AXI4-Lite is slower than data processing by the hardware accelerator. This would also increase the activity factor leading to higher overall efficiency. Another approach to reduce the size of the hardware accelerators is to utilize DSP and BRAM tiles that are commonly available on many FPGAs [16]. Integrating these optimization strategies into the concept of tinyHLS, the translation of larger CNN architectures into reasonable sized hardware accelerators suitable for deployment on standard FPGA boards can be facilitated. For more efficient data transmission, an interrupt signal can be implemented.

As tinyHLS is constrained regarding different CNN architectures, it is essential to develop layer templates for other types of layers such as average-pooling, max-pooling or global-average-pooling in future work. Furthermore, parameters like zero padding or stride can be implemented to provide more flexibility. Average-pooling and max-pooling layers as well as stride are particularly important as they reduce the overall computational effort of the inference calculation.

## Acknowledgements

This research has been funded in part by the project CLEVER (Project ID 101097560), which is supported by the Key Digital Technologies Joint Undertaking and its members (including top-up funding by the German Federal Ministry of Education and Research (BMBF)).

This manuscript was edited with the assistance of OpenAI's language model to enhance clarity, readability, and consistency. All suggestions were critically reviewed and accepted or modified by the authors, who take full responsibility for the final content. No AI tools were used to create, alter, or manipulate original research data or results.

## References

[1] AMD, AMD Vivado$^{TM}$ High-Level-Design. [Online]. Available: https://www.amd.com/de/products/software/adaptive-socs-and-fpgas/vivado/high-level-design.html (accessed: Sep. 19 2025).

[2] D. Baptista, S. Abreu, F. Freitas, R. Vasconcelos, and F. Morgado-Dias, "A survey of software and hardware use in artificial neural networks," (in En;en), Neural Comput & Applic, vol. 23, 3-4, pp. 591–599, 2013, doi: 10.1007/s00521-013-1406-y.

[3] M. Imani, R. Garcia, S. Gupta, and T. Rosing, "Hardware-Software Co-design to Accelerate Neural Network Applications," J. Emerg. Technol. Comput. Syst., vol. 15, no. 2, pp. 1–18, 2019, doi: 10.1145/3304086.

[4] D. Milojicic, "Accelerators for Artificial Intelligence and High-Performance Computing," Computer, vol. 53, no. 2, pp. 14–22, 2020, doi: 10.1109/mc.2019.2954056.

[5] I. Kuon and J. Rose, "Measuring the gap between FPGAs and ASICs," in Proceedings of the 2006 ACM/SIGDA 14th international symposium on Field programmable gate arrays, New York, NY, USA, 2006, pp. 21–30.

[6] C. Qian, L. Einhaus, and G. Schiele, "ElasticAI-Creator," in Proceedings of the 20th ACM Conference on Embedded Networked Sensor Systems, New York, NY, USA, 2022, pp. 941–946.

[7] I. Hoyer, A. Utz, C. Hoog Antink, and K. Seidl, "tinyHLS: a novel open source high level synthesis tool targeting hardware accelerators for artificial neural network inference," Physiol. Meas., vol. 13, no. 1, p. 15002, 2025, doi: 10.1088/1361-6579/ada8f0.

[8] AXI4-Lite Interface MIPI D-PHY LogiCORE IP Product Guide (PG202) Reader AMD Technical Information Portal. [Online]. Available: https://docs.amd.com/r/en-US/pg202-mipi-dphy/AXI4-Lite-Interface (accessed: Sep. 19 2025).

[9] Amir Gholami, Sehoon Kim, Zhen Dong, Zhewei Yao, Michael W. Mahoney, and Kurt Keutzer, "A Survey of Quantization Methods for Efficient Neural Network Inference," in Low-Power Computer Vision: Chapman and Hall/CRC, 2022, pp. 291–326. [Online]. Available: https://www.taylorfrancis.com/chapters/edit/10.1201/9781003162810-13/survey-quantization-methods-efficient-neural-network-inference-amir-gholami-sehoon-kim-zhen-dong-zhewei-yao-michael-mahoney-kurt-keutzer

[10] M. Nagel, M. Fournarakis, R. A. Amjad, Y. Bondarenko, M. van Baalen, and T. Blankevoort, "A White Paper on Neural Network Quantization," Jun. 2021. [Online]. Available: http://arxiv.org/pdf/2106.08295v1

[11] L. Wei, Z. Ma, C. Yang, and Q. Yao, "Advances in the Neural Network Quantization: A Comprehensive Review," Applied Sciences, vol. 14, no. 17, p. 7445, 2024, doi: 10.3390/app14177445.

[12] TensorFlow, Keras: The high-level API for TensorFlow  |  TensorFlow Core. [Online]. Available: https://www.tensorflow.org/guide/keras (accessed: Sep. 19 2025).

[13] AMD, AMD KR260 Robotics Starter Kit. [Online]. Available: https://www.amd.com/de/products/system-on-modules/kria/k26/kr260-robotics-starter-kit.html (accessed: Sep. 19 2025).

[14] R. Conlin, K. Erickson, J. Abbate, and E. Kolemen, "Keras2c: A library for converting Keras neural networks to real-time compatible C," Engineering Applications of Artificial Intelligence, vol. 100, p. 104182, 2021, doi: 10.1016/j.engappai.2021.104182.

[15] P. Jiang, D. Ergu, F. Liu, Y. Cai, and B. Ma, "A Review of Yolo Algorithm Developments," Procedia Computer Science, vol. 199, pp. 1066–1073, 2022, doi: 10.1016/j.procs.2022.01.135.

[16] P. Goswami and D. Bhatia, "Floorplanning of Partially Reconfigurable Design on Heterogeneous FPGA," in Proceedings of the 2016 ACM/SIGDA International Symposium on Field-Programmable Gate Arrays, New York, NY, USA, 2016, p. 275.

# 10

# Fair AI Experimentation on Edge Device Clusters via Distributed Orchestration in dAIEdge-VLab

**Baptiste Dupertuis, Maïck Huguenin, Dorvan Favre, Grégoire Rebstein, Margaux Divernois, and Nuria Pazos**

HES-SO, Switzerland

## Abstract

Efficient orchestration and scheduling are essential for managing hardware resources in clusters of edge devices, especially when benchmarking their ability to run AI models, perform on-device training, and engage in federated learning. Coordinating benchmarking requests must be responsive, consistent, and resource efficient.

The distributed nature of such clusters adds complexity, particularly in the absence of a central server for resource allocation. Each node must communicate directly with others, increasing overhead—especially when devices are dispersed across different networks.

Open-source orchestration frameworks such as Kubernetes and Nomad (with Consul) offer robust foundations, yet their distributed deployment and effective integration remain challenging.

This work presents the design of a distributed orchestrator and scheduler for fair and efficient execution of AI experiments on remote edge device clusters. The proposed approach combines priority awareness, resource sensitivity, completion awareness, and a FIFO mechanism to optimize task execution. Integration into dAIEdge-VLab—a distributed virtual laboratory for AI experimentation—will enable coordinated benchmarking and workload distribution across heterogeneous edge devices.

DOI: 10.1201/9788743815211-10

An implementation using Nomad and Consul demonstrates the system's ability to meet performance and fairness requirements, validating its effectiveness for scalable AI experimentation in decentralized, resource-constrained environments.

**Keywords:** Edge AI, Benchmarking AI Model, Distributed Cluster, Orchestration, Scheduling, Nomad.

## 10.1 Introduction

The dAIEdge-VLab is a distributed framework for fair, efficient, and reproducible benchmarking of AI workloads on heterogeneous edge devices. Built on Nomad and Consul, it orchestrates resources across a decentralized cluster and provides a flexible foundation for testing new scheduling algorithms focused on fairness, efficiency, and resource management in realistic edge environments.

### 10.1.1 Motivations

The rise of edge computing has created a need to evaluate diverse hardware platforms, from microcontrollers to GPU-enabled boards. The dAIEdge-VLab was developed to meet this need by providing a shared benchmarking environment where researchers can test models and training procedures directly on representative edge devices.

Its goal is to make AI benchmarking on the edge fair, efficient, and reproducible. The platform operates within a decentralized cluster architecture, where each host participates as part of the cluster. This structure improves scalability and robustness but also introduces coordination and scheduling challenges. To address them, the framework implements dedicated scheduling mechanisms that fairly allocate devices, balance workloads, and ensure consistent, comparable results across users and experiments.

### 10.1.2 Challenges in fairness, efficiency, and resource sensitivity

Designing a scheduler for the dAIEdge-VLab requires balancing three core challenges in a shared, heterogeneous, and decentralized environment:

Fairness: Ensure equitable access to limited devices, prevent monopolization, and maintain reproducible conditions regardless of cluster load.

Efficiency: Maximize utilization and minimize waiting time or wasted computation while keeping global coordination consistent despite decentralization.

Resource sensitivity: Account for diverse benchmark types and device capabilities by enforcing device affinity, one-job-per-device isolation, and adapting to real-time health states.

Together, these factors define the core scheduling problem: achieving fair, efficient, and resource-aware benchmarking across a decentralized, heterogeneous cluster.

### 10.1.3 Contributions of the paper

The dAIEdge-VLab orchestrator is designed for AI experimentation, embedding priority-, resource-, and completion-aware scheduling to ensure fair and reproducible benchmarking across heterogeneous edge clusters. Built on Nomad and Consul, it adopts a lightweight, semi-distributed model that balances coordination and decentralized execution.

### 10.1.4 Structure of the paper

This paper presents the dAIEdge-VLab, a distributed framework for fair, efficient, and reproducible benchmarking of AI workloads on heterogeneous edge devices. It outlines the motivation, key challenges, and main contributions of the work, then reviews existing orchestration systems such as Kubernetes, K3s, and Nomad, highlighting their limitations for heterogeneous edge environments.

Building on this analysis, the paper introduces the architecture developed for the dAIEdge-VLab, along with its scheduling framework and algorithms for equitable resource allocation. Finally, it presents experimental results demonstrating fairness and reproducibility and discusses future directions.

## 10.2 Background and related Work

This section reviews existing orchestration and scheduling approaches in cloud and edge computing.

### 10.2.1 Overview and research gaps

Distributed orchestration and scheduling manage workloads across computing resources. In clouds, Kubernetes [1] and Apache Mesos [2] run on large, mostly homogeneous clusters optimized for throughput, scalability, and efficiency. By contrast, edge computing spans heterogeneous, resource-limited devices, from microcontrollers to GPU boards, with constrained compute, memory, energy, and often intermittent connectivity [3, 4], so scheduling must account for device capabilities, availability, and workload diversity.

While mature frameworks like Kubernetes and Nomad offer robust orchestration, they are not designed for launching benchmarking experiments on clusters of heterogeneous edge devices: Kubernetes (and its lightweight and edge-oriented variants such as KubeEdge [5] and OpenYurt [6]) assumes cluster-native, containerized resources, while Nomad supports containerized and standalone workloads via a scalable client-server architecture; both assume stable, continuously connected clusters and lack native mechanisms to handle wide device diversity [7].

Recent research addresses these edge-specific challenges with multi-resource-aware and load-balanced scheduling strategies. Liu et al. [8] propose dynamic multi-resource allocation in heterogeneous edge clusters, improving task throughput while reducing latency by considering device heterogeneity and load balancing. Similarly, the LR2Scheduler framework [9] introduces layer-aware, resource-balanced, and request-adaptive container scheduling, optimizing resource usage and startup time by adapting allocation based on workload demands and container image layer dependencies. Furthermore, multi-cluster layer-sharing scheduling strategies [10] exploit shared image layers across cloud-edge clusters, significantly reducing container startup latency and improving load balancing through algorithms like Probabilistic Relaxation Container Scheduling and Greedy Layer Sorting.

Despite these advances, current frameworks and research still fall short in supporting fair benchmarking in edge scenarios. Key missing features include integration of peripheral devices managed through host nodes, strict one-job-per-device isolation, reproducibility under variable load, and fair access control, all critical for evaluating scheduling policies across clusters of heterogeneous edge devices.

## 10.3 Architecture

The dAIEdge-VLab addresses the limitations of existing orchestration frameworks through a decentralized, scalable architecture built on Nomad, featuring dedicated scheduling mechanisms that ensure fair, isolated, and reproducible benchmarking across heterogeneous edge platforms.

It integrates distributed orchestration, service discovery, and custom scheduling to provide scalability, robustness, and transparency.

### 10.3.1 Assumptions

The architecture of the dAIEdge-VLab is designed using the following assumptions: each edge devices are managed by a host, a host can leave the network at any time, an edge device can become unresponsive or failing, and a benchmark running on an edge device can estimate and advertise its completion and state.

### 10.3.2 Topology

The dAIEdge-VLab uses a distributed topology across hosts [12] that improves scalability and reliability by removing single points of failure. These advantages come at the cost of greater system complexity and increased communication between nodes.

Figure 10.1 shows the overall topology, composed of hosts, edge devices, and users. Users can access the cluster through any reachable host, which

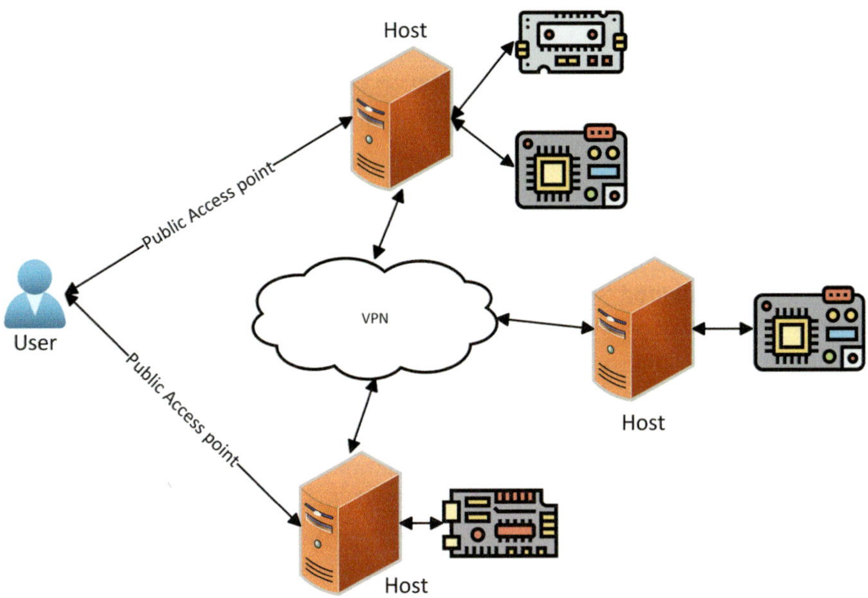


**Figure 10.1** dAIEdge-VLab Topology.

serves as their entry point. Hosts are connected through a mesh VPN layer, ensuring secure and resilient communication. Each host can manage multiple edge devices, but every edge device is assigned to a single host, ensuring clear ownership.

### 10.3.3 Tasks

The dAIEdge-VLab supports three benchmarking services: synthetic model evaluation (TYPE 1), data-driven model evaluation (TYPE 2), and on-device training benchmarking (TYPE 3). Each task is submitted by remote users and scheduled across a shared pool of heterogeneous edge devices.

Users specify the device family (e.g., Raspberry Pi 5) on which their benchmark should run. The scheduler then assigns the job to a compatible, available device of that family.

Execution time depends on factors such as model complexity, dataset size, and device capability, but an empirical duration pattern can be observed: synthetic benchmarks typically complete fastest, followed by data-driven inference, while on-device training is the most time-consuming.

Benchmarks are non-preemptive; if a job is stopped, it must restart from the beginning to preserve a consistent device state.

### 10.3.4 Host architecture

Each host acts as a bridge between its local edge devices and the rest of the cluster, advertising their capabilities and current state to the network. Every host runs a VPN layer ensuring secure and persistent connectivity among all hosts. On top of this layer, Consul and Nomad instances are deployed, as illustrated in Figure 10.2.

Consul provides service discovery and cluster integrity management, ensuring that distributed services such as the *Benchmark API*, and web interface server remain reachable across the network.

Nomad handles orchestration, maintaining service health, deploying jobs, and tracking their status throughout the cluster. A custom *EdgeDevices* plugin extends Nomad to recognize and manage attached edge devices, enabling precise resource utilization and controlled benchmark deployment.

Each host runs the core services required for cluster operation and may also host application-level services such as the Web Interface or the *Benchmark API*.

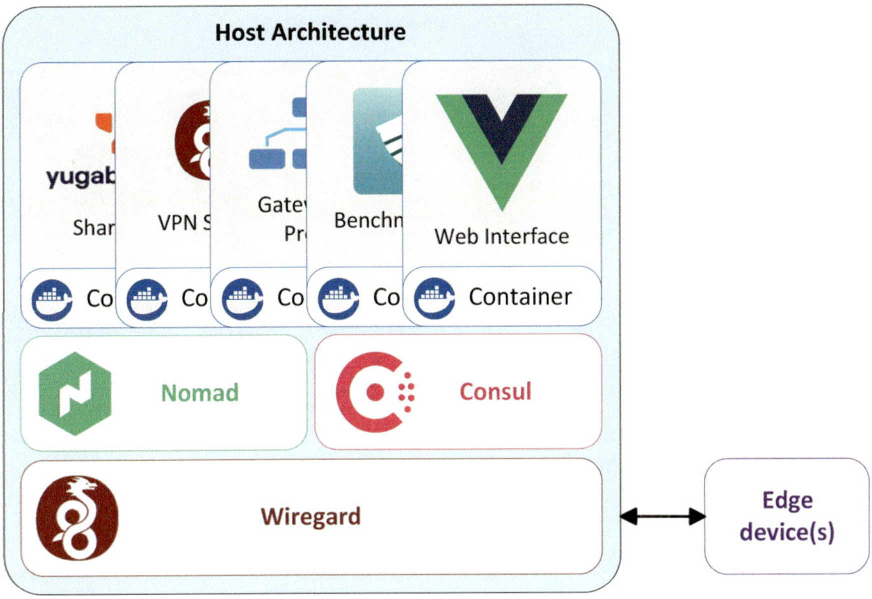


**Figure 10.2** Host architecture.

### 10.3.5 Orchestrator and Scheduler

Scheduling decisions are handled by a dedicated scheduler integrated within the *Benchmark API*. Both components are co-located in the same service: the API acts as the entry point for user interactions, while the scheduler processes validated requests to determine job placement and execution timing. Figure 10.3 illustrates the conceptual interactions between the cluster components.

Once a job is ready for execution, the scheduler submits it to the Nomad cluster, which coordinates deployment across available hosts. Scheduling decisions rely on the aggregated cluster and edge device state (the *resource pool*) advertised by Nomad, ensuring placement only on compatible and available devices.

Before scheduling, the *Benchmark API* validates requests against available resources and user permissions. Infeasible or unauthorized submissions are rejected early.

In summary, users interact solely with the *Benchmark API*: it validates and forwards requests to the scheduler, which plans execution, while Nomad manages deployment and lifecycle operations on the target hardware.

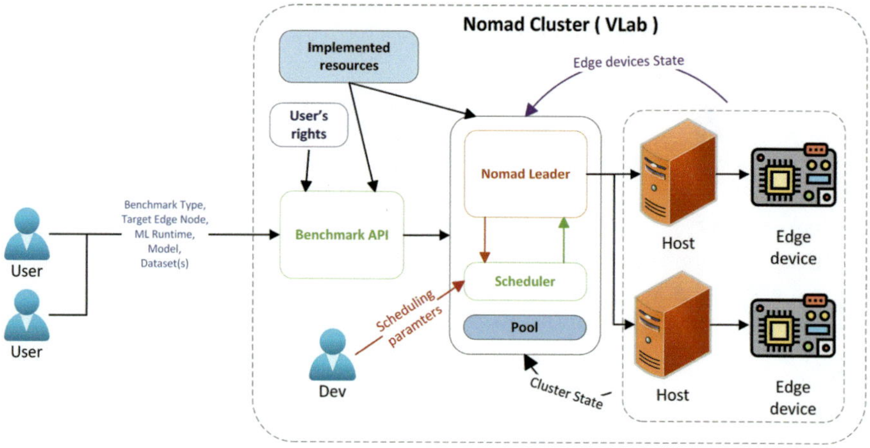


**Figure 10.3** Conceptual interaction diagram.

## 10.4 Scheduling

The dAIEdge-VLab requires efficient scheduling of diverse benchmark workloads on its Nomad cluster. The scheduling design must therefore reconcile heterogeneity, fairness, and efficiency, while maintaining the flexibility to evolve with future workload types.

### 10.4.1 Requirements

The dAIEdge-VLab scheduling framework is built around functional and non-functional requirements derived from the core challenges of fairness, efficiency, and resource sensitivity, ensuring reproducible and consistent benchmarking across heterogeneous edge devices.

#### 10.4.1.1 Functional requirements

The system must provide the following capabilities:

- **Job submission:** Users shall be able to submit one-time benchmark jobs to the cluster.
- **Job management:** Users shall be able to cancel submitted jobs and monitor their execution status.
- **Non-preemptive execution:** Running benchmarks shall not be preempted once started, to preserve consistency of results.

- **Job eviction**: Jobs may be stopped and rescheduled only if they have not yet been completed. This can be used to serve high priority job by evicting lower running ones.
- **Hardware dispatching:** The scheduler shall dispatch jobs only to hosts that provide the hardware explicitly requested by the benchmark.
- **Exclusive execution:** At most one benchmark shall run on an edge device at any given time to ensure the best performance and consistency.
- **Priority handling:** The scheduler shall consider job priorities when allocating scarce edge resources.
- **Advanced scheduling:** The system may support more advanced scheduling features, such as dynamic adaptation of priorities or user quota management.

#### 10.4.1.2 Non-Functional requirements

In addition, the system must satisfy the following considerations:

- **High availability:** The system shall be fault-tolerant and free of single points of failure. If a host fails, jobs and services shall be rescheduled to another compatible host if available.
- **Low latency:** Jobs shall be scheduled and dispatched with minimal delay to avoid long idle times on available devices.
- **Consistency:** Jobs shall be executed only once, and benchmark results shall remain consistent and reproducible across repeated runs.

### 10.4.2 Objectives

The objectives of the scheduling framework can be summarized as follows:

- **Efficiency:** Maximize utilization of cluster resources without unnecessary idle times or avoiding wasting too much computation time.
- **Fairness:** Ensure equitable access for multiple users and competing benchmark submissions.
- **Scalability:** Support a growing number of benchmarks and diverse resource types as the platform evolves.
- **Flexibility:** Accommodate different scheduling policies (e.g., priority-based, resource-sensitive) depending on workload characteristics.
- **Reproducibility:** Enable consistent allocation strategies and environments, so benchmark results are comparable across runs and independent of cluster load variations.

### 10.4.3 Metrics

The evaluation of scheduling performance in the dAIEdge-VLab relies on a set of metrics that quantify both resource usage and user satisfaction.

- **Resource Utilization**: The ratio of total computation time spent executing jobs (including restarts) to the total available device time.

$$RU = \frac{total\ active\ compute\ time}{total\ available\ device\ time}$$

- **Resource usefulness:** The ratio of useful computation time that directly contributed to completing the benchmark to the total computation time (i.e. restarted jobs reduce this ratio, especially if the job was stopped after a long period of time).

$$RUF = \frac{Useful\ computation\ time}{Total\ computation\ time}$$

- **Latency / Wait Time**: The elapsed time between benchmark submission and the start of the execution that produced the result. This reflects user-perceived responsiveness, especially important for short-running tasks.
- **Stress ratio**: The stress ratio defines a dynamic waiting allowance for each job, assuming users tolerate longer waits for longer tasks. It compares actual waiting time $W_j$ to an allowed delay proportional to the job's execution time $T_j$:

$$S_j = \frac{W_j}{\alpha_k \cdot T_j}$$

Where $\alpha_k$ is a type-specific scaling factor (e.g. 3 for TYPE 1) it adapts the waiting allowance time for each type. When $S_j$ is $<= 1$, this means that the waiting time of the job was within its waiting allowance. For $S_j$ $> 1$, this means that the job waited longer than its allowance.
- **Compliance rate**: This metric simply counts the percentage of jobs that waited a time within their allowance.
- **Average service score for a user and benchmark type:** The service score quantifies how well a job was served relative to its allowed waiting time. It is derived from the stress ratio $S_j$ and bounded between 0 and 1.

$$Q_j = \min\left(1, \frac{1}{S_j}\right)$$

A value of $Q_j = 1$ indicates the job was executed within its allowance (good service), while lower values reflect increasing delay beyond the acceptable threshold.

The Average service score for a user and benchmark type is simply the average service score that a user experienced for a given type of benchmark.

$$\overline{Q}_u = \frac{1}{n_u} \sum_{j \in user\ u,\quad type\ t} Q_j$$

Where $n_u$ is number of benchmarks type that the user has in the considered experiment.

- **Fairness Index:** A Jain's index [11] is then computed from per-user average service scores for a benchmark type to assess equality of treatment across users:

$$J\left(\{\overline{Q}_u\}\right) = \frac{\left(\sum_u \overline{Q}_u\right)^2}{n \cdot \sum_u \overline{Q}_u^{\,2}}$$

Where $Q_u$ is the mean service score of user u for the considered benchmark type and $n$ the number of users that has at least one benchmark of the considered type.
This index measures fairness, not absolute performance. Values close to 1 indicate that users were treated evenly.

- **Job Completion Success Rate**: The percentage of benchmarks that complete successfully without eviction or restart due to resource contention.

These metrics provide both a system-level view (efficiency and resource use) and a user-level view (responsiveness and fairness) of scheduling performance within the dAIEdge-VLab.

### 10.4.4 Techniques

The dAIEdge-VLab ensures efficient, fair, and hardware-aware scheduling across heterogeneous edge devices through three key principles:

- Resource sensitivity: The scheduler tracks cluster and device states in real time, considering availability, health, and progress. Only one benchmark runs per device to prevent interference and ensure reproducibility.
- Priority awareness: Jobs are prioritized by urgency and duration, with priority aging to prevent starvation and maintain fair access.
- Heterogeneity handling: Each device is managed by a host that abstracts hardware differences and reports capabilities, enabling consistent benchmarking across diverse platforms.

## 10.5 Scheduling Algorithms

The scheduler receives a job description from the Benchmark API containing key information such as the edge device family, runtime, and benchmark type. It then uses this data together with the current state of the edge nodes, including their capabilities, unique IDs, and dynamic attributes like job progress, to compute a scheduling plan. Once the plan is determined, the scheduler submits or removes jobs through Nomad using its deployment interface.

### 10.5.1 Baseline algorithm

The baseline scheduler uses a FIFO queue per edge device family within the dAIEdge-VLab *Benchmark API*, with Nomad as the backend executor.

Submitted benchmarks are queued by device family. The dispatcher selects the oldest compatible job when a suitable device becomes available, converts it into a Nomad job specification, and submits it for execution.

The scheduler subscribes to the Nomad event stream, a key component that provides real-time updates on job completions and node availability. Running in a separate thread from the dispatcher, this mechanism keeps the scheduler continuously aware of the cluster state without requiring redundant polling.

### 10.5.2 Explored Algorithms

The next sections will describe the different algorithms tested for the scheduler logic.

#### 10.5.2.1 Algo 1 - FIFO with Type-Based Fixed Priority (No Job eviction)

This algorithm extends the baseline by introducing fixed priorities per benchmark type while preserving FIFO order within each category.

Priority classes (static; higher value = higher priority):

- Type 1 - synthetic model benchmarking: 80
- Type 2 - data-driven model benchmarking: 60
- Type 3 - on-device training benchmarking: 50

The dispatcher always selects the highest non-empty priority class and, within that class, the oldest job that matches an available edge device. There is no interruption or restart of running jobs; once a job starts, it runs to completion.

#### 10.5.2.2 Algo 2 - FIFO with Type-Based Fixed Priority and Job eviction

This algorithm extends Algo 1 by introducing job eviction. When no capacity is available, a running job may be evicted only if a waiting task has higher priority within the same device family. The newest eligible lower-priority job is selected to minimize wasted computation, while jobs of equal priority are never evicted. Displaced jobs are requeued in FIFO order.

This approach improves responsiveness for short, high-priority tasks but may lead to starvation under sustained load due to the absence of priority aging.

#### 10.5.2.3 Algo 3 FIFO with Type-Based Fixed Priority, Bounded eviction and Aging

This algorithm builds on Algo 2. When all devices are busy, a bounded eviction policy applies: a running job can be evicted only if a waiting job has higher priority and the running job's progress is below a set threshold (e.g., progress $< X\%$). Progress is reported via the *EdgeDevices* Nomad plugin. Among eligible candidates, the newest lower-priority job is selected to minimize wasted work.

To prevent starvation, the scheduler adds priority aging, allowing long-waiting or repeatedly evicted jobs to gradually gain priority up to a defined limit.

### 10.5.3 Algorithm evaluation

A heterogeneous cluster including three Raspberry Pi 5 devices was used to evaluate the scheduling algorithms. For simplicity, only the Raspberry Pi 5 devices were used as benchmark targets. Since users select the resource type, the results remain representative of overall algorithm performance.

A test bench ensured repeatable and fair evaluation by replaying a fixed sequence of job requests from multiple users and benchmark types under identical conditions. Four jobs were defined per benchmark type, each with a unique Experiment ID. The test bench tracked job states, generated execution timelines, and computed performance metrics.

Two evaluation scenarios were considered:

- Realistic workload: assessing waiting times, useful resource utilization, and user experience.

- High contention: evaluating fairness, waiting times, completion rate, and resource utilization with all devices fully loaded.

All metrics are defined in Section 1.4.4.

#### 10.5.3.1 Base test-bench

The first test bench is summarized in Table 10.1. Three users submit different types of benchmark requests, making this setup representative of a typical dAIEdge-VLab use case. The parameter $\alpha$, used to compute each job's waiting allowance, was set to 1 for all benchmark types.

#### 10.5.3.2 Contention test-bench

The Table 10.2 describes a test bench designed to create contention within the cluster. Three users simultaneously submit identical sets of benchmarks, mixing different types in quantities exceeding the available resources.

Job waiting allowances were computed using scaling factors of $\alpha = 3$, 4, and 5 for TYPE1, TYPE2, and TYPE3 benchmarks, respectively. These values were tuned to produce meaningful results and prevent all jobs from exceeding their waiting allowance.

### 10.5.4 Algorithms performances

Each figure shows the evolution of job states over time, including four main statuses:

- Queued: waiting in the scheduler's internal queue until selected for submission to Nomad.
- Pending: accepted by Nomad but not yet placed on a suitable resource.

**Table 10.1** Base test-bench definition

| User | Time | Type | Edge device | Runtime | Experiment ID |
|---|---|---|---|---|---|
| 1 | T+0 | TYPE3 | Rpi5 | tflite | 3-2 |
| 2 | T+2 | TYPE3 | Rpi5 | tflite | 3-3 |
| 3 | T+2 | TYPE3 | Rpi5 | tflite | 3-3 |
| 1 | T+1 | TYPE1 | Rpi5 | tflite | 1-1 |
| 2 | T+8 | TYPE1 | Rpi5 | tflite | 1-2 |
| 3 | T+8 | TYPE1 | Rpi5 | onnx | 1-0 |
| 1 | T+76 | TYPE1 | Rpi5 | tflite | 1-1 |
| 2 | T+83 | TYPE1 | Rpi5 | tflite | 1-2 |
| 3 | T+83 | TYPE1 | Rpi5 | onnx | 1-0 |
| 1 | T+12 | TYPE2 | Rpi5 | onnx | 2-0 |
| 2 | T+90 | TYPE2 | Rpi5 | onnx | 2-0 |

**Table 10.2** Contention test-bench definition

| User | Time | Type | Edge device | Runtime | Experiment ID |
|---|---|---|---|---|---|
| 1-2-3 | T+0 | TYPE1 | Rpi5 | tflite | 1-1 |
| 1-2-3 | T+0 | TYPE1 | Rpi5 | tflite | 1-1 |
| 1-2-3 | T+0 | TYPE2 | Rpi5 | onnx | 2-0 |
| 1-2-3 | T+0 | TYPE3 | Rpi5 | tflite | 3-3 |
| 1-2-3 | T+15 | TYPE1 | Rpi5 | tflite | 1-1 |
| 1-2-3 | T+15 | TYPE1 | Rpi5 | tflite | 1-1 |
| 1-2-3 | T+15 | TYPE2 | Rpi5 | onnx | 2-0 |
| 1-2-3 | T+15 | TYPE3 | Rpi5 | tflite | 3-3 |
| 1-2-3 | T+30 | TYPE1 | Rpi5 | tflite | 1-1 |
| 1-2-3 | T+30 | TYPE1 | Rpi5 | tflite | 1-1 |
| 1-2-3 | T+30 | TYPE2 | Rpi5 | onnx | 2-0 |
| 1-2-3 | T+30 | TYPE3 | Rpi5 | tflite | 3-3 |

- Running: actively executing on an assigned device.
- Evicted: interrupted to free a resource for a higher-priority job and rescheduled later.

Timestamps follow the test-bench configuration, showing when users initiated requests, while time zero marks their arrival at the API. Small offsets stem from upload time, latency, or polling. Figures therefore reflect actual API arrival times, showing how network and upload delays affect order.

#### 10.5.4.1 Base algorithm

The Figure 10.4 illustrates the timeline generated by the baseline algorithm using the Base test-bench. The behaviour is straightforward: jobs are executed strictly in their order of arrival.

The median waiting time for TYPE1 benchmarks is 3 seconds, with a standard deviation of 14.33 seconds. This suggests that while most jobs start quickly, some experience significantly longer delays, indicating uneven scheduling among jobs of the same type and a potential impact on user experience. If TYPE3 benchmarks were hour-long experiments, shorter jobs could be delayed for an hour before execution.

The usefulness of performed computations and the clean success rate both reach 100%, as this algorithm does not support job restarts.

#### 10.5.4.2 Algo 1

Figure 10.5 shows the timeline produced by the Algo 1, which prioritizes short-running jobs in the queue. Overall, it resembles the baseline algorithm's

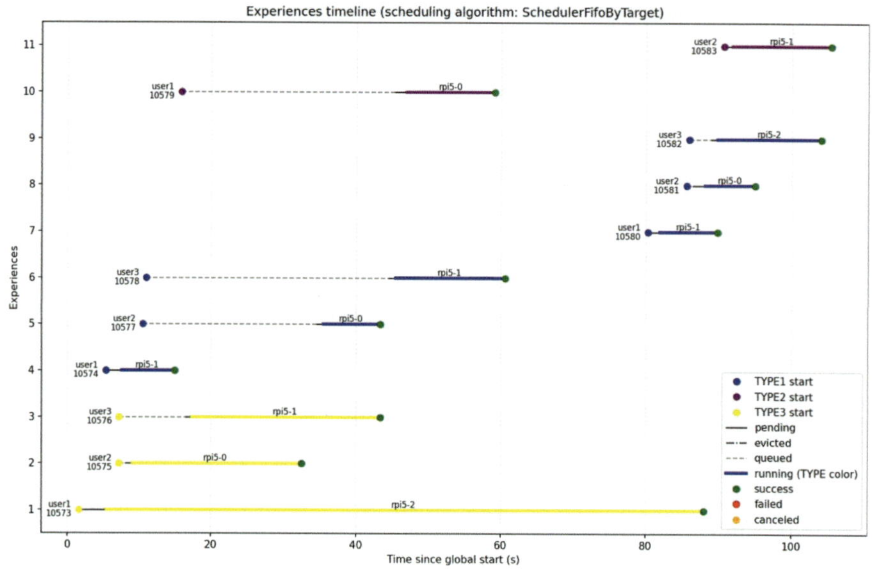


**Figure 10.4** Base test-bench timeline base algorithm.

**Table 10.3** Metrics base test-bench – Base Algo

| Metrics | Base | | |
|---|---|---|---|
| **TYPE** | **1** | **2** | **3** |
| Wait time mean [s] | 11.39 | 15.93 | 5.06 |
| Wait time median [s] | 3.00 | 15.93 | 3.60 |
| Wait time standard deviation [s] | 14.33 | 21.17 | 4.37 |
| Average stress ratio | 1.05 | 1.28 | 0.16 |
| Average service score | 0.80 | 0.70 | 1 |
| Compliance rate [%] | 66.7 | 50.0 | 100 |
| Jain (user service) | 0.97 | 0.85 | 1 |
| Clean success rate [%] | 100 | 100 | 100 |
| Resource usefulness [%] | 100 | | |

timeline, except that the three first short jobs are executed before the single long job submitted by User 3.

The median waiting time for TYPE1 benchmarks is 2.68 seconds, with a standard deviation of 6.45 seconds, indicating fairer waiting times compared to the baseline algorithm, as also reflected in the Jain's fairness index. However, if all resources were occupied with TYPE3 benchmarks, the standard deviation would increase significantly. This prioritization improves responsiveness but is still limited by the absence of an eviction mechanism.

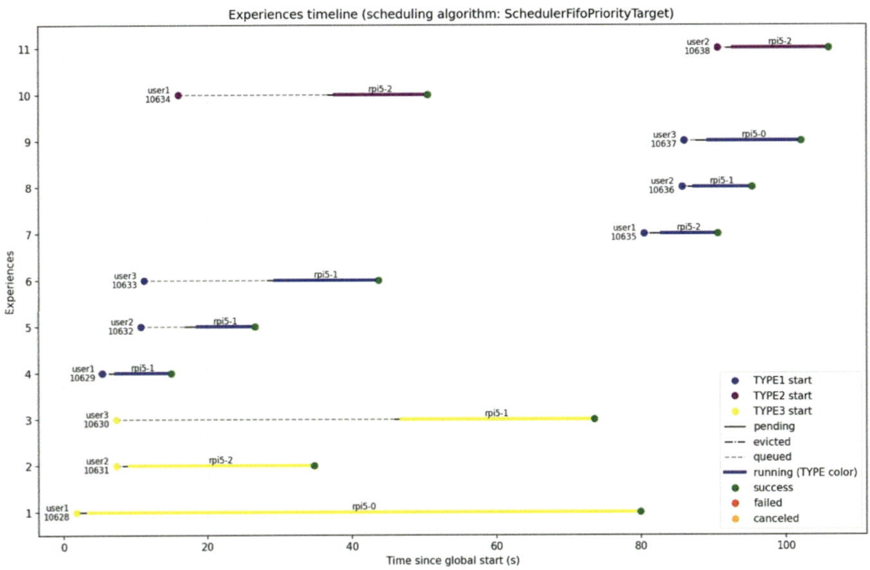


**Figure 10.5** Base test-bench timeline Algo 1.

**Table 10.4** Metrics base test-bench – Algo 1

| **Metrics** | **Algo 1** | | |
|---|---|---|---|
| **TYPE** | **1** | **2** | **3** |
| Wait time mean [s] | 5.71 | 11.70 | 14.11 |
| Wait time median [s] | 2.68 | 11.70 | 1.64 |
| Wait time standard deviation [s] | 6.45 | 13.86 | 21.74 |
| Average stress ratio | 0.52 | 0.90 | 0.51 |
| Average service score | 0.98 | 0.80 | 0.87 |
| Compliance rate [%] | 83.3 | 50.0 | 66.7 |
| Jain (user service) | 1 | 0.94 | 0.97 |
| Clean success rate [%] | 100 | 100 | 100 |
| Resource usefulness [%] | 100 | | |

#### 10.5.4.3 Algo 2

This algorithm introduces job eviction capability as illustrated in Figure 10.6. Thus, the short running jobs are always placed as soon as they arrive.

In this case, the median waiting time for TYPE1 jobs is 2.12 seconds, with a standard deviation of 0.67 seconds, indicating consistent scheduling.

However, the clean success rate drops to 81.8%, as two long-running jobs were stopped and restarted. This also reduces the useful computation ratio to 77.7%, meaning 22.3% of the total computation was wasted.

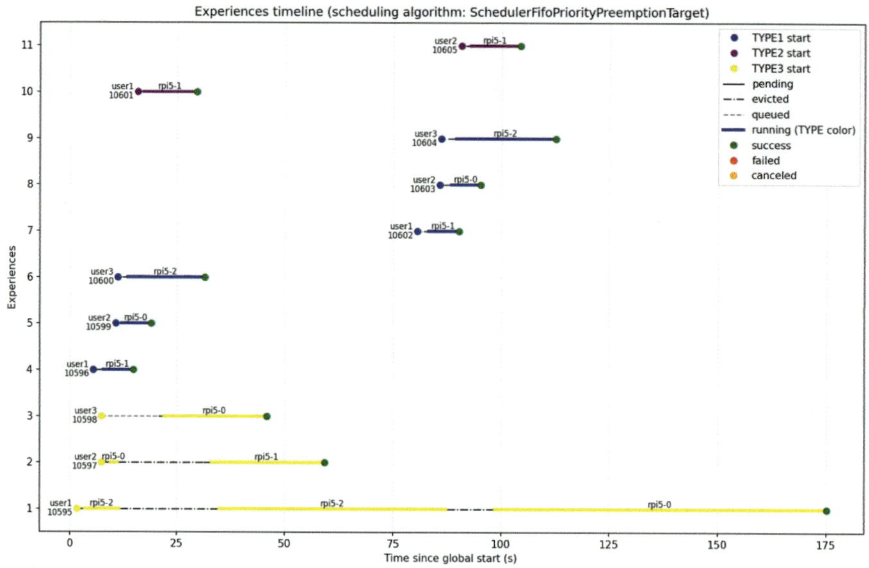


**Figure 10.6** Base test-bench timeline Algo 2.

**Table 10.5** Metrics base test-bench – Algo 2.

| **Metrics** | **Algo 2** | | |
|---|---|---|---|
| **TYPE** | **1** | **2** | **3** |
| Wait time mean [s] | 2.14 | 1.45 | 45.40 |
| Wait time median [s] | 2.12 | 1.45 | 25.37 |
| Wait time standard deviation [s] | 0.67 | 0.52 | 44.70 |
| Average stress ratio | 0.22 | 0.12 | 0.93 |
| Average service score | 1 | 1 | 0.93 |
| Compliance rate [%] | 100.0 | 100.0 | 66.7 |
| Jain (user service) | 1 | 1 | 0.99 |
| Clean success rate [%] | 100 | 100 | 33.3 |
| Resource usefulness [%] | 77.7 | | |

#### 10.5.4.4 Algo 3

Finally, the last algorithm considers job progress before eviction, preventing near-completion jobs from being stopped and thus reducing computational waste. As shown in Figure 10.7, the first long-running job is not evicted by later short-running requests, with only a slight delay of a few seconds for one of them. Overall, the test bench completes noticeably faster than with Algo 2.

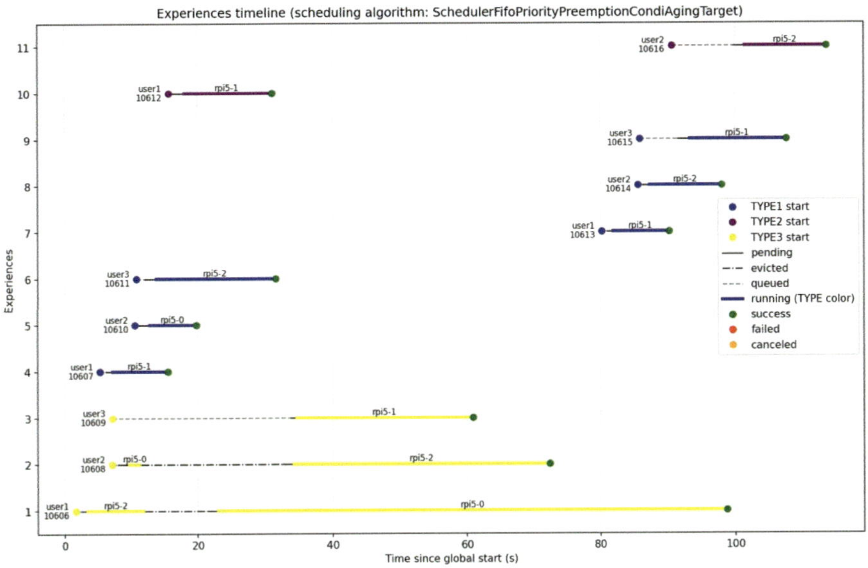


**Figure 10.7** Base test-bench timeline Algo 3.

**Table 10.6** Metrics base test-bench – Algo 3

| **Metrics** | **Algo 3** | | |
|---|---|---|---|
| **TYPE** | **1** | **2** | **3** |
| Wait time mean [s] | 2.78 | 6.40 | 25.10 |
| Wait time median [s] | 1.82 | 6.40 | 26.85 |
| Wait time standard deviation [s] | 2.25 | 6.02 | 3.39 |
| Average stress ratio | 0.24 | 0.51 | 0.67 |
| Average service score | 1 | 1 | 0.99 |
| Compliance rate [%] | 100.0 | 100.0 | 66.7 |
| Jain (user service) | 1 | 1 | 1 |
| Clean success rate [%] | 100 | 100 | 33.3 |
| Resource usefulness [%] | 95.6 | | |

For this final algorithm, the median waiting time for short-running jobs is 1.82 seconds, with a slightly higher standard deviation of 2.25 seconds.

While the clean success rate remains at 81.8%, the amount of useful computation increases significantly to 95.6%, meaning only 4.4% of the total computation was wasted due to the eviction mechanism.

**Table 10.7** Metrics contention test-bench - 1

| **Metrics** | **Base** | | | **Algo 1** | | |
|---|---|---|---|---|---|---|
| **TYPE** | **1** | **2** | **3** | **1** | **2** | **3** |
| Wait time mean [s] | 59.91 | 71.80 | 84.78 | 11.99 | 63.32 | 119.88 |
| Wait time median [s] | 57.84 | 74.97 | 87.81 | 12.48 | 63.16 | 120.37 |
| Wait time standard deviation [s] | 40.60 | 44.07 | 44.62 | 6.91 | 1.09 | 11.28 |
| Average stress ratio | 2.65 | 1.46 | 0.66 | 0.52 | 1.30 | 0.96 |
| Average service score | 0.50 | 0.69 | 0.98 | 0.99 | 0.78 | 0.98 |
| Compliance rate [%] | 27.8 | 33.3 | 66.7 | 94.4 | 0.0 | 66.7 |
| Jain (user service) | 0.99 | 1 | 1 | 1 | 0.99 | 1 |
| Clean success rate [%] | 100 | 100 | 100 | 100 | 100 | 100 |
| Resource Utilization [%] | 82.4 | | | 83.0 | | |
| Resource usefulness [%] | 100 | | | 100 | | |

**Table 10.8** Metrics contention test-bench - 2

| **Metrics** | **Algo 2** | | | **Algo 3** | | |
|---|---|---|---|---|---|---|
| **TYPE** | **1** | **2** | **3** | **1** | **2** | **3** |
| Wait time mean [s] | 11.32 | 62.24 | 119.10 | 40.86 | 67.94 | 96.3 |
| Wait time median [s] | 11.6 | 62.58 | 119.19 | 14.41 | 43.32 | 84.93 |
| Wait time standard deviation [s] | 7.03 | 1.36 | 10.83 | 47.06 | 39.15 | 28.62 |
| Average stress ratio | 0.54 | 1.29 | 0.95 | 1.76 | 1.40 | 0.77 |
| Average service score | 0.98 | 0.78 | 0.99 | 0.74 | 0.78 | 0.98 |
| Compliance rate [%] | 83.3 | 0.0 | 55.6 | 66.7 | 44.4 | 66.7 |
| Jain (user service) | 1 | 0.99 | 1 | 1 | 1 | 1 |
| Clean success rate [%] | 100 | 100 | 100 | 100 | 100 | 100 |
| Resource Utilization [%] | 81.2 | | | 83.7 | | |
| Resource usefulness [%] | 100 | | | 100 | | |

### 10.5.5 Algorithms performances under heavy starvation

The following tables present the results of all algorithms under the Contention test-bench, designed to evaluate their behaviour under starvation conditions. No figures are presented due to the large number of jobs.

Under contention, all algorithms maintain fairness across users, but their compliance rates differ. Algos 1 and 2 favour short benchmarks due to the absence of priority aging, causing longer TYPE2 and TYPE3 jobs to risk starvation over time.

The base algorithm avoids starvation by serving jobs strictly in arrival order, but this leads to higher waiting times and lower compliance for short jobs. Algo 3 provides the best balance by raising the priority of long-waiting jobs, improving fairness. Its median waiting time for TYPE1 jobs is about

14.4 s, with the highest compliance across all types, though with higher variance.

All schedulers achieve roughly 83 % utilization within the test window. Remaining inefficiencies arise from network latency and short synchronization delays, which could be mitigated by more frequent scheduler updates or event-driven triggers.

### 10.5.6 Results analysis

Algo 3 proves to be the most adaptable and effective across diverse conditions. Under normal circumstances, it enhances user experience by prioritizing short-running jobs while avoiding wasted computation through the non-eviction of jobs nearing completion. Its priority-aging mechanism prevents starvation of lower-priority tasks, and by selecting the oldest job among those with equal priority, it reduces uneven treatment across users.

Under severe resource scarcity, Algo 3 behaves similarly to a FIFO strategy, maintaining fairness but at the cost of increased waiting times for all users. This results in a uniformly degraded experience rather than one favouring specific users or workloads, demonstrating the algorithm's balanced approach to fairness and performance.

### 10.5.7 Limitations of the current implementation

The scheduling logic remains simple, focusing on priorities, device availability, and fairness through priority aging. This design ensures robustness and transparency but lacks user-quota mechanisms to balance long-term resource access and prevent unfairness under heavily unbalanced user requests.

## 10.6 Conclusion

This work introduced the dAIEdge-VLab, a distributed framework for fair, efficient, and reproducible benchmarking across heterogeneous edge devices. By combining Nomad's orchestration capabilities with a custom scheduler and Nomad plugin, it enables device-aware, priority-based execution while ensuring balanced resource allocation and consistent results.

Among the evaluated strategies, Algo 3 achieved the best balance between responsiveness, fairness, and resource utilization through its priority-aging mechanism and adaptive behaviour under varying load conditions. The resulting architecture is scalable, resilient, and flexible, uniting the robustness of cloud orchestration with the adaptability required for decentralized edge environments.

### 10.6.1 Future Work

Future work on the dAIEdge-VLab will aim to enhance scheduling intelligence, fairness, and scalability. Planned developments include a predictive scheduler using historical data for runtime estimation, and support for federated learning requiring coordinated multi-device execution. Further research will address dynamic user quotas and broader hardware support to improve responsiveness and sustainability.

## Acknowledgements

This work has been funded by the European Union's Horizon Europe project dAIEdge under grant agreement No. 101120726.

## References

[1] B. Burns, B. Grant, D. Oppenheimer, E. Brewer, and J. Wilkes,"Borg, Omega, and Kubernetes," *Commun. ACM*, vol. 59, no. 5, pp. 50–57, May 2016, doi: 10.1145/2890784.

[2] B. Hindman *et al.*, "Mesos: a platform for fine-grained resource sharing in the data center," in *NSDI'11: Proc. 8th USENIX Conf. Networked Systems Design and Implementation*, Boston, MA, USA, Mar. 2011, pp. 295–308, doi:10.5555/1972457.1972488.

[3] M. Satyanarayanan, "The Emergence of Edge Computing," *Computer*, vol. 50, no. 1, pp. 30–39, 2017.

[4] Y. Mao, C. You, J. Zhang, K. Huang, and K. B. Letaief, "A survey on mobile edge computing: The communication perspective," *IEEE Commun. Surveys Tuts.*, vol. 19, no. 4, pp. 2322–2358, 2017, doi: 10.1109/COMST.2017.2745201.

[5] KubeEdge, "kubeedge/kubeedge," *GitHub repository*. [Online]. Available: https://github.com/kubeedge/kubeedge. Accessed: Dec. 10, 2025.

[6] OpenYurt, "OpenYurt: extending your native Kubernetes to edge," *GitHub repository* openyurtio/openyurt. [Online]. Available: https://github.com/openyurtio/openyurt. Accessed: Dec. 10, 2025.

[7] HashiCorp, "Nomad: A Simple and Flexible Scheduler and Orchestrator for Cloud and Edge Workloads," [Online]. Available: https://www.nomadproject.io Accessed: Oct. 17, 2025.

[8] X. Li, E. Zhu, J. Qin, W. Xu, and Y. Wu, "A Multi-Resource-Aware and Load-Balanced Scheduling Strategy for Heterogeneous Edge Clusters," *J. Grid Comput.*, vol. 23, art. no. 32, 2025. Available: https://doi.org/10.1007/s10723-025-09817-2

[9] W. Peng, Z. Tang, J. Guo, J. Lou, T. Wang, and W. Jia,"$LR^2$Scheduler: layer-aware, resource-balanced, and request-adaptive container scheduling for edge computing,"*CCF Trans. Pervasive Comput. Interact.*, Online First, 2025.Available: https://doi.org/10.1007/s42486-025-00186-z

[10] Y. Cao, S. Hu, Z. Qu, L. Hao, and B. Ye, "Multi-cluster layer-sharing container scheduling in cloud-edge collaboration," in *Advanced Intelligent Computing Technology and Applications*, D.-S. Huang, C. Zhang, Q. Zhang, and Y. Pan, Eds., *Lecture Notes in Computer Science*, vol. 15856, Singapore: Springer, 2025, pp. 16–27, doi: 10.1007/978-981-96-9914-8_2

[11] R. Jain, D.-M. Chiu, and W. Hawe, "A quantitative measure of fairness and discrimination for resource allocation in shared computer systems," *arXiv preprint* arXiv:cs/9809099, 1998. Available: https://arxiv.org/abs/cs/9809099.

[12] B. G. S. Costa, J. Bachiega Jr., L. R. de Carvalho, and A. P. F. Araujo,"Orchestration in fog computing: A comprehensive survey," *ACM Comput. Surv.*, vol. 55, no. 2, Art. 29, pp. 1–34, Jan. 2022, doi:10.1145/3486221.

# 11

# Physics-Informed Kalman Filtering for Multi-Step Bias Correction in Indoor Temperature Forecasting

**Georgios Daoutis[1], Othon Tomoutzoglou[2], George Kornaros[3], and Marcello Coppola[4]**

[1]Hellenic Mediterranean University, Greece
[2]Neotera, Italy
[3]Hellenic Mediterranean University, Greece
[4]STMicroelectronics, France

## Abstract

Indoor temperature prediction is often utilized to maintain the right environment in which wine can be fermented or stored. However, forecasting these indoor microclimates is challenging due to inaccuracies in outdoor temperature predictions combined with the difficulty of modelling a building's thermal inertia, which changes due to unpredictable environmental factors. This paper proposes a two-stage machine learning and state-estimation pipeline to predict temperatures inside a winery up to an 18-hour horizon. First, feature extraction is performed to train an Autoregressive with eXogenous inputs (ARX) model. Then, to mitigate the drift caused by factors such as noise in the API predictions or errors caused by the model, a Two-State Kinematic Kalman Filter (KKF) is introduced. The proposed KKF lies in its dual-state formulation which tracks both the magnitude of the prediction error and its latent velocity. In this way, the filter effectively models the building's thermal inertia and identifies the steady, low-frequency velocity of the thermodynamic drift, resulting in a stable and physically realistic forecast.

DOI: 10.1201/9788743815211-11

**Keywords:** Microclimate forecasting, Kinematic Kalman Filter, ARX modelling, smart agriculture, building thermal inertia, time-series error correction, winery climate control.

## 11.1 Introduction and Background

Fermentation processes in viticulture and winemaking are highly sensitive to thermal fluctuations and extreme temperatures; therefore, indoor temperatures must often be maintained within specific limits [1]. To prevent detrimental thermal instability and maintain ideal conditions, facility managers or IoT infrastructure need reliable, multi-hour forecasts of indoor microclimates to proactively manage indoor conditions [2]. Meteorological APIs powered by global atmospheric models, such as Open-Meteo, can supply baseline predictions of future outdoor conditions that will eventually affect indoor temperature. Despite these advantages, predicting indoor microclimates using external macro-weather data with standard ARX models presents challenges. These challenges arise because forecasts made by API often contain inaccuracies for the specific area of interest. As these global models operate on wide spatial grids, they often fail to capture localized temperature and solar radiation anomalies that impact the building's exterior and eventually the indoor temperature [3]. Furthermore, the agricultural buildings have thermal inertia often influenced by unpredictable circumstances such as open doors or windows [4]. Consequently, when predicting iteratively several hour horizons, this macro-weather noise cascades into the indoor thermal model. The small, step-by-step prediction errors can compound causing the base model to drift significantly from the actual indoor temperature trajectory [5]. If left uncorrected this cumulative drift results in significant control latency and can trigger HVAC activations, undermining the energy efficiency and stability goals of smart agricultural Edge AI systems [6].

### 11.1.1 Contribution

This paper proposes a hybrid, two-stage forecasting pipeline to alleviate the problems arising from noise in the data.

- An ARX model was developed using Ridge Regression. To train this model correctly, we created and tested several features related to the inertia of the winery and identified the most valuable ones using L1 regularization (LassoCV). This feature selection was performed seasonally to capture shifting thermal dependencies, such as the increased impact of solar radiation during summer or the dominance of indoor thermal mass in winter.

- To correct the multi-step drift inherent in recursive ARX predictions, a Two-State Kinematic Kalman Filter (KKF) is introduced. Unlike traditional filters that treat error as random noise, the proposed KKF models the prediction bias as a dynamic state with both position and latent velocity components. By focusing on the velocity of the temperature drift, the filter effectively respects the building's thermal inertia and ignores transient observation noise. A Differential Evolution algorithm is utilized to optimize the baseline noise matrices, the decaying bias parameters, and a thermal anchoring weight $\beta$. This ensures that the correction filter identifies genuine thermodynamic trends, providing a stable and physically realistic forecast up to 18-hour horizons.

## 11.2 Data Preprocessing and Feature Engineering

To implement the base prediction model, we must collect data for the winery that we are interested in, along with the corresponding meteorological predictions for the particular area from the external API. After the acquisition of the raw IoT and API datasets, it is important to construct and select features designed to capture the building's thermal inertia without overparameterizing the ARX model. This section outlines the data acquisition, feature engineering, and dimensionality reduction steps required to build the forecasting ARX baseline.

### 11.2.1 Data Sources

To test our model, we retrieved historical 24-hour-ahead predictions for solar radiation and outdoor temperature from the Open-Meteo API [8]. These forecasts were generated by the AROME France model [7] for the specific location of the winery.

The dataset used consists of indoor temperature measurements collected from an IoT sensor deployed within a winery facility.

### 11.2.2 Feature Construction and Thermal Lag Analysis

To find how exogenous drivers such as outdoor temperature and solar radiation affect the indoor temperature, we must quantify the temporal behaviour of the winery and explore how the indoor temperature responds, and with what delay, to these external influences. Therefore, we implemented a statistical analysis of the dataset for both indoor and outdoor data to find minimum, maximum, and average measurements, along with cross-correlation analysis to quantify the exact physical delay or thermal lag between external forcing and internal response in three representative intervals of the year:

- **Summer (June 3 – July 21):** During this interval outdoor API temperatures averaged 20.63 °C reaching peaks of 39.40 °C and exhibited an average daily temperature swing of 11.25 °C and a maximum of 19.90 °C. The solar heat peaked at 918.00 W/m$^2$ driving the average indoor daily swing to 7.47 °C and pushing the absolute maximum indoor temperature to 31.50 °C. Using Pearson cross-correlation, we found a delay of about 6 hours for the outdoor temperature to completely affect the indoor temperature with r = 0.947, and an 8-hour delay for the penetration of solar radiation with r = 0.805.
- **Autumn (Sep 10 – Nov 17)**: In the autumn period, the mean API outdoor temperature dropped to 13.23 °C, reaching an absolute peak of 29.70 °C, while the indoor mean was maintained at 16.87 °C with an absolute maximum of 26.68 °C. The average outdoor daily swing of 7.27 °C, a maximum daily swing of 17.30 °C, and solar radiation peaking at 720.00 W/m$^2$ the indoor microclimate experienced only moderate average diurnal swings of 3.55 °C. As the external thermal load decayed, the thermal resistance of the facility shifted accordingly, reducing the optimal cross-correlation lags to 5 hours for outdoor temperature r = 0.869 and 7 hours for solar radiation r = 0.737.
- **Winter (Dec 9– Jan 31)**: Conversely, the winter dataset demonstrated internal stability as the mean API outdoor temperature dropped to 3.49 °C, reaching an absolute peak of 11.60 °C, with an average daily swing of 4.65 °C and a maximum daily swing of 11.10 °C. External solar radiation was minimal, averaging just 32.48 W/m$^2$ and peaking at only 319.80 W/m$^2$. Because of the building's massive thermal persistence and the lack of external solar pressure, the indoor temperature was stable, maintaining a mean of 11.24 °C with an absolute maximum of only 15.30 °C and a mere 1.51 °C average daily swing. The temperature lag reduced to 4 hours and the correlation for solar radiation collapsed entirely r = 0.246 at a 5-hour lag, proving that direct solar heat transfer is negligible during the winter months.

### 11.2.3 Feature Construction

Driven by these empirical lag variables, three distinct sets of temporal features were engineered from the API data to enable the linear ARX model to capture the winery's specific thermal profile:

- **Lagged Variables:** To model the thermal inertia, discrete lagged versions of the raw API data outdoor temperature and solar radiation were generated. Specifically, we explored a discrete interval of 4, 5, 6, 7, and 8 hours, as this represents the established time required for exogenous variables to noticeably penetrate the building. Furthermore, an immediate previous-step indoor temperature $t - 1$ and a 24-hour lagged indoor temperature $t - 24$ were included to capture the facility's daily autoregressive thermal persistence.
- **Rolling Windows:** To capture long-term environmental heat accumulation, moving average windows of 8 hours were calculated for both solar radiation and outdoor temperature. This effectively aligns the immediate API predictions with the building's broader thermal envelope.
- **Interaction and Non-Linear Terms:** High ambient heat combined with direct sunlight impacts the heating of the building non-linearly. To ensure the standard linear ARX model could capture these dynamic non-linear interaction features were constructed. First, an interaction term was created by multiplying the predicted outdoor temperature with shortwave solar radiation to capture their combined thermal load. Second, squared solar intensity was calculated. Finally, Boolean flags were engineered to isolate specific solar states: a baseline daylight flag (taking the value 1 when solar radiation exceeds 20 W/m$^2$ and a flag extreme (taking the value 1 when radiation exceeds 600 W/m$^2$. These flags isolate extreme solar events, which have a particularly disruptive impact on the building's thermal response.

### 11.2.4 Feature Selection

To identify the most important features affecting the winery's microclimate and avoid redundant variables, we applied Lasso L1 regularization [9] independently for each season, implemented via the scikit-learn library [10]. The winery facility exhibits shifting physical thermodynamics across the year. For instance, during the summer period, the optimizer selected a stronger penalty of $\alpha = 0.00336$, and the dataset was reduced to just 9 out of 19 features. In contrast, during the stable autumn and winter periods, the model retained

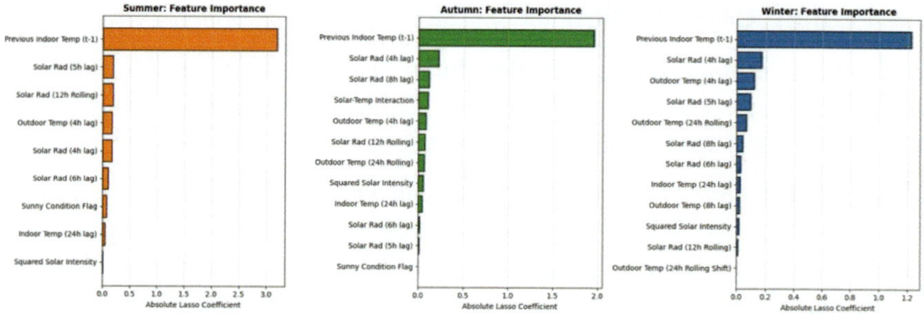


**Figure 11.1** Magnitude of retained feature coefficients following Lasso L1 regularization.

more features (12 active variables in winter) using weaker environmental signals, as seen in Figure 11.1. In all seasons, however, the building's thermal mass was the dominant predictive factor, with the immediate previous indoor temperature (t-1) exerting the highest influence by a wide margin. Crucially, this influence scaled with the seasonal thermal load: Lasso coefficients peaked at 3.18 in summer, dropped to 1.95 in autumn, and reached their lowest point at 1.22 in winter. Beyond this internal baseline, the seasonal coefficient shifts directly quantify the building's structural thermal delay. The 4-hour to 5-hour lagged external variables specifically solar radiation and outdoor temperature emerged as the strongest exogenous predictors across all three datasets. This proves that peak external heat loads require a minimum of 4 to 5 hours to have a noticeable effect on the indoor microclimate. Furthermore, the autumn and winter models prioritized complex interaction terms and long-term rolling averages (such as the 24-hour rolling outdoor temperature). In winter specifically, the model compensated for the lack of intense, direct solar heat by leaning on these slower diurnal heat transfers to anchor the autoregressive forecast.

## 11.3 Methodology

A machine learning and state-estimation pipeline combination is proposed that first utilizes an autoregressive linear forecast to predict the baseline of the temperature trajectory and then introduces a dynamic error-correction Rolling-Window Adaptive Kalman Filter (AKF).

### 11.3.1 The Base ARX Model

The initial predictions are generated by an AutoRegressive with eXogenous inputs (ARX) architecture, formulated using the specific subset of features isolated by the L1 algorithm discussed in Section 3.4. The intrinsic properties of the ARX model are highly suited for modelling building thermodynamics: the autoregressive (AR) component natively captures the winery's massive thermal inertia by leveraging lagged historical indoor temperatures, while the exogenous (X) inputs integrate external meteorological driving forces, such as API-derived outdoor temperatures and solar radiation. To stabilize this architecture against the residual multicollinearity of overlapping temporal features, the model is constructed via Ridge Regression with an L2 penalty. While these linear properties provide a mathematically interpretable and physically grounded baseline for the winery's thermal trajectory, the static nature of the ARX structure cannot dynamically adapt to real-time microclimate disturbances or unmeasured API inaccuracies. Consequently, recursive multi-step predictions remain susceptible to compounding predictive drift.

### 11.3.2 Two-State Kinematic Kalman Filter

To tackle the cumulative prediction drift discussed in this chapter, a Two-State Kinematic Kalman Filter (KKF) was implemented. Traditional adaptive filters often treat ARX prediction errors as purely stochastic noise. However, in agricultural buildings, temperature errors compound through slow, continuous thermodynamic drift driven by the facility's thermal inertia. To physically model this behaviour, the proposed pipeline employs a kinematic state-space architecture that tracks both the magnitude of the prediction bias and its rate of change. First, to account for continuous meteorological volatility, the model estimates the real-time ARX prediction error as a two-dimensional state vector $X_t$, containing both the bias position $X_{\text{pos}}$ and the latent bias velocity $X_{\text{vel}}$. For a given time, step $t$ , the raw ARX prediction error is calculated as:

$$\mathbf{y}_{\mathbf{err,t}} = \mathbf{y}_{\mathbf{actual,t}} - \mathbf{y}_{\mathbf{pred,t}} \tag{11.1}$$

The KKF defines the state transition matrix F and the observation matrix H to model a constant-velocity kinematic system. Because the ARX model outputs at regular hourly intervals, the transition matrix assumes the error position updates linearly based on its velocity, while only the position error is directly observable:

$$\mathbf{F} = \begin{bmatrix} \mathbf{1} & \mathbf{1} \\ \mathbf{0} & \mathbf{1} \end{bmatrix}, \quad \mathbf{H} = [\mathbf{1}\ \mathbf{1}] \tag{11.2}$$

A critical, physics-informed enhancement in this architecture is the structural formulation of the process noise covariance matrix, Q. Rather than dynamically reacting to all outliers equally, the algorithm isolates the noise into a diagonal matrix where the position variance $Q_{\text{pos}}$ and velocity variance $Q_{\text{vel}}$ are optimized independently:

$$\mathbf{Q} = \begin{bmatrix} \mathbf{Q_{pos}} & \mathbf{0} \\ \mathbf{0} & \mathbf{Q_{vel}} \end{bmatrix} \tag{11.3}$$

By isolating these parameters, the Differential Evolution optimizer is allowed to actively constrain $Q_{\text{pos}}$ toward zero in high-inertia environments. When this occurs, the filter acts as a mathematical lock against non-physical, instantaneous temperature shocks. All thermodynamic volatility is strictly routed through the velocity variance, ensuring that the filter ignores high-frequency sensor noise and actively tracks the smooth, slow-moving drift inherent to passive building heat loss. During the iterative execution of the filter, the a priori state estimate $X_{\text{pred,t}}$ and error covariance $P_{\text{pred,t}}$ are projected forward in the predict step:

$$\mathbf{X_{pred,t}} = \mathbf{FX_{t-1}} \tag{11.4}$$

$$\mathbf{P_{pred,t}} = \mathbf{FP_{t-1}F^{T}{+}Q} \tag{11.5}$$

Once the new ARX prediction error is observed, the innovation and Kalman Gain $K_t$ are calculated to optimally update the state vector, governed by the optimized measurement noise R:

$$\mathbf{innovation_t{=}y_{err,t}{-}HX_{pred,t}} \tag{11.6}$$

$$\mathbf{K_t{=}P_{pred,t}H^{T}\left(HP_{pred,t}H^{T}{+}R\right)^{-1}} \tag{11.7}$$

Finally, the state vector and covariance matrix are updated (a posteriori) to be utilized in the subsequent time step:

$$\mathbf{X_t{=}X_{pred,t}{+}K_t{\cdot}innovation_t} \tag{11.8}$$

$$\mathbf{P_t{=}\left(I{-}K_tH\right)P_{pred,t}} \tag{11.9}$$

### 11.3.3 Multi-Step Prediction Correction with Bias Decay

Because facility managers require reliable forecasts up to 18 hours in advance, iterative multi-step forecasting is performed. As the model predicts further into the future ($j$ steps ahead), projecting the error velocity in a continuous straight line from the Two-State Kinematic Kalman Filter (KKF) can lead to severe overcorrection, as environmental thermodynamics naturally fluctuate rather than drift infinitely. To safely project the state error, the KKF applies an optimized exponential decay factor $\gamma$ to the kinematically projected bias. The corrected bias at future step $j$ is calculated using the estimated error position $X_{\text{pos}}$ and error velocity $X_{\text{vel}}$ components of the state vector

$$\mathbf{Bias_{corr,j}} = (\mathbf{X_{pos}} + \mathbf{X_{vel}} \cdot \mathbf{j}) \cdot \gamma^{\mathbf{j}} \tag{11.10}$$

Finally, recognizing that agricultural buildings possess massive thermal mass, the prediction output must be physically anchored. The final forecast is formulated as a weighted blend controlled by the optimized thermal persistence parameter $\beta$ of the simulated indoor temperature from the previous time step $y_{\text{sim,t}+j-1}$ and the newly bias-corrected ARX forecast:

$$\mathbf{y_{final,t+j}} = \beta \cdot \mathbf{y_{sim,t+j-1}} + (-\beta) \cdot (\mathbf{y_{ARX,t+j}} + \mathbf{Bias_{corr,j}}) \tag{11.11}$$

## 11.4 Experimental Setup and Results

This section details the training of the ARX model and the finetuning of the KKF via Differential Evolution (DE). In addition, we compare the hybrid ARX-KKF architecture against the standard ARX baseline for each season to display the predictive accuracy improvement of the system and its dynamic physical adaptation to the winery's shifting thermodynamics.

### 11.4.1 Hyperparameter Optimization

To validate the proposed pipeline and to test its adaptability, we trained the model for each specific season interval independently. For each season, we took the first 70% of the data to train the ARX model, used the next 15% of the data to calibrate the Kalman filter parameters, and used the rest as unseen samples to test the performance of the model. Specifically, the input features were normalized using standard scaling before being fitted to a Ridge Regression algorithm with a fixed regularization parameter of $\alpha = 1.0$. After that, we calibrated the Kalman filter using the validation dataset by employing DE to implement a global search in the multidimensional parameter space to find the optimal combination of hyperparameters that minimizes the multi-step prediction error. As the parameter space specifically the tuning of the noise covariance matrices is non-convex and prone to local minima, DE was selected for its proven ability to locate global optima in continuous spaces without relying on gradient information [11]. The DE algorithm was deployed to simultaneously optimize five KKF parameters: the physical thermal anchoring weight $\beta$ , the process noise variances for both the error position $Q_{\text{pos}}$ and error velocity $Q_{\text{vel}}$ the baseline measurement noise, $R_{\text{base}}$ and a kinematic projection decay factor $\gamma$.

### 11.4.2 Multi-Horizon Performance Analysis

The results of running the experiments described in Section 4.1 are outlined in Table 4.1. They confirm the efficacy of the proposed framework, but also the hyperparameters that the DE chose reveal how the filter shifts its behaviours for each specific season. By analysing the optimal thermal anchoring weights $\beta$, kinematic process noise variances $Q_{\text{pos}}$ and $Q_{\text{vel}}$, and projection decay factors $\gamma$ selected across the three seasons, a physical narrative emerges regarding how the algorithm adapts to shifting thermodynamics through the seasons.

- Summer: In the summer interval, the Hybrid KKF provided a 15.02% improvement at the 6-hour mark, though performance degradation accelerated at the 12- and 18-hour horizons. The aggressive diurnal solar loads caused the baseline trajectory to drift so significantly that traditional thermal persistence became a liability. To compensate for this extreme volatility, the optimizer practically eliminated the thermal blending weight $\beta < 0.08$, maximized the velocity process noise $Q_{\text{vel}}, > 0.08$, and raised the decay factor $\gamma > 0.56$ for extended horizons. The DE acknowledged that large, sudden temperature swings in summer are true physical realities not transient observation noise and therefore shifted the forecasting weight entirely onto the active kinematic tracking of the thermodynamic drift.
- Autumn: In the autumn interval, the architecture achieved the highest relative improvements of the entire study, peaking at 22.89% for the 12-hour horizon. Because the external weather was not as violently volatile as mid-summer, yet not as static as winter, the KKF was able to successfully track and update the state bias without becoming saturated. The optimizer manages to balance moderate thermal anchor $\beta \approx 0.20$ with active velocity tracking $Q_{\text{vel}}, \approx 0.01$ to $0.04$ and an elevated decay factor $\gamma \approx 0.55$. This configuration allowed the kinematic projection to confidently ride out the steady, predictable seasonal drift while maintaining a physically realistic anchor, yielding the most robust and stable multi-step forecasts of the year.

**Table 11.1** Predictive Performance Comparison (MAE) and Optimized KKF Hyperparameters Across Seasonal Forecasting Horizons

| Season | Forecast horizon | ARX MAE °C | KKF MAE °C | Impr.% | $\beta$ | $Q_{pos}$ | $Q_{vel}$ | $R_{base}$ | $\gamma$ |
|---|---|---|---|---|---|---|---|---|---|
| Summer | 6h | 0.2623 | 0.2029 | **22.65** | 0.029 | 0.0704 | 0.0001 | 0.000 | 0.50 |
| | 12h | 0.3607 | 0.2782 | **22.89** | 0.063 | 0.0284 | 0.0826 | 0.002 | 0.51 |
| | 18h | 0.3912 | 0.3154 | **19.39** | 0.074 | 0.0661 | 0.0813 | 0.000 | 0.56 |
| autumn | 6h | 0.2623 | 0.2029 | **22.65** | 0.190 | 0.0538 | 0.0159 | 0.223 | 0.50 |
| | 12h | 0.3607 | 0.2782 | **22.89** | 0.222 | 0.0873 | 0.0408 | 0.857 | 0.55 |
| | 18h | 0.3912 | 0.3154 | **19.39** | 0.200 | 0.0000 | 0.0172 | 0.161 | 0.51 |
| Winter | 6h | 0.2314 | 0.2069 | **10.61** | 0.459 | 0.0000 | 0.0000 | 0.593 | 0.50 |
| | 12h | 0.3191 | 0.2917 | **8.59** | 0.416 | 0.0892 | 0.0000 | 0.686 | 0.50 |
| | 18h | 0.3754 | 0.3420 | **8.90** | 0.361 | 0.0000 | 0.0000 | 0.969 | 0.50 |

- Winter: During the winter months, external thermal loads and overall absolute temperatures are lower. To adapt to this low-energy, highly persistent environment, the optimizer selected a remarkably high thermal blending weight $\beta \approx 0.46$ at the 6-hour mark) while mathematically neutralizing the velocity tracking $Q_{\text{vel}}, \approx 0.0$. Furthermore, the kinematic decay factor hit the absolute lower boundary $\gamma = 0.500$ across all time horizons. Because the winter indoor microclimate strongly resists rapid change, the filter essentially learned to distrust noisy, high-frequency errors from the ARX baseline. By setting the decay to its maximum dampening effect relying instead on the building's massive physical inertia to anchor the forecast.

## 11.5 Conclusion

To address the drift that often affects indoor temperature autoregressive predictions, we proposed a two-stage hybrid pipeline. We did this by integrating an ARX model with a Two-State Kinematic Kalman Filter (KKF) and a thermal smoothing anchor to correct the cascading errors caused by noise in the API data or other unpredictable events. We evaluated the model across three distinct seasonal intervals. For each interval, we trained the model from scratch and optimized the kinematic and thermal persistence parameters via Differential Evolution. The proposed pipeline was able to reduce multi-step forecasting errors by up to 22.89% across forecast horizons of up to 18 hours. Future work will explore replacing the linear ARX baseline with advanced recurrent neural network (RNN) architectures. Transitioning to deep learning could allow the base model to better capture the extreme, non-linear thermal dynamics observed during peak summer solar loads, thereby enhancing the framework's overall accuracy.

## References

[1] I. Kovačević, I. Aleksi, T. Keser, and T. Matić, "Winnie: A sensor-based system for real-time monitoring and quality tracking in wine fermentation," Appl. Sci., vol. 15, no. 21, p. 11317, Oct. 2025, doi: 10.3390/app152111317.

[2] S. Kontogiannis, M. Tsoumani, G. Kokkonis, C. Pikridas, and Y. Kotseridis, "Proposed SmartBarrel system for monitoring and assessment of wine fermentation processes using IoT nose and tongue devices," Sensors, vol. 25, no. 13, p. 3877, 2025.

[3] A. Worthy, M. Ashayeri, J. Marshall, and N. Abbasabadi, "Bridging the simulation-to-reality gap: A comprehensive review of microclimate integration in urban building energy modeling (UBEM)," Energy and Buildings, vol. 331, p. 115392, 2025, doi: 10.1016/j.enbuild.2025.115392.

[4] R. Felez and J. Felez, "Advanced energy management for residential buildings optimizing costs and efficiency through thermal energy storage and predictive control," Appl. Sci., vol. 15, no. 2, p. 880, 2025, doi: 10.3390/app15020880.

[5] A. Benechehab, G. Paolo, A. Thomas, M. Filippone, and B. Kégl, "Multi-timestep models for model-based reinforcement learning," arXiv preprint arXiv:2310.05672, 2023, doi: 10.48550/arXiv.2310.05672.

[6] K. Almazam, O. Humaidan, N. M. Shannan, F. M. Bashir, T. Gammoudi, and Y. A. Dodo, "Innovative energy efficiency in HVAC systems with an integrated machine learning and model predictive control technique: A prospective toward sustainable buildings," Sustainability, vol. 17, no. 7, p. 2916, 2025, doi: 10.3390/su17072916.

[7] Demortier A, Mandement M, Pourret V, Caumont O. Assimilation of temperature and relative humidity observations from personal weather stations in AROME-France. Nat Hazards Earth Syst Sci. 2025;25:429–449. https://doi.org/10.5194/nhess-25-429-2025

[8] Zippenfenig P. Open-Meteo.com Weather API [Internet]. Zenodo; 2023 [cited 2026 Mar 13]. Available from: https://doi.org/10.5281/ZENODO.7970649

[9] R. Tibshirani, Regression shrinkage and selection via the lasso, Journal of the Royal Statistical Society: Series B (Methodological) 58 (1) (1996) 267–288. https://doi.org/10.1111/j.2517-6161.1996.tb02080.x

[10] F. Pedregosa, G. Varoquaux, A. Gramfort, V. Michel, B. Thirion, et al., Scikit-learn: Machine learning in Python, *Journal of Machine Learning Research* 12 (2011) 2825–2830.

[11] R. Storn, K. Price, Differential evolution – A simple and efficient heuristic for global optimization over continuous spaces, Journal of Global Optimization 11 (4) (1997) 341–359. https://doi.org/10.1023/A:1008202821328

# Index

# About the Editors

**Dr. Ovidiu Vermesan** holds a PhD degree in microelectronics and a Master of International Business (MIB) degree. He is Chief Scientist at SINTEF Digital, Oslo, Norway. His research interests are intelligent systems integration, mixed-signal embedded electronics, analogue neural networks, edge artificial intelligence and cognitive communication systems. Dr. Vermesan received SINTEF's 2003 award for research excellence for his work on implementing a biometric sensor system. He is currently working on projects addressing nanoelectronics, integrated sensor/actuator systems, communication, cyber-physical systems (CPSs) and the Industrial Internet of Things (IIoT), with applications in green mobility, energy, autonomous systems, and smart cities. He has authored or co-authored over 100 technical articles and conference papers. He is actively involved in the activities of the European partnership for Key Digital Technologies (KDT) Joint Undertaking (JU), now the Chips JU. He has coordinated and managed various national, EU and other international projects related to smart sensor systems, integrated electronics, electromobility and intelligent autonomous systems such as E3Car, POLLUX, CASTOR, IoE, MIRANDELA, IoF2020, AUTOPILOT, AutoDrive, ArchitectECA2030, AI4DI, AI4CSM. Dr. Vermesan actively participates in national, Horizon Europe and other international initiatives by coordinating and managing various projects. He is a member of the Alliance for AI, IoT and Edge Continuum Innovation (AIOTI) board. He is currently the coordinator of the Edge AI Technologies for Optimised Performance Embedded Processing (EdgeAI) project.

**Dr. Luca Valcarenghi** is a Full Professor at the Scuola Superiore Sant'Anna of Pisa, Italy, since 2024. He received the Laurea in Electrical Engineering in 1997 from Politecnico di Torino and the M.S.E.E. and Ph.D. in Electrical Engineering Major Telecommunications from UTD in 1999 and 2001, respectively. He published more than three hundred papers in International Journals and Conference Proceedings. Dr. Valcarenghi received a Fulbright Research Scholar Fellowship in 2009 and a JSPS "Invitation Fellowship

Program for Research in Japan (Long Term)" in 2013. He coordinated, as a PI or local PI, several National and International projects, among which Collaborative edge-cLoud continuum and Embedded AI for a Visionary industry of thE futuRe (CLEVER) project. His main research interests are optical networks design, analysis, and optimization; communication networks reliability; energy efficiency in communications networks; optical access networks; zero touch network and service management; 5G technologies and beyond; networking for the edge-cloud continuum.

For Product Safety Concerns and Information please contact our EU representative GPSR@taylorandfrancis.com Taylor & Francis Verlag GmbH, Kaufingerstraße 24, 80331 München, Germany